SEATTLE CITIZENS AGAINST FREEWAYS, 1968-1980

FIGHTING FIERCELY and WINNING SOMETIMES

PART 1, TRANSPORTATION DECISIONS IN SEATTLE, 1968-1972
PART 2, THE STATE LEGISLATURE, 1970-1978
PART 3, 1-90, THE MERCER ISLAND PLAN, 1971-1979

MARGARET CARY TUNKS
with drawings by DAVID LEFEBVRE

Published by the author, Margaret Cary Tunks

First Edition

First Printing • 200 • December 1996

Library of Congress Catalog Card Number: 96-90929

ISBN 1-57502-387-3

Copies may be obtained for a two dollar mailing charge from the author,

Margaret Cary Tunks
4201 Via Marina #183,
Marina Del Rey, CA 90292

Printed in the USA by

Morris Publishing
3212 E. Hwy 30
Kearney, NE 68847
800-650-7888

Beware of the many typing errors in this book-try to ignore them and just keep reading!

FOREWORD

This is my book. It is self-published; I wrote it and paid for the printing. It is a history of an important period in Seattle, and I will give it away with the hope that people will read it and resolve not to repeat this history.

The drawings are Dave Lefebvre's, and most of them headed letter-sized flyers that he planned and lettered—he alone knew how to illustrate what we wanted people to know.

The quotations from the newspapers record factual descriptions of what took place as the history developed. I could not have written the book without them.

I want to thank many people who made our part of this history from 1968 to 1980, but the reader should remember that this book is really a record of what citizens' organizations did together: CARHT (Citizens Against the R.H. Thomson); C.A.F. (Citizens Against Freeways); the Washington Coalition for Sensible Transportation (WCST); Put Transit Across; the I-90 Majority; and many other community and other citizens' organizations. I need to thank an enormous list of people but some particularly: Virginia Gunby, who I kept phoning to ask about governmental structures, transportation laws, and history; Nancy Hevly, who edited the manuscript early on—she is not responsible for all the mistakes I made years later; the people we remember with fondness—Joan Lefebvre, who was with me all the way, and Bill and Laura Dawson.

The reader will find frequent mistakes and discrepancies. The quotations from the newspapers give factual descriptions of what actually took place, and I could not have written this history without them. Capitalization differs because the Washington state statutes do not capitalize legislature, house of representatives, senate, (and senator and representative only before their names), federal, etc. I tried to use State, capitalized, for the state of Washington's highway department (later the transportation department) although the decisions are supposed to be made by the highway or transportation commissioners. The U.S. Transportation Department people capitalize Federal and Secretary, and they call the State everything, even the WSHD (the Washington State Highway Department).

Many quoted materials will seem to be too long, too often repeated, or generally uninteresting, but remember what and where they are because they may be important source materials later. I did not change any of the quoted material.

I hope that much reference material will be in the University of Washington Archives. I will leave: my *300-page Critique of the I-90 4(f) and Environmental Impact Statement*; the I-90 Moment of Truth, a compilation of the writing submitted to the State after the 1996 Hearing; the *Newsletter of the Washington Coalition for Sensible Transportation* and the many flyers used in the 1970's legislative sessions for information and lobbying. I will offer the following items to the Archives, (if they do not keep them, I will have copies of the most important): important letters; my analysis writings; flyers we used in lobbying in Seattle, etc.

Please let me know if you learn anything from this book!

SEATTLE CITIZENS AGAINST FREEWAYS, 1968 - 1980

FIGHTING FIERCELY and WINNING SOMETIMES

PART II — Page 100

THE WASHINGTON STATE LEGISLATURE
THE CITIZENS' ROLE

PART III — Page 136

INTERSTATE 90, THE MERCER ISLAND PLAN
1969 to 1980

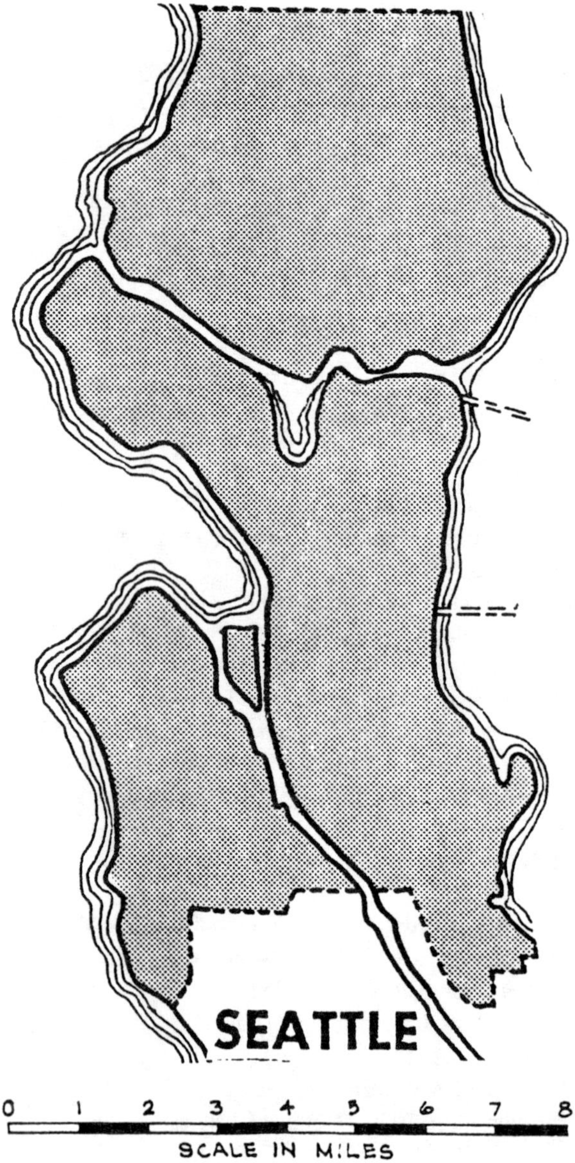
SEATTLE
0 1 2 3 4 5 6 7 8
SCALE IN MILES

PART I
TRANSPORTATION DECISIONS IN SEATTLE, 1968 - 1980

Introduction

I've been typing for two long years, and when visitors come they invariably go over to look at the piles of paper, file boxes, notebooks, and newspaper clippings—and the conversation always starts like this:

"*What* are you working on?"

I answer, "I'm writing a book."

And the visitor always says, "Oh ... that's good. What's it about? When can I read it? Can I have a copy?"

I answer, "I'm working on a history of transportation in the Seattle area in the 1970's."

The visitor's enthusiasm has clearly diminished, "Hmmm. But *why* do you write that?"

I answer, "I write it because no one else has, and someone has to."

"Oh ... well ... but *who* will read it?"

I answer, "Maybe five people will read it," (realizing that I can no longer include my husband and my mother), "but a whole lot of people should read it if they are interested in the future here. Remember, those who do not know history are doomed to repeat it."

Seattle area maps will show streets, bridges, highways, and freeways. It's fairly easy to evaluate them to see what effects they have had both as transportation facilities and as factors which set the development of the whole area. But records of often incomplete and inaccurate, and some important decisions were purely political and deliberately hidden in a barrage of misinformation. I want this book to be a record of what I learned when people were trying to bring sensible transportation to Seattle—from 1968, when we thought we could be effective, until 1980, when we knew what we had won and lost.

This history is especially important because new plans for transportation systems for the area are being formulated right now, systems which will be very costly both in money and in the effects of the construction and the traffic in Seattle. If we are to make good choices in the future, we must study the records of the 1970's to learn how decisions were made, what we got in both benefits and detriments, and measure that evaluation against what we needed and might have done then—and what we have to do now. It's important for us to find out what we did wrong in order to find out how to do it right.

A transportation expert said to me recently, "We think that public transportation in Los Angeles is 20 years behind Portland and that Seattle is 20 years behind Los Angeles." She didn't need to tell me how obsolete transportation is in the Seattle area compared to Vancouver B.C., San Francisco, and San Diego.

I really began this history in 1968 in the writing I did at the time the first events I knew about were taking place. When I began to write in 1993, I found that I had 96 cartons of materials—now winnowed down to this book and some essential substantiating materials. This history will be recorded in the major decisions as they were made and in the important decisions which were never made at all. This history will be a record of the activities of the citizens as they tried to influence those decisions. My objective is to find the relevant facts in these processes and to make them available to everyone. This history will consist of the facts as I discovered them and my knowledge of what happened from 1968 to 1980.

1. THE BEGINNING

We had just moved into a new neighborhood, in northeast Seattle in 1968, when a neighbor came to ask us to go with him to a meeting at our school where a state highway department engineer would talk about the new freeway which would be built through our area. I agreed to go, and when we walked to that meeting on that lovely evening in

September, 1968, I had no premonition that I would hear a presentation which would start me on a twelve-year, full-time fight for sensible transportation in the Seattle area.

The speaker that evening was Mr. Wallace Foster, and he showed maps of possible corridors for the new freeway—there were eight of them, labeled from "A" to "H".

He presented these astonishing facts: Seattle had adopted the Planning Commission's highway plan for the city; three north/south freeways and four bridges across Lake Washington; the whole system was planned as a package and everything must be built!

The highway he was discussing that night was to be State Route 522, (SR 522), a new road from I-405 east of Bothell, around the north end of Lake Washington and through the Lake City area of Seattle to connect to Interstate 5 at Northeast 75th Street in Seattle. I asked who would use this new highway, and *he said that 90% of the people who would travel on it would be living in North Bothell and Woodinville and that they did not live there yet!*

When someone asked how long this six-to-eight lane freeway would serve the area, Mr. Foster said that *the planned-for roads and bridges were going to be obsolete—used beyond capacity—when finished!*

Mr. Foster concluded his presentation with an announcement that a route or corridor hearing would be held in December or in January to chose one route or corridor from the eight routes. My neighbor and I were alarmed when we looked at the maps and saw that Route H would go within two blocks of our houses, but Mr. Foster had not even mentioned any adverse effects of the freeway.

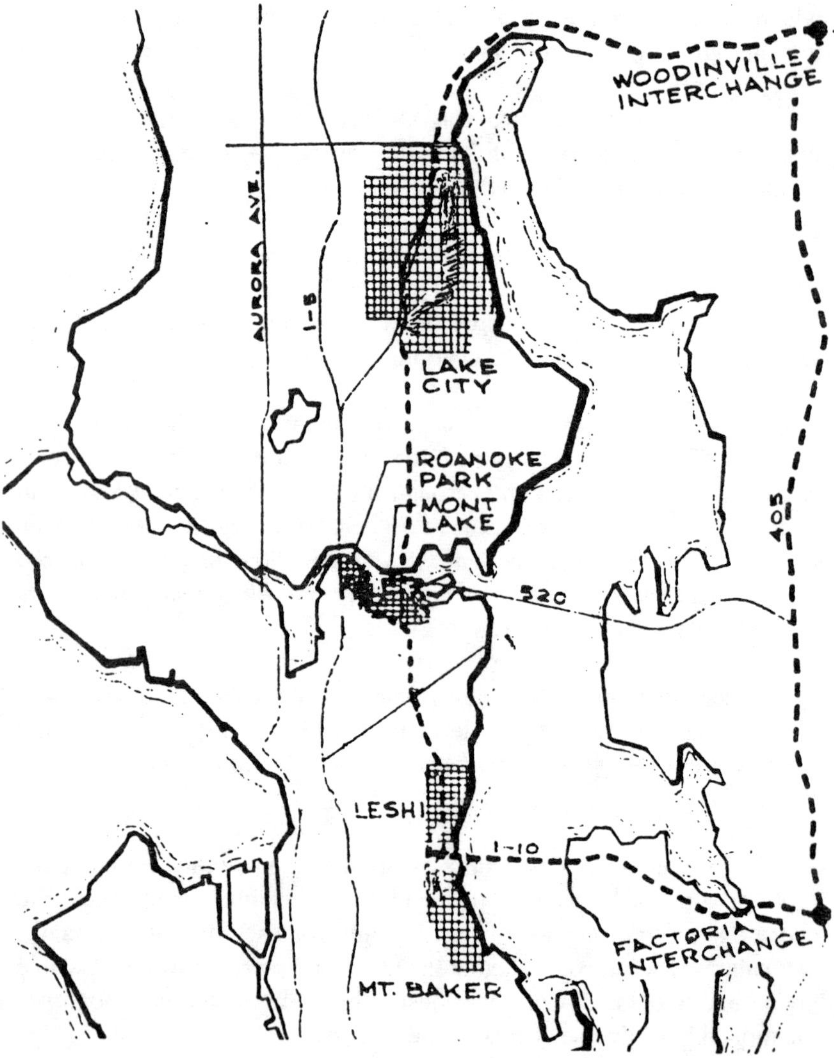
WOODINVILLE
INTERCHANGE
AURORA AVE.
I-5
LAKE
CITY
ROANOKE
PARK
MONT
LAKE
520
405
LESHI
I-10
FACTORIA
INTERCHANGE
MT. BAKER

The maps showed that suburban areas to be served by the proposed freeway were east of Lake Washington and even east of Interstate 405! I couldn't believe that these non-existent persons, way off there, might need to split our town with another enormous freeway on which they would commute, one to a car. I couldn't believe that their right to travel could be so overwhelming that our right to live in our city would not be important.

By the time I got home, I had decided to find out why we had not known about this freeway before. What had happened before I came to Seattle? What was planned? I would try to get the facts I would need to test the validity of the SR 522 freeway proposal.

The Origin of the Highway

My first discovery was that the proposed SR 522 freeway was supposed to bring traffic into Seattle to connect to both the Seattle Freeway and to a long-planned and funded project, the Empire Expressway. The Seattle Municipal Library election files showed that the Empire Expressway had first been funded by a Seattle bond issue in 1956, and again by a bond issue in 1960. The project was a north/south freeway from an intersection with Interstate 90 north to a junction with SR 522 at Northeast 85th Street; it was to be a six lane divided expressway about seven-and-a half miles long. The expressway was described in sections between interchanges; there was to be a tunnel under the Ship Canal.

In 1961, the city had authorized the acquisition of property in the corridor, and the demolition of buildings and the opposition to the Expressway began. Lawsuits were filed in 1961 as the people whose homes would be destroyed tried to get the route to go through the University Arboretum while the plant lovers wanted to protect it from invasion. The State began buying property, and the Expressway corridor was marked by the poor condition of that property. Houses had been demolished and the lots left vacant; houses had been bought and left vacant and deteriorating. "For Sale" signs in both Montlake and Ravenna communities showed the pressure on property owners along the route. As opposition grew to the Empire Expressway, someone had a brilliant idea of an easy way to make it more palatable—call it the R.H.Thomson Expressway (the RHT), after Seattle's first city engineer, who master-minded such early infrastructure as the water department and was considered an honored founder of the city.

The acquisition, demolition of property, and the construction of Interstate-5 was really damaging the city and its residents, but the elected officials and the voters had confirmed the decision to build the Empire Expressway without any consideration of the effects it might have on Seattle and upon the development of the suburbs.

The fault lay in the process by which transportation decisions were made. The planners were traffic engineers, and the process was managing traffic, not transportation planning. The projects had been selected by the city's traffic engineers, who determined the present vehicular traffic, predicted the future "need" for more highway capacity, and tried to meet that "need" by enlarging streets and roads and building bigger new ones. (We later were to call the process "moving the bottlenecks around"). The process was not transportation planning. In fact, Seattle did not have transportation planning or a transportation department.

Traffic engineering did not include any process or policies for determining the environmental effects of projects. When Mr. Foster presented the SR 522 project at Cedar Park School, he had not mentioned any adverse effects of the project because the engineers had not paid any attention to them.

One can well wonder how the decisions to build the Expressway originated. The city of Seattle is a double peninsula between Lake

Washington on the east and Puget Sound on the west. The city is narrow—at the south end of the central business district, the city is slightly over two miles wide. In 1960, when the Empire Expressway bonds were voted, the main road from Canada to Mexico was Highway 99 (Aurora Avenue in Seattle); the parallel north/south interstate freeway, Interstate 5, had been started, and it was obvious that it was bisecting the city. The Empire/R.H.Thomson project would be the third north/south freeway in Seattle, built less than a mile from Interstate-5 where it connected to the I-90 intersection. It would be only one mile from I-5 in Ravenna and Montlake.

As the "For Sale" signs on houses and the general deterioration of property moved north to mark the corridor of the R.H. Thomson along 25th Avenue Northeast in the Ravenna area, some of us in Lake City in northeast Seattle began to criticize the methods being used by the State and the City to push through the Thomson freeway—both in the way they made their decisions and in the ways they carried them out. We began to examine what had happened in the Montlake and Ravenna neighborhoods as the Empire/RHT project moved north. We had begun to realize that the traffic from that project would have to come through Lake City on some new highway. We began to realize that it was happening to us.

After the 1960 Bonds: the "Noose"

I began to unearth other records—to find out what had happened after the big bond issue in 1960. Following a tip from a friend, I found an incredible statement of Seattle's transportation policy. On March 24, 1963, the *Seattle Times* had printed a map of the "Seattle Central Area (CBD) Plan" with a headline, "FREEWAY PATTERN TO EASE TRAFFIC PROBLEM FOR SUBURBIA RESIDENTS." The development of the Plan had been paid for half by the city of Seattle and half by the Downtown Association, an organization of business and real estate people.

Freeway Pattern to Ease Traffic Problem for Suburbia Residents

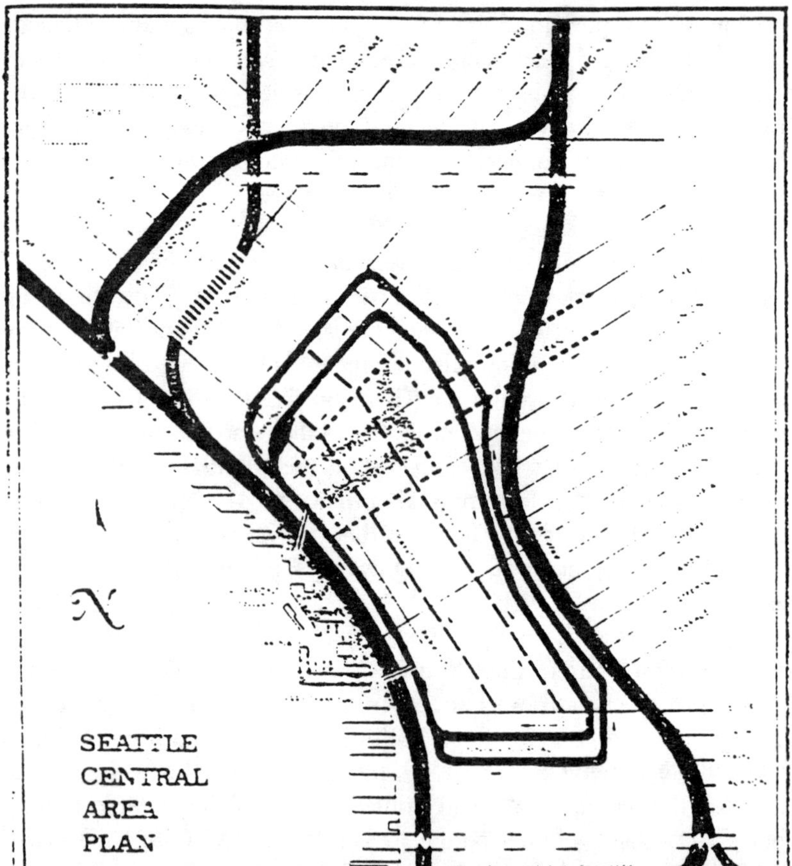

THIS MAP PLAN shows downtown Seattle surrounded by a loop of freeways. Traffic will flow easily and through-traffic w not have to enter the downtown area.

The map showed an outer freeway ring road around the Seattle Central Business District. It consisted of Interstate 5 on the east, the unbuilt Connecticut Connector (also funded in the 1960 bond issue) on the south, Alaskan Way on the west, and an unbuilt Broad Street Connector on the north, (this became the Bay Freeway, and it was also funded by the 1960 bonds). The plan showed an inner freeway loop, all to be built except on the west side of the Noose, and parking was planned between the two loops.

The *Seattle Times* explained, "This map plan shows downtown Seattle surrounded by a loop of freeways. Traffic will flow easily, and through traffic will not have to enter the downtown area.... What does all this mean to you as a homeowner? It means you can work in downtown Seattle, but enjoy the benefit derived from living outside the regular city limits. You can buy a home in whichever area appeals to you and still travel back and forth to work without difficulty."

The *Times* was merely printing the policies and goals which had led to the planning of the CBD loop, but some people noted its suburban slant and were appalled enough to call it, more appropriately, "The Noose."

The Puget Sound Governmental Conference: Federally Required Urban Planning

I found that the adopted Seattle highway plan had been confirmed by the *Puget Sound Governmental Conference Report*, which was published in preliminary form in March, 1966. PSGC had been organized in 1960 to fulfill new federal law requirements for areawide planning in urban areas as a condition for receiving federal funds for capital projects. PSGC was made up of representatives of the four counties in the Seattle urbanized area: King, Kitsap, Snohomish, and Pierce, and of the local jurisdictions in them. The study had begun in 1960-61, and it had cost some \$3.5 million by 1969: \$2.5 million in Federal Bureau of Public Roads, (BPR) funds; \$400,000 from Federal

Housing and Urban Development Funds (HUD); and the remainder from Washington State motor vehicle funds, restricted to use for motor vehicle purposes as were the BPR funds. The policy decisions throughout the study had no known origin; they were not made by the elected officials who were the PSGC. The planners were hired professionals, educated and skilled in transportation planning, but they had been controlled by the sources of the funding and by political pressure.

When the preliminary report was unveiled, the public and the media immediately rejected the plan because it was for a massive highway network designed to bring commuters into the Seattle Business District (CBD)—one editorial called it the "Design for Disaster." The Report immediately vanished; I could not find a copy in the PSGC Library, or in the Seattle Municipal Building or Public Libraries. I finally found one in the University of Washington Library, and my reading confirmed the criticism. No one in these studies had considered the effect of the massive freeway and bridge system on Seattle. The basic information had been obtained by "young men lolling in armchairs" in 1961; they had stopped each vehicle on the corridors leading into Seattle and asked the driver where the trip had originated and where it would end. PSGC then estimated how much the population in the area would increase by 1990 and predicted the number of trips in each corridor; the *Report* showed the total added highway capacity which would be "needed" in each corridor in 1990, and the Plan included these additions. There had been no mention or consideration of the adverse social, economic, and environmental effects of the planned system. There had been no consideration of transportation alternatives nor of the possibility of basing suburban development on any kind of transportation except the use of private automobiles.

Seattle Citizens Against Freeways

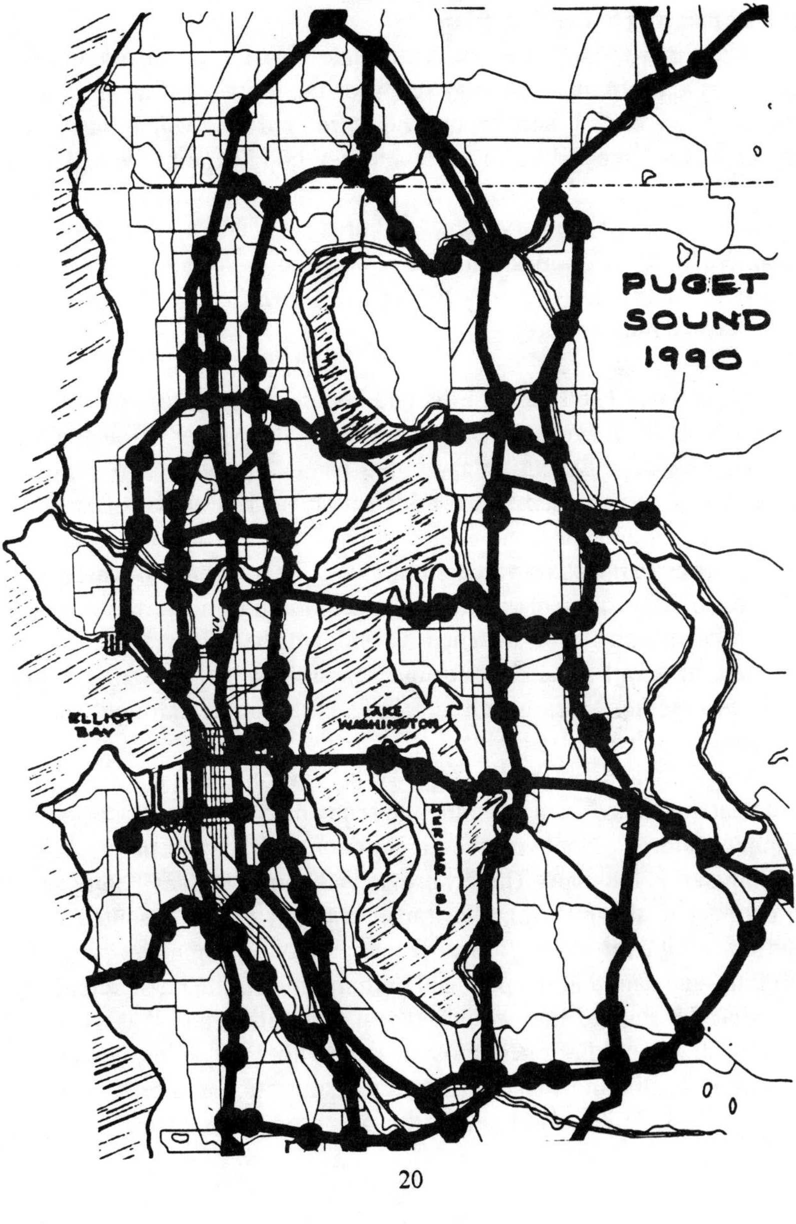

The Forward Thrust Rail Plan

The Final PSGC Report was circulated in 1967; it differed not at all from the preliminary report except for the drawing of a rail system proposed by an ad hoc group, Forward Thrust, which had been organized by James Ellis, a Seattle attorney bond expert. He had been called "the father of Metro" because he had recognized the need for and had organized the very successful area-wide effort to establish the Lake Washington drainage district sewage control agency, Metro, to "clean up Lake Washington"—to stop local jurisdictions from pouring their sewage into the Lake.

In the later 1960's, Mr. Ellis had begun an effort to obtain funds for needed capital projects in King County. The Mayor of Seattle and the King County Executive appointed some 200 people to form an organization to be called "Forward Thrust"; by 1967 a list of projects was prepared, and the bond issues to pay for them were placed on a King County ballot to be voted on in 1968. There were two categories of transportation projects in the package: Funding for arterial roads; and $385 million (to be matched by $775 million Federal funds) for the start of a rail system: one line across Lake Washington; a line from the Renton area south of the Seattle north through central business district into Ballard.

People examined the Forward Thrust rail plan and many of them said that it existed in a vacuum—it seemed to have no past and no planned future. None of the jurisdictions in the Metro area had participated in the plan. There were no viable public transit companies to connect to the rail—Seattle transit was not to be "rescued" until Metro took it over in 1972. Seattle people looked at the two proposed rail lines and said that the plan had nothing in it for them; suburbanites said that the Ballard line wouldn't help them at all and that the Lake crossing line would not help most of them either—it didn't connect to anything. Furthermore, there was no transportation authority with the power to tax, build, and operate the proposed rail system. Forward

Thrust was an ad hoc organization of business people and local leaders—it had no elected officials, no electorate.

The Forward Thrust proposal came at a climax during the anti-freeway movement in Seattle, and Mr. Ellis was supporting more highway and bridge construction in *addition* to the planned rail system. He said that the need now is obvious for eight additional lanes at the proposed third crossing [of Lake Washington] parallel to the Mercer Island floating bridge; another bridge similar in size to the Evergreen Floating Bridge, probably built parallel to that bridge, is also needed. He said that the need for a fifth span, somewhere near Sand Point in Seattle, possibly could be deferred by an accepted mass transit system.

When I tried to put the PSGC plans for highways and the Forward Thrust rail plan together to see if the rail were an alternative, a supplement, a complement to or a substitute for the highway system, I found that it surely was not an alternative, and it surely hadn't been planned as a supplement or a complement, or a substitute either.

The rail bond proposal was rejected by the voters in the 1968 Forward Thrust election.

2. CITIZENS ORGANIZE, The Background for Citizens' Actions

When I look back to the time of Mr. Foster's presentation of the Empire/SR 522 Expressway in September, 1968, I realize that I was already prepared for what I was going to try to do. I had a basis for setting a course of action.

In 1963, we had moved to Seattle from Essex County, New Jersey, where we had lived only six miles from the city of Newark. I was interested in housing problems in Seattle, and I began to notice that Seattle was showing signs of Newark's deterioration. On October 28, 1967, I had written this letter to Seattle Councilman Ted Best:

"Fourteen years ago we moved to Essex County, New Jersey. We saw the upper and middle class residents pull out of the city, we saw its housing deteriorate until it was the most dilapidated in the United States, and we saw Newark as a city of slums without hope as the unwanted poor and disadvantaged were forced into its crowded ghettos. The gap between the city and the suburbs became wider as the suburbs walled off the city's problems and continued to pour their undesirable residents into the city. We could predict what was going to happen in Newark, and it happened in the summer of 1967 in the residents' massive and damaging riots.

"I had watched one family of five move into two rooms in Newark because none of us could find decent housing for them elsewhere. When we moved to Seattle, I resolved to begin to work for better housing for the poor.

"We came to Seattle four years ago. It is a city of unrivaled natural beauty and resources in its climate, the Lake and the Sound, and its proximity to the high mountains. Its beauty was already marred by the scar of a freeway so obvious that it seems incredible that there are plans for another freeway and three more bridges across the Lake Washington.

"Seattle is only four-and-a-half miles wide at its northern boundary, N.E. 145 Street, and it is only two miles wide at Yesler Street at the south end of the central business district; it is a double peninsula, not as wide as San Francisco Peninsula. The adopted Seattle highway plan shows a city cut by freeways, bridge approaches, interchanges, and ramps that would imprison its residents in impenetrable concrete pens less than a mile square.

I wrote further to purpose, "No one should contemplate pouring another single yard of concrete for a new freeway or bridge until the most exhaustive process of finding facts, drawing conclusions, and making plans has been completed."

[I wish I could report that my letter changed Mr. Best's views in the slightest, but it didn't—he never acknowledged my letter, and he always voted for whatever had been planned, long ago.]

In 1967, Seattle already showed the symptoms of the Newark decay: The middle class was moving into the suburbs (especially away from the proposed freeway routes); the rents for the disadvantaged and poor living in the Central District were 150% higher than in the rest of the city while Newark similar rents were only 125% higher—one might conclude that our ghetto housing was already twice as scarce as Newark's. Stores were moving out of the downtown retail section.

I thought that the questions to be resolved in Seattle then were: What had the highway planners and the elected officials thought would be the effect of these planned routes on Seattle? Was I right in believing that these planned projects would be harmful? Had the planners and the elected officials concluded that the benefits to the suburbanites outweighed the detriments to Seattle? Or had the elected officials ever considered the effects of their choices?

In 1967, I was working with two communities in the Thomson corridor, Ravenna and Montlake, that had already suffered damage from the proposed Thomson freeway. Bill Frantilla, president of the Ravenna Community Council, asked me if I would do a bibliography of marterials available on the subject, "The Freeway and the City". By the middle of the summer I had spent four months of my free time in the University of Washington Library, I had typed up a notebook full of references and quotes, and I was hooked on fighting freeways in Seattle.

I joined CARHT, Citizens Against the R.H. Thomson, which had been started by the President of the Montlake Community Club, Maynard Arsove. The history of CARHT is well-documented by Peggy Johnson in her excellent Seattle University paper, "The Montlake Community and the R.H. Thomson. Case of a Successful Freeway Fight." It is available in the local libraries, and I will try to have my copy shelved with this history.

CARHT immediately made two decisions of great importance, and we were to follow them throughout:

"We would not try to change the routes of the freeways in order to protect our areas because we were against freeways wherever they might be placed;

"We would follow this resolution passed on June 4, 1968:

"We oppose use of the R.H. Thomson route as a major traffic corridor.

"We are against the proposed Third and Fourth Lake Washington Bridges.

"We support a comprehensive mass transit system.

"We would oppose any further urban highway construction in the Seattle area until a comprehensive mass transit system has been authorized by the voters."

On March 17, 1968, the *Seattle Times* published a map showing "Proposed Thomson, I-90 routes." The reporter wrote, "This map shows the proposed routes of the R.H. Thomson Way and Interstate 90. No date has been set for completion of Thomson Way, and the completion of the I-90 link between South Bellevue and Interstate 5 in Seattle has been moved back to 1973. A route hearing that established a 'corridor' ranging from two to five blocks wide has been held for the Thomson segment between Northeast 85th Street and the north shore of Union Bay. A joint study is under way of the tube crossing of the bay. The Arboretum interchange has been constructed from south of the Bay to East Calhoun Street, but the project is tied up by a court suit. A route hearing has been held on the section from East Aloha to East Empire Way. An access hearing to fix the Thomson route from Lake City Way northeast to Union Bay is pending the outcome of a proposed urban-design study of the entire Thomson alignment. The entire I-90 corridor has been established in route hearings. Access hearings probably will be held this fall on the Seattle section of I-90, at which time the Thomson interchange design will be considered."

L.I.F.T., Lake City Improves for Tomorrow

In the spring of 1968, the Lake City Chamber of Commerce announced that they had formed a community organization which would meet regularly at lunch time to discuss plans to improve our area, Northwest Seattle. I went to the Chairman to say that many residents were gone during the day, and I asked him to consider changing the meeting time to evening. He refused so abruptly that I realized that they had intended to exclude everyone who didn't belong to the Chamber of Commerce.

Obviously Lake City needed a real community group, and obviously we were going to have to organize our own. I had read about the University of Washington's Bureau of Community Development, which was working throughout the state to help people determine the essential changes they needed in their areas. The process used was: determine the borders of the area with which people identified; formulate a questionnaire to find out what changes people wanted; call on every household to get answers to the questions; and read and classify the answers and submit them to committees for analysis and a written report. A public meeting would then be held, where the reports were read and accepted or rejected by vote.

I telephoned Andrew McCall, the Director of Field Services for the Bureau, and asked him if he would speak to a meeting in Lake City if I got together a group of interested people. He asked me, "Who's with you?" I answered truthfully that I had to call the meeting myself because I was new in the area and didn't know anyone yet, we needed an active citizens' group, and I thought that if the people were given an opportunity to talk about the problems in Lake City, they would come. Mr. McCall lived in the area and agreed to speak to us.

I had flyers printed, and I delivered them around town. People did respond, 78 attended the meeting on the evening of May 28, Mr. McCall outlined the process for us in an excellent speech, and the group voted to ask the Bureau for help. A man I did not know, Oscar Verlo, stood up and nominated me for chairman and himself for vice-chairman of the group, and the group so voted. At the next meeting he suggested and we adopted the name for the organization, L.I.F.T.—Lake City Improves for Tomorrow. We met through the summer to write our questionnaire, and by fall we were ready to begin to canvass the residents.

In September, the Washington State Highway Department announced the planned freeway throughout Lake City. I concluded that our state and city were planning transportation backwards, and I wrote this outline of what I thought the process should be to clarify my own goals.

Transportation Planning for People
by Margaret Tunks, September, 1968

I

"Transportation is the movement of goods and people. The systems needed for this movement are determined by the process of recording the places where the movement begins and ends. The greatest demand for urban systems consists of the movement of people between the place where they live and the place where they work.

"When people are already employed in one place and living at one place, the designing of a transportation system is easy, but it usually also is not necessary—obviously a system already exists to take people to work. Transportation planning must begin, then, with the determining of the places of residence and of employment of the people who are not in the area yet—the people who are not working at a specific place or residing at a specific place.

"The places of residence and employment of the people who are not here yet will be determined by a definite process of choice. Their opportunity to live at a certain place and to work at a certain place will depend upon earlier decisions made to put residences and jobs at those places. Each time residence, education, business, recreation, and employment sites are determined or buildings are placed, land use is being determined—a definite choice has been made. These choices constitute land use plans for the area they encompass.

"Therefore: Land use for any given area must be determined before transportation planning can begin. Where land use has not been determined, a process for the best choice of land use should be carried out.

II

"Transportation and land use planning should be carried out for an area which is geographically determined and of sufficient size to encompass the area of growth for the foreseeable future. The Federal Departments of Housing and Urban Development, Health Education and Welfare, Agriculture, Commerce, Interior, Transportation, and even Defense are now requiring the fulfillment of certain urban area planning requisites as conditions for qualification for federal funding. Plans for area-wide systems of transportation and water and sewer lines, for land use, open spaces, and law enforcement must all be submitted to the Federal Government by 1971. The area-wide planning agency should be a voluntary association of governmental bodies within the area fairly and equally represented; it should have the full sanction of the state, and it should have its own and uncommitted sources of funds.

"Therefore: Land use and transportation planning by any governmental body within an area should be consistent and coordinated with area-wide planning.

III

"Land use plans can be expedited and maintained by the planning of and control of the lines of communication between places in the area. These lines of communication are: the utilities—the water, sewer, electric, and gas lines; and the various transportation facilities—sidewalks, streets, highways, airports, transit systems. These communication systems must be planned to carry out the desired land use plans—to determine and maintain the sites to be used for each purpose. The insistence of both the federal and state governments on this area wide planning will be effective in strengthening area planning agencies, and incompatible smaller utility lines and transportation systems will not be built.

"Therefore: Transportation systems and utility lines should be planned to expedite and control land use choices made for the area.

IV

"Transportation planning will involve a study of all the alternative choices of transportation for a certain desired system or corridor. This study should distinguish the various transportation choices according to their effect on the land uses of the place where the system begins, where it ends, and on the areas it transverses. The study should distinguish between the choices on the basis of cost and benefits to the users, to the public, and on the basis of convenience and travel time. The studies must be made fairly and by persons with no bias or commitment to any one of the possible choices or alternatives possible. Funding for the studies should be from sources with no particular commitment to any particular choice of transportation system or alternative, and neither studies nor plans should be made by any persons interested in executing any particular plans. All policy decisions in the study and planning process should be made by elected officials responsible to the people with full disclosure of every step of the process.

"Therefore: Transportation planning should be based upon studies made by unbiased personnel and financed by uncommitted funds; all policy decisions in the study and planning process should be made by the elected officials, with full disclosure to the people.

V

"The choices of transportation systems cannot be made in a climate in which only one alternative can be studied or funded. Transportation systems greatly overlap—each system is dependent upon others. Too great an emphasis on one type of transportation by funding it to the exclusion of every other type will result in an overbalancing of the system. Similarly, no one type of transportation can be planned or built without planning supporting systems."

"Therefore: All transportation user funds in a given area should accrue to one fund regardless of source, and this fund should be used for all the transportation systems of the area, dispensed through a single agency."

VI

"CITIZEN PARTICIPATION IS NEEDED AT ALL STAGES OF THE PLANNING PROCESS."

"Principles for Citizen's Participation in Decisions, (Plans for Capital Improvement Projects of Governmental Bodies)

Seattle Citizens Against Freeways

1. Citizens should be involved in the processes before the objectives and goals have been determined.

2. Citizens should have the power and the duty to extend the study scope of the projects so that all related information and issues may be considered.

3. Citizens should have the power and the duty to enlarge the group of citizens participating to include all who can help with the process or need to enter into it. Participants should form one group in order that everyone can work together to reach conclusions which will be common to all.

4. Citizens should be brought into the process early. They should prepare a realistic time schedule for their participation and should be allowed to follow the schedule.

5. The governmental agencies should provide citizens with essential facts, answer their questions without deception, and make all reasonable efforts to provide requested information. Citizens should have their own staff.

6. The participating citizens and governmental agencies should work out together a method of publicizing the details of the on-going process. This method should include public meetings, media publicity, and circulation of citizens' reports.

7. Citizens should set up their own process for reaching decisions which should include finding the relevant facts, determining the issues, delineating and evaluation of alternatives, and reaching a conclusion by voting in order to get a consensus.

8. The citizens should write an entire history of the consideration process on which their conclusions and consensus are based; they should also write a summary of the essential parts. These two writings should be copied and disseminated by the governmental agency which will make the final decision, to the news media, to the participants, and to all interested persons requesting copies.

9. The officials who will make the final decisions should meet with the citizens during the process. They should meet with the citizens

after the written report is submitted and then begin the process of trying to reconcile citizens' views to theirs.

10. Public hearings on the proposal must include full testimony and the full report of the citizens who participated in the planning process."

3. CITIZENS AGAINST FREEWAYS IN ACTION

C.A.F.'s Program on SR 522 at Jane Addams School

When Mr. Foster presented the SR 522 project at the September, 1968, school meeting, some of the people working in L.I.F.T. began to discuss the threat of the freeway through our area and how we could oppose the project. We thought that the Lake City people should be organized to fight the freeway, but if we were to act through L.I.F.T., we would be prematurely focusing on just one issue before the process of determining all the needs was completed.

We got together to talk about forming a new organization. We were: David and Joan Lefebvre; Gary and Laurie Ness; Jack and Lois Brooks; Jean Godden; and I, Margaret Tunks. We decided to form an organization and that it would be called Citizens Against Freeways (C.A.F.).

We were immediately forced into action on November 13 when the Seattle newspapers announced that a corridor had been selected for a "NEW SIX LANE BOTHELL FREEWAY LINK." W.C. Bogart, district highway engineer, said, "because of the spiraling traffic needs from the expected population explosion in the area, he hoped to call for route hearings before the end of the year." (*Seattle Times*, November 13, 1968, page 1.) This announcement was particularly revealing because in it Bogart announced that a route hearing to select a route would be held *after* the Highway Commission had selected the route and that the project was being built for the suburbanites who didn't live there yet.

We hastily called a meeting—each of us asked Lake City people we thought would be interested, 24 people came, and we passed these motions:

"C.A.F. should call an open public meeting as soon as possible to disseminate information about the proposed Thomson-Bothell Freeway in order that the people in our area could be prepared for their participation in the route or corridor hearing in January.

"We should select an attorney to speak at the meeting to give us the information we would need about the federal laws and administrative regulations under which the hearing would be held and how we could participate in the route-selection process.

"A committee of four should set the time and place for the meeting and ask the speakers to come. The meeting would be held the week of December 9. Margaret Tunks was to be the acting chairman of C.A.F.; Laurie Ness volunteered to be treasurer and collected $15."

We hoped to get CARHT's participation in and co-sponsorship of the meeting we were going to hold, and Jean Godden and I went to talk to CARHT President Maynard Arsove, and Vice President Bill Frantilla. They thought that we had set the meeting date, December 11, too soon; they said we didn't have time to plan such a meeting and to get out enough notice to the public, and besides, people were too busy to come to a meeting so close to Christmas; they said we should change our meeting date to some time after the New Year. We told them that since the hearing date was supposed to be in January, we couldn't possibly delay giving the people the information we thought was needed before the hearing. They then promised that CARHT would help us, but that CARHT would not co-sponsor the meeting.

C.A.F. immediately went to work: We had to begin a really effective campaign to get the people to the meeting, to get the essential publicity; we had to decide what we would try to do at our meeting, the speakers we should ask and what we would ask them to talk about. We decided:

— We would ask Robert Beezer, an attorney well-experienced in administrative law, to explain the state and federal hearing processes so that people would know what the guide rules were and what their rights were under the laws.

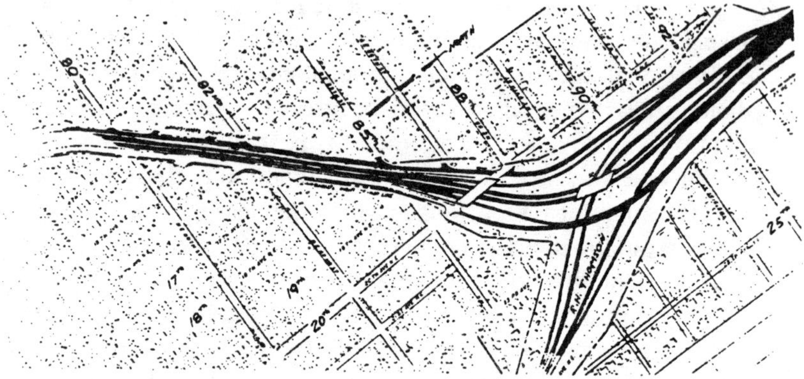
R.H. THOMSON

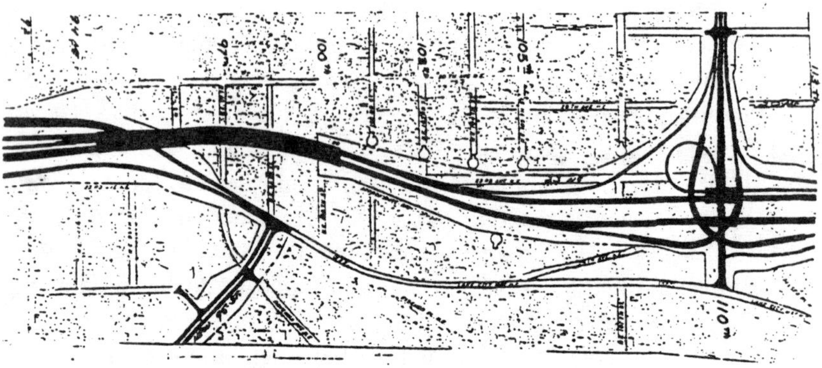
100th
105th
110th

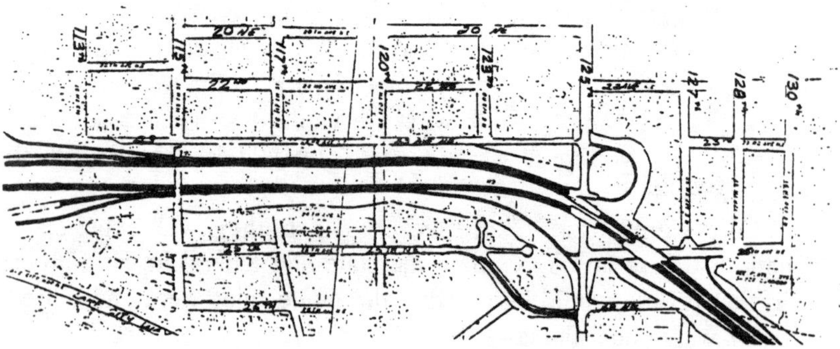
20 NE
120th
125th
127th
128th
130th

— We would ask Brock Evans, a spokesman for environmental groups, to speak on damage caused by freeway construction and use.
— We would ask Bill Frantilla, the vice-president of CARHT, to talk about the Thomson Freeway project in Seattle and to describe how it is part of the SR 522 proposed project.
— We would ask Sam Wood, editor of the publication *Cry California* and consultant to California Tomorrow, a non-profit organization dedicated to the preservation of California, to tell us that freeways had been stopped and how the people in San Francisco had successfully quashed the Embaracadero Freeway there.

Everyone we asked to speak agreed to come!

We really worked hard and fast preparing for the meeting. We posted notices in store windows and on telephone poles. We prepared information flyers and mailed them to lists of people we got from other organizations. We got notices in all the newspapers.

We had a bonanza when someone surreptitiously lent us the Highway Department's large publication of September, 1968, "The Advance Planning Study State Route 522 Junction I-5 to I-405" done by VISTA, a consulting firm. It had complete drawings of the proposed freeway copied over aerial photographs of the entire corridor, and we copied the Lake City pages to distribute them at our meeting so that people could tell exactly where the six or eight lane freeway would go through their neighborhoods.

The night of December 11, 1968, was dark and stormy, but people came to Jane Addams School and just kept coming until all the seats on the main floor were filled. (I didn't think about checking the balcony audience). Jack Brooks presided; the speakers were both interesting and informative and exactly provided the basis for our future decision-making and action. Hundreds of people signed our mailing lists.

Then, on December 28, the Seattle newspapers published an announcement by W.C. Bogart, Seattle District Highway Engineer, that the Bothell SR 522 hearings originally scheduled for late January, would be indefinitely postponed! His explanation was amazing

Margaret Cary Tunks

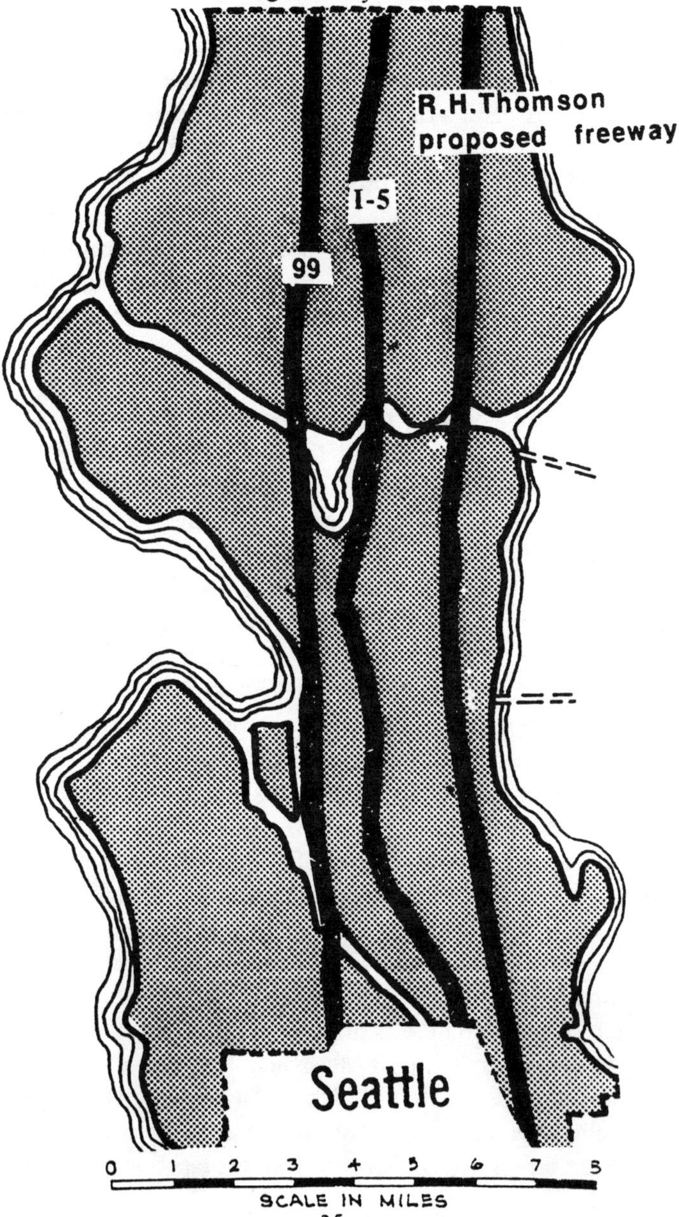

because he gave the impression that the State was going to meet with the local people to try to work out problems which were causing their anxiety. But he never did schedule any public meeting anywhere that we knew of.

On December 31, we sent, "NEWS and NOTICES FROM C.A.F.—CITIZENS AGAINST FREEEWAYS" to our members, and we announced the next meeting to be on January 6. Again it was a dark and stormy night; I had another appointment and was a half-hour late. I walked into the ground-floor rooms of the Lake City Presbyterian Church where the meeting was to be held, and no one was there. Someone came down to tell me that the meeting had been moved upstairs to the chancel, and when I got there I found that all of the pews were filled! It was our first C.A.F. meeting, and at least 250 people came. We had started to promote intelligent transportation planning in Seattle, the meeting ended with some really good questions, and we were pleased.

With our immediate crisis over, we began to realize that the "design team approach" for SR 522 that Bogart had announced on December 29, 1968, was all too similar to what Seattle was doing to try to build the R.H. Thomson. The elected officials of Seattle, especially Mayor Braman, had decided to plan a new, more palatable Thomson project by hiring firms to devise methods to conceal the RHT and convert it into a "parkway" by building it below grade and surrounding it with plantings. On October 8, 1968, the city had signed a $700,000 contract with the Okomoto/Liskamm firm to explore "beautification" possibilities. The city also hired the Worthington firm to plan an underwater crossing from the Arboretum to the landfill northeast of the stadium—in a tunnel with three artificial islands in the Lake to hide ventilation outlets. I looked at their drawings and called it the "Bali Hai" portion of the RHT, after the fictional South Pacific Island.

Employees of the Okomoto/Liskamm firm began to hold public meetings at which they seemed to be salesmen, presenting designs for the "RHT Parkway," but they said they were working to determine whether or not the RHT should be built and if so how.

The Tudor Report On Lake Washington Bridges

In December, 1968, the Tudor Engineering Company had published a report on work done under a contract with the State. It was titled: *"Legislative Reconnaissance and Feasibility Report Lake Washington Bridge Crossings Parallel Evergreen Point Bridge North Lake Bridge."*

This report was an incredible doozy—it found the "needs" for and proposed an additional Evergreen Bridge and two parallel bridges across the north end of Lake Washington from Juanita Park in Kirkland to Matthews Beach Park in Seattle.

On April 30, 1969, the *Seattle Times* published this explanation: "A consulting firm's report prepared for the State Highway Commission gives an up-to-date version of the latest official thinking on the often-studied matter of Lake Washington Bridges.

"In addition to recommending a parallel span beside the Evergreen Point Bridge, the report envisages still another crossing on a north Lake Washington route...

"All in all, though, the North Lake Bridge would be part of a new 9-mile east-west expressway extending from a couple of miles north of Redmond to Aurora Avenue North, just south of Washelli cemetery.

Tudor said that the timing of the bridge construction would depend upon the transit implementation schedule—if only "limited bus transit" were developed, the need for the North Bridge could be delayed five years.

The accompanying map and description showed that the Windermere University areas were "spared" the bridge to Sand Point because of their "anxiety" at the prospect of having a big expressway cut a swath to the central freeway and Aurora Avenue through their neighborhoods. "Madison Park has been spared, too, by the shelving of an alternative bridge route that would have entered Seattle near the Seattle Tennis Club—to tunnel under the hills to join the central freeway at the critical Mercer Street interchange. However, the reaction of neighborhoods along the North Lake route is yet to be heard."

Seattle Citizens Against Freeways

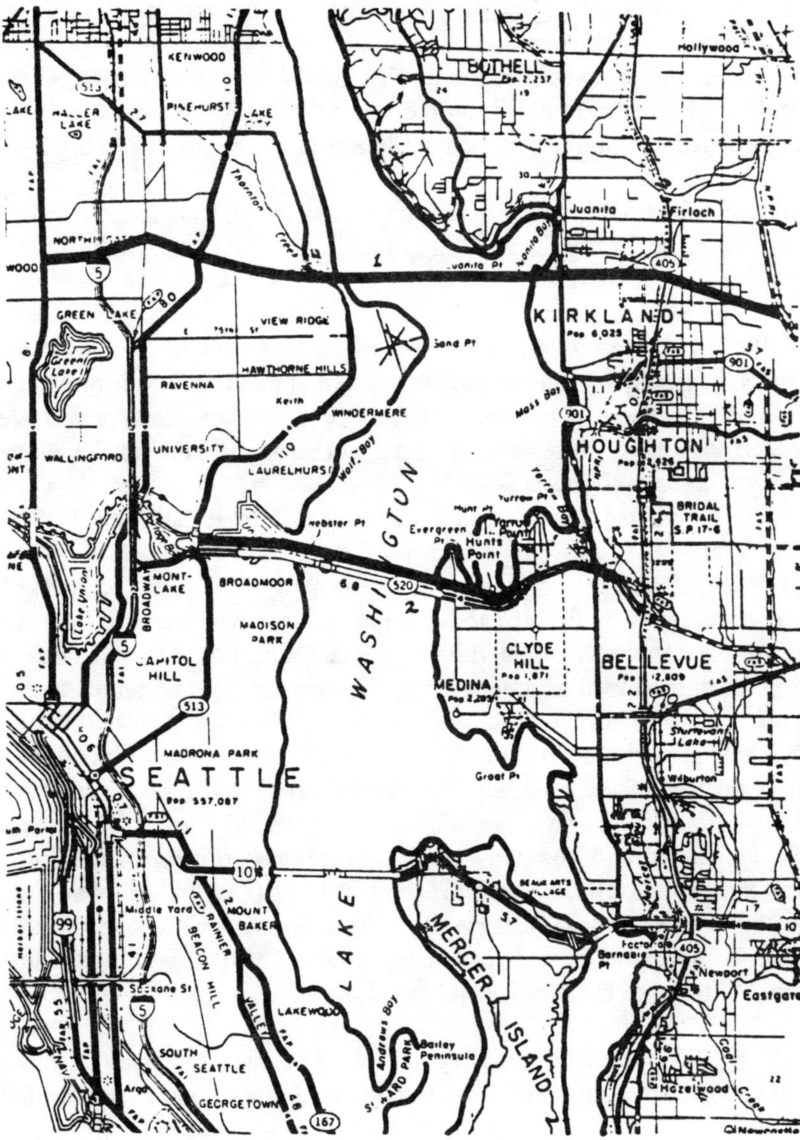

[I can only say, "How true, how true!" for the people in Lake City hadn't known of the plan.]

The map showed that the north cross-lake freeway bridge would be built from Juanita Beach on the east side into Matthews Beach, our city-owned swimming and boating beach in Lake City. The highway would take land from the north side of the Nathan Hale High School athletic field en route to a connection to Interstate-5, (already gridlocked at Northeast 95th Street), and on to Federal Highway 99, Aurora Avenue in Seattle.

The plan was ridiculous. Tudor would send all the cross-lake traffic into Seattle to funnel into existing highways already used far beyond capacity. Tudor warned that building the R.H. Thomson would *not* help, because it was predicted to be full when completed. We found also that Tudor was planning not just one but *two four-lane bridges to be built in sequence.*

We obtained a copy of the Tudor report to find that projects were taking park and school lands because they thought that would solve the problem of people's objecting to their taking homes and businesses. But Congress had decided to save the nation's parks by passing two laws, NEPA, the National Environmental Protection Act and Section 135 of the Federal Highway Act, both containing the same section known as "4(f)" which prohibited the taking of parklands for federally-funded projects unless the Secretary of Transportation signed a statement that there was *"no feasible and prudent alternative and that all possible measures were taken to minimize harm."* The North Bridges faded into oblivion—because there was no capacity in Seattle for the proposed bridge traffic?—because all parts of the plan were prohibitively costly?—because of the sure opposition from the Seattle neighborhoods to be destroyed and damaged?—Because the Juanita and Matthew's Park Beaches had to be saved?

But like everything else on any existing plan for bringing more Eastside suburbanites into Seattle, the north bridges plan keeps coming back.

The proposal to add a bridge parallel to SR 520, the Evergreen Point Bridge route, or additional lanes to the existing bridge, has never really died, and the battle against it continues despite the very obvious fact that there is no place for more Evergreen Bridge traffic to go in Seattle—I-5 is still gridlocked and so are all the streets in the University and Mercer Street areas.

The Tudor Bridge Report should be embalmed as a monument to the demise of the single goal upon which the ridiculous proposals were founded—predict the "needs" for commuters of the future in their private cars, draw lines across parks, lakes, school grounds, and residential districts for the "essential" highways and bridges which must be built to provide capacity for those cars, turn those lines into highways, and those "needs" are met!

4. THE BEGINNING OF THE END OF THE R.H. THOMSON EXPRESSWAY

The Okomoto/Liskamm Contract on the Thomson

In January, 1969, I found time to work on the R.H. Thomson riddle: Could the Okomoto/Liskamm firms be paid with 1960 bond funds if part of their work entailed studies to determine whether or not the RHT should be built? I went back to the Seattle Municipal Building Library's big book of clippings about elections, where we had found information about the 1960 bond issue and the Empire Expressway; and sure enough, those bond funds could be used ONLY FOR IMPROVEMENTS AS DESCRIBED TO THE VOTERS which included the Empire Way projects, now called the R.H. Thomson Expressway or Parkway. The funds could *not* be used for any work which would not result in the construction of the project.

I went to the city clerk's office to look at the monthly records of work done as submitted by Okmoto/Liskamm and found this statement at the top of each one, "For planning and urban design services incidental to the final alignment and location of the Thomson Way in the corridor extending from SSH 1 K. [SR 509, at the south end of Seattle] to Lake City Way NE, [the new name for the Lake City part of the Bothell Highway, SR 522]." The contract between O/L and Seattle repeated these words.

Our April 1969 C.A.F. newsletter, *The Interchange*, said:

'RECENT CITY COUNCIL ACTION:

"On March 21, the C.A.F. Steering Committee discovered that the City Council was to vote, on March 24, for a $3.2 million appropriation for the Okomoto/Liskamm firm to perform and direct "studies incidental to the establishment and final alignment of Thomson Way." The contract was to be financed with the state highway funds and with money from the 1960 Thomson bond issue. We thought that the $3.2 million contract looked almost exactly like Okomoto/Liskamm's contract of October, 1968, which authorized the firm to determine <u>how</u> the Thomson would be built (<u>not if it should be built</u>). It seemed to us that the work they were to do under both contracts was intended to try to sell Seattle the Thomson.

"C.A.F. members' campaign that weekend encouraged the City Council to postpone their vote for a week to allow the public to make statements at a meeting on March 31, 1969. To our surprise, the Council came in that day with a substitute request—not $3.2 million for the study, but $25,000 to give to the firms which were to make the study so that they could tell us how they would spend the $3.2 million!

"After the Council had discussed the appropriation, I stood up to say that since the Okomoto/Liskamm contract was for work "incidental to the final alignment and location" of the R.H. Thomson, and since the work was being paid for with Empire Way bonds voted for the Empire Way in 1960, the city could not use the bond funds for any studies which might result in a decision not to build the freeway. Councilwoman Lamphere asked City Engineer Morse if this were true, and he said it was, to the absolute amazement of everyone there, Council and audience alike."

Again quoting *The Newsletter*, "The statements and argument which followed this request led to a hung vote by the Council, 4 against 4, and the $25,000 appropriation lost (and the $3.2 million with it). Engineer Morse warned that the Okomoto/Liskamm contract should then be canceled if no decision to continue on with the Thomson was made (and the contract was voidable by the City with 10 days notice), but O/L continued to work and to be paid with Thomson bond funds. This is how it was done."

"Right after the Council turned down the $3.2 million for the study of the R.H. Thomson, and then the $25,000 for the study on whether to do a study, City Engineer Morse came up with another fiction. He wanted a "Task Force" appointed to begin "The Eastern Corridor Study" from the I-90 Bridge north to NE 85th Street in Lake City. It had been adopted from a plan by Okomoto/Liskamm and was obviously the old RHT study in camouflage. Here's how it was done:

"At the March 31, 1969, hearing, C.A.F. had asked for a transportation study of Seattle; it was obvious that these attempts to implement obsolete highways should end and planning for sensible transportation should begin. The C.A.F. Board wrote this letter to Mayor Miller:

"We have just received a copy of your letter to the City Council recommending that a task force be appointed to make a study of the scope and cost of an approach to the question of whether or not the design of the R.H. Thomson Parkway should proceed. We well agree that such basic determinations for the provision of transportation facilities in the east part of the city should be made. We think, however, that no one part of the city can be studied independently of the whole of the city and that the limited study you propose on incomplete facts and conclusions would not be acceptable to Seattle residents.

"We enclose our suggestions for proceeding with such a study. We believe that it would take several years to make such a study which would include all of Seattle if not the whole region. We think that much of the work has already been done in piecemeal planning which, although it was not done by Seattle for Seattle, can be re-evaluated and used. We think that Seattle planners could rather speedily reach the stage in the process where a valid transportation plan for the city could be proposed and adopted.

Transportation Planning for Seattle, 1969
[submitted by board of Citizens Against Freeways]

A.

"The current comprehensive plan for the City of Seattle is based on an assumption of an infinite capacity of land to provide for any likely uses which might arise in the foreseeable future. Our future now indicates than there is more demand for such land space on our isthmus than there is land available. We must move from an assumption of abundance to a realization of scarcity.

"We must therefore reconsider the entire comprehensive plan for the City of Seattle, identifying the areas in which comparative freedom to plan remains. In regard to the entire city, we must determine the finite population of various kinds which the isthmus can accommodate, the general locations of their employment and residence, and then connect them with a transportation system that leaves us a city and gives us general principles on which to act in planning and zoning matters. We must reconsider—determine what we have left which will yield to planning to provide the best urban environment on scarce land.

"After we are well into our study, we are willing to consider a system of connections which will provide the needed intra-city population movement in such a way as to preserve both convenience of necessary movement and the amenities of a city whose future has arrived now. Neighborhoods, as population and other pressures develop, should not be changed as a matter of expediency, but should be developed and redeveloped in relation to the entire community goals. A process that does not continuously consider community goals may lead to decisions which will be capricious or arbitrary and destructive to individuals.

"In execution of these objectives, certain principles should be borne in mind:

"(1) As far as possible, the reconstruction of a comprehensive transportation plan should be carried out by a group of experts employed full time by the city and free from the routine short term problems of the planning department.

"(2) Neither they nor any experts hired on a temporary basis to assist in the process should have any stake beyond production of the general planning structure in order that none will be distracted from any type of planning by a possible vested interest in executing the plan.

"(3) The city of Seattle should fund the planning process. Since transportation, in particular, will involve only a small part (Seattle) of a much larger area, we should, after our limitations and recommendations are known, try to convince the other cities, towns, and counties in this area to participate in the planning with Seattle, sharing both the funding and the responsibility for it. Under no circumstances should any part of the planning be funded from any immediate source other than the cities, towns and counties involved in the planning process; the participants may use funds received for planning from such neutral sources as uncommitted Federal or foundation bodies, but no source of funds can have any interest in the execution of any part of the plan.

"(4) Although all previous plans may be studied (and they should be), the planners should review all previous studies and plans from the standpoint of how special interests may have influenced the plans; indications of such interests may be found in studying the funding of the previous plans, the given parameter of the plan or study when it was begun (what they were told to do), and the goals of the body for whom the study or plan was made. The planners must study and analyze these previous plans most carefully, evaluate them honestly, and decide what additional information they will need to make their own study.

"(5) Citizens of Seattle can participate in this planning process mainly by providing a proper climate for the City Council to establish and conduct such a planning process. Full and honest disclosure of every part of the planning process will enable the citizens to provide the proper support to the City Council in order that the planning process should proceed in a climate free from possible outside pressures; an informed citizenry can see that the City Council has the proper financial support for such a process. It is vital that the disclosure to and education of the citizens follow the process as it proceeds in order that the final plan, when it is finished, can be accepted by the citizens.

"(6) The work should be undertaken with the realization that its outcome will be determinative of the character of the city for work and living. In short, the undertaking of a transportation plan for Seattle now will determine whether paleontologists of the year 3000 will find an abandoned city or a healthy, urban society."

The Parking Commission

On April 29, 1969, Mayor Miller said that the Council refusal to appropriate money for a study of the Thomson project had effectively set it back until a comprehensive study of balanced transportation could be made. He said, however, that the road was not dead as long as it remains on the comprehensive plan. He got permission from the Council to appoint a task force to work on the formation of a Seattle Parking Commission.

At the same time they were discussing the Eastern Corridor Study, the Mayor and the City Council exposed their priorities for transportation planning in Seattle by establishing a Parking Commission and paying for it from the city's general funds. The three appointed commissioners set a salary of $24,000 per year for a director, fixed an annual budget of $69,000 for the year, and the Council approved it. (Note that they never did use general funds for the Eastern Corridor Study—1960 Empire/Thomson bonds were illegally used for that, like the Okomoto/Liskamm R.H. Thomson activities).

C.A.F. sent a telegram protesting bitterly to the elected officials:

"The City of Seattle should not establish such a Parking Commission because:

"1. The creation of another autonomous commission is not good government. Power and responsibility in the public domain must rest with our directly elected officials, not abdicated to an unresponsive commission with a narrow, specialized focus of interest.

"2. The creation of a separate parking commission would further fragment Seattle's transportation planning.

"3. The creation of a separate parking commission runs counter to strongly emerging environmental concerns for the quality of life in Seattle ... The critical decision as to whether Seattle will develop into another Los Angeles or into a city more like San Francisco or Vancouver, B.C. is really the result of many small actions.

"4. The creation of a parking commission would represent a further city subsidy of the automobile and a setback for public transportation. This commission would use city funds for the acquisition and maintenance of parking property and for the planning for development and financing of parking lots. This sort of a city subsidy of the automobile would be both a blow to public transportation and a step in committing Seattle to a Los Angeles-type of sprawl development."

Neither Mayor Uhlman nor any of the Council members ever answered our telegram. We never received any reaction to our protests.

The Parking Commission hired engineer Victor Gray to study parking, and his studies are available in the Seattle Public Library. His basic planning turned out to be almost the only transportation planning the city did. He prepared an inventory of all the vacant lots in the Central Business District that could be used for construction, predicted that high-rise buildings would be built on them, and *people who worked*

⁄ould want to drive to work and park in downtown Seattle. Th. mostly what we have today because the elected officials of Seattle refused to provide for adequate transportation studies and plans (particularly for commuter trips). Victor Gray's work became the actual land use plan for downtown Seattle! The City's traffic engineers planned transportation, implementing their goals and policies to provide more street capacity for vehicles. This is how Seattle missed the great opportunity to manage the commuter car demand when I-90 was approved and built.

[I find it difficult to believe that any city on this planet is planning to pour more cars into its center, but Seattle is still moving backwards. In 1994, the voters of Seattle decided to again allow vehicles on Seattle's only promenade area on Pine Street. In 1995, the City Council and Mayor voted for councilman bonds (no vote by the people required) to build downtown parking garages including a 1,500 car parking garage in the middle of the shopping area, almost over the place where the bus tunnel below turns north. This is surely evidence that the elected officials of Seattle do not intend for the tunnel to work well as a substitute of private car transportation.]

The Eastern Corridor Study and Okomoto/Liskamm

The Mayor's Task Force for the Eastern Corridor Study consisted of four council members, and one person each from the mayor's office, the engineering department, the planning department, and the Model Cities agency. We began to be anxious and sent this telegram to the city officials on August 6, 1969:

"THE TASK FORCE APPOINTED BY THE MAYOR TO MAKE DECISIONS CONCERNING A TRANSPORTATION PLAN CANNOT ACT UPON ANY ADVICE GIVEN BY PROFESSIONALS UNLESS THESE PROFESSIONALS ARE FREE TO CONSIDER ALL ALTERNATIVES, INCLUDING WHETHER THE R.H. THOMSON SHOULD BE BUILT OR NOT. OKOMOTO/LISKAMM IS CURRENTLY WORKING ACCORDING TO A SUBSTANTIAL CONTRACT FOR A STAGE

IN THE BUILDING OF THE THOMSON. IF THEY MAKE ANY PROPOSALS, STUDIES OR PLANS WHICH MIGHT RESULT IN NOT BUILDING THE THOMSON AS STATED IN THE CONTRACT, THEY WILL BE BREACHING THAT CONTRACT."

We never got any acknowledgment of that telegram, either.

When the Council announced the study plan on August 14, it considered ONLY the proposal outline prepared by the firm of Okomoto/Liskamm, and the study also would be done by that firm.

From the August, C.A.F. Newsletter, *The Interchange*:

"We have seen the proposed study which will be presented to the public at a hearing on September 8, and we will get clarification on several of the items. If you would like to help us worry 'till then, here are some ominous points to consider:

"(1) The study is being managed by the same people in city government who were dedicated to building the R.H.Thomson.

"(2) It will be done by Okomoto/Liskamm, apparently under a modified version of the same contract they had before, which called for them to establish the final alignment and location of the Thomson.

"(3) The attitude of these two groups toward the study may be contained in a report from Okomoto/Liskamm to the city engineering department in which they say, 'We have been refining our ideas regarding strategy and participants for any possible revision of the study, in order to generate sufficient community participation and support currently lacking in the present program.'

"(4) Although the new study is supposed to be impartial and unbiased toward a solution favoring construction of the Thomson, that freeway is still on the Seattle Comprehensive Plan, and the city at present has no plans to remove it."

Okomoto/Liskamm continued to be paid with money from the 1960 bonds—$58,206.43 for work done in May, June and July. On

July 27, I had written to the Council, "Their bills list the hours each employee worked and what the work was. I am familiar with their contract, and there is no doubt but what they are doing, what they contracted to do—determining the final alignment and location of the Thomson. I also wrote that it is presumed that the tunnel studies being done by the Worthington firm are of the type which are done AFTER the decision to build the tunnel is made, and note that Worthington was paid $26,924.54 in May and June from the Thomson funds.

It is interesting to note that the Okomoto/Liskamm firm was paid with 1960 bond funds until it was hired in the fall to work on bus transit plans to supplement the rail transportation proposal for the 1970 Forward Thrust bond issue. All the payment they had received from the 1960 bond funds was illegal, and the City should have canceled its contract after the Council refused to authorize spending any additional Thomson funds in their March 31 vote. The payments for the so-called Eastern Corridor Study were also illegal.

A report was finished, but nothing ever came of it. The Eastern Corridor Study faded into oblivion, quietly.

The Transportation Coordinating Committee

By the summer of 1969, many of us were having difficulties in obtaining the information we needed about transportation. I telephoned Ben Fiegenbaum, a lawyer who had worked on the Omnibus Budget lawsuit and in CARHT. I told him that we needed an area-wide citizens' organization to meet to exchange information, and he agreed to act as chairman if I were to organize it. I scheduled the first meeting in July, and people from thirteen organizations came.

We named the group the Transportation Coordinating Committee (TCC), and we decided that we would not act on any issues as an organization, but that organizations could present items at meetings to be sent to other organizations.

The TCC originally met monthly, with extra meetings when necessary, and it became a lively medium for keeping up with what was happening. The chairmanship changed from time to time. When information began to be more available due to the requirements of new federal laws, TCC met sporadically, but it remained an available vehicle for exchange of information.

"Thomson Way Project Tottering"

The November 23, 1969, *Seattle Times* published a story by Dave Suffia under the headline: "Thomson Way Project Tottering." Suffia wrote, "Seattle's long-suffering proposal to build the R.H. Thomson Way may just be on its last legs.

"A survey of five City Council members reveals that all of them, a majority of the council, will not vote any funds to the $100 million north/south project now or in the future.

"Their stand makes it probable that no further action will be taken on the Thomson Way proposal until a comprehensive study of transportation is made for Seattle and vicinity.

"Councilman Don D. Wright said he will vote against any money for the Thomson because of concern for the Seattle neighborhoods that will be disrupted and Seattle residents who would be displaced. ... Wright said that the Council must consider the needs of Seattle residents and neighborhoods, not the needs of East Side residents who congest Seattle streets and then go home to suburbia after work.

"Councilwoman Phyllis Lamphere said she is not convinced we need the R.H. Thomson. She said, however, she wants very much to see a comprehensive study of Seattle's transportation needs undertaken. She said more weight would be placed on environmental factors involved with highways than had been given in past studies. Mrs. Lamphere said the Thomson is dead until the Council is satisfied it has been properly planned to serve people in a way they want to be served.

"Councilman Sam Smith said he would continue to vote against the $3.2 million request. However, he would vote for a comprehensive study. 'The Thomson is not dead yet,' Smith warned. 'The present situation will just make it more likely to die. One more negative vote and the State Highway Department may just throw up its hands and give up,' he said.

"Councilman Charles Carroll said, 'We realize that traffic has to be moved, but the time has come to quit cutting swaths through neighborhoods and disturbing peoples' lives.' He said that the present proposals on the Thomson probably are dead because of citizens' and Council's concern over them.

"Councilman Tim Hill, who also voted last time against the $3.2 million appropriation, was unavailable for comment. However, he had indicated he opposes the Thomson until further is completed on an area-wide basis."

5. THE FEDERAL HIGHWAY HEARINGS

The Right to Information

The State Highway Department announced that federal hearings would be held on I-90 in North Bend on December 3, 1969, and on SR 522 in Bothell on December 17, 1969. I immediately went to the district highway offices to get the information I would need for my participation in the hearings. I didn't want to make any mistakes about the facts.

The Federal Policy Procedure Memorandum (PPM) for highway hearings, records and approval spelled out our rights precisely:

"B. Conduct of public hearing: ... (3) At each required corridor public hearing ... alternatives studied by the State Highway Department shall be made available."

I went to the State Highway District Office that would hold the hearings on the North Bend section of I-90. To my utter amazement, the people at the highway office refused to let me see anything at all! I went back, with a copy of the Federal PPM, and this time I was allowed to stand at the counter and look at some papers. I was greatly hampered because the counter was flush to the floor, there was no place to put my feet, and it was very difficult to stand there, sideways, trying to read and take notes. The third time I went to the District Office, they did let me sit down at a desk, but they stationed a man to stand three feet behind me to watch what I did! I read for several hours in a complete, professional, large book with colored illustrations. Surely it had been available to be passed around for some time.

The North Bend I-90 Hearings

In November, 1969, the Washington State Highway Commission announced that it would hold hearings on the North Bend portion of I-90 in the town of North Bend on December 3, in a notice that said that there would be a route or corridor hearing in the morning and a design hearing in the afternoon, both being held under the Federal rules in PPM 20-8, the administrative regulations for hearings on federally funded highways. The announced procedure was scary, for it was so clearly contrary to the regulations stipulating that a corridor or route hearing "(1) is held *before* the route location is approved and before the State Highway Department is committed to a specific proposal" and that a highway design hearing "is held *after* the route location has been approved, but *before* the State Highway Department is committed to a specific design." [Emphasis added.]

It was obvious that the State was totally ignoring the rights of the people at the North Bend hearing to record their information about options in the highway route selection because the state already had a design for a specific chosen corridor. Early that year I had written about the new PPM in *The Interchange*, the C.A.F. newsletter:

"*NEW FEDERAL LAWS - A NEW ERA!* Until January 17 of this year, the federal government required state highway departments to fulfill only one requirement for the benefit of citizens—to notify them of the so-called "corridor" or "route" of the road on which federal funds were to be used. This was called a hearing, but the citizens had no right to speak, to present any statements or materials, to have a record made, or to be heard. The new PPM [20-8] for public hearings and location approval changes all this: It 'provides for a two-hearing procedure designed to give all interested persons an opportunity to become fully acquainted with highway proposals of concern to them and to express their views at those stages of a proposal's development when the flexibility to respond to those views still exist.'

"The PPM sets forth 23 social, economic and environmental effects which must be considered and these are 'the direct and indirect benefits or losses to the community and the highway users.' Each step of the process is stated—notice of the public hearing is now to be changed from 30 to 40 days; any person can participate; a record is kept; the highway department must analyze all information submitted, etc. The PPM is four pages of extremely fine print, all of it boiling down to a much better deal for citizens against freeways."

The North Bend announced procedure was scary also because we knew that the State had scheduled a corridor hearing on SR 522 in Bothell, and we didn't want them to try to use this illegal procedure again. I decided that I must go to the North Bend hearing with the federal laws and regulations in hand and protest the State's procedures.

I went to my husband to get help—he had taught administrative law before he became dean of the law school. I asked him for advice, and he said, "You can do it yourself—you can read."

I tried to get help from Professor Bill Andersen, who was then teaching administrative law, and he said, "It's easy, you can do it yourself."

Thus, I began a decade of what became a very time-consuming but extremely interesting avocation: finding the facts of an issue; finding the applicable laws and regulations and applying them to the facts; writing and speaking clearly and concisely on what I had discovered.

The little town of North Bend was bisected by the Interstate-90 highway to Snoqualmie Pass, the lowest pass through the Cascade Mountains. Traffic on the highway mushroomed with the greatly increased use of automobiles and trucks, with even more traffic during the holiday, hunting, and ski seasons. The town had installed a traffic light right in the middle of the business district so that people could get across the busy highway, and this stop created the famous North Bend bottleneck.

I found that the State's chosen route went south of the existing

I-90 route and that the principal alternatives to it were routes south of town. The townspeople and elected officials had not chosen any route, and they held different opinions about the alternatives. Some people wanted the route in the middle of the town—my friend who had an office in North Bend assured me that if the State put the highway out of town, the business section would die. Some people wanted the highway south of town; others wanted to get rid of the highway forever.

I was an absolute stranger to the people of North Bend, who gathered for the hearing the cold winter morning of December 3, 1969. After State Highway District Engineer Roberts had made his introductory speech, I stood up and said, "This hearing is not a bona fide hearing to determine the corridor as set forth in the notice because the Highway Department has already announced its intention to hold a design hearing on a portion of a specific corridor on the same day. The Highway Department is already committed to a specific corridor, the citizens have been denied their rights as outlined in the PPM, the purpose of the hearing cannot be fulfilled, and no corridor hearing as defined in the PPM can be held. Even if the Highway Department should state today that it will not have the scheduled design hearing, this corridor hearing should not continue because by its acts prior to today, the Department has shown that it is committed to a specific corridor and has led the public to so believe."

Then I asked if this were the corridor hearing on this section of I-90 held under federal laws. When the answer was yes, I said that this hearing was illegal because it did not conform to federal law, and I read the PPM sections pertaining to corridor hearing. Immediately the audience began to object, "Sit down! We want our hearing!" And then Mr. Roberts proceeded with the hearing as if I had never spoken.

After lunch, the same procedure was repeated with Mr. Roberts' introduction to the design hearing on the already-chosen corridor of I-90. I objected again. When the hearing was over, I handed in my written comments, went home, and wrote to the State Highway Commission and to the Secretary of the U.S. Department of Transportation to tell them of the illegalities of both hearings and that neither a route (corridor) or a design could be approved.

The *Seattle Times* story on December 4, 1969, about the hearings said, "Speakers also questioned whether yesterday's combined hearing on design and route of the freeway was legal and whether they defeated the intent of federal rules designed to give residents a voice in plans before they were complete. District Engineer Roberts said after the meeting that he wished now that he had not had the hearings combined."

On December 11, the *North Bend Record* reported, "The materiality of the hearing itself, and even its legality, were left in doubt as a result of statements by Department of Highway's engineers and a number of critics.

"Highways District Engineer D. I. Roberts opened the hearing by announcing that a cross-town freeway route was officially selected back in 1957, when he said, a corridor hearing was held, and the route formally determined."

"Before Roberts had got even that far, however, Mrs. Margaret Tunks of Seattle, an active foe of freeways that cut across towns, interrupted him and charged that the Wednesday hearing was illegal because it had been announced as a corridor and design hearing. The State can't, under Federal rules, combine the hearings, she said."

"Mrs. Tunks' interruption disturbed both Roberts and the audience. Both encouraged her to sit down and shut up, and she did, rising later at the proper moment to read the PPM and to get her objections in the record."

"At the end of last Wednesday's state hearing on the route and design of the North Bend freeway bypass, two North Bend officials charged that the state had not fully informed local government on the possibility of routes other than the State-supported cross-town route."

My letter to the Secretary of the U.S. Department of Transportation, objecting to the hearing, was answered by Bureau of Public Roads official Bartlesmeyer. He said that the State had held a route or corridor hearing in 1957, that the corridor had been selected then, and that the State had not needed to hold another. His letter completely ignored the contradictory facts—the State that had decided to hold the December 3, 1969, hearing and could hardly now say that it wasn't necessary!

This U.S. Transportation Department reply was important because from it we learned that there was no federal review of the State's conforming with federal laws. Ever afterward, when we wrote objections to the U.S. Department of Transportation, it would always merely confirm the State's action. The federal officials never intended to review the decision the State had reached, regardless of any change in circumstances or in the federal laws, administrative regulations, or relevant court opinions interpreting them.

The final choice of the route of the North Bend portion of I-90 was to be far in the future. There was another corridor hearing, with federal approval of that corridor. Later, there was another design hearing.

The I-90 route finally chosen went quite a bit south of North Bend, along the foot of the hills. The business people in North Bend had wanted the corridor to run down the center of town so that they would get highway-users as customers. I never knew if they decided (when peace and quiet was restored to their town) that the procedures and the decisions were right, after all.

To my knowledge, the Washington State Highway Commission never repeated the North Bend hearing errors.

6. THE SR 522 HEARING, DECEMBER 17, 1969

Available Hearing Arterials

Our district highway office refused to give us any information about SR 522 until just days before the hearing, and then they gave us the absolute minimum—the things they knew we already had: The VISTA book (we had copied the route for the people at our December 11 meeting the year before), and drawings of the corridors which had been given to the media and published.

What were they *not* showing us? What were they doing that we didn't know about? When we finally got access to a few records (which I am sure were only a small part of those filed), I made these notes; it was information we should have had all along:

"March 7, 1969, meeting of Seattle school officials with Schlater from VISTA. The purpose was to review the status of the Advance Planning Study for SR 522. VISTA is investigating a shift in the line from NE 115 to NE 145 Streets to take the Lake City School.

"This investigation was undertaken as a result of the City of Seattle's request to the State Highway Department." The school officials apparently agreed to consider phasing out Lake City School if given five years' notice to rebuild in Victory Heights. No mention was made of the destruction of the library across the street and the community center building next to it or to the play field adjacent to the school. No citizens had been consulted about any of this. [Note that the State is referring to the part of SR 522 which would be built in Lake City contradicting their later statements that they are concerned only with SR 522 at Bothell.]

September 16, 1969, Citizens Committee of Bothell, appointed by the Mayor, meeting with representatives of the State Highway Department. "System #2, the main Bothell corridor, would be contracted for first (within four years); in System #3, this portion would be constructed by 1980." On page five, the "facility would probably be converted to six lanes." On page six, the State disowns the comments made by the design team relative to mass transit. I interpreted these statements to mean that Lake City would be waiting in limbo from six to eleven years for the freeway to start; and the Highway Department was in no way going to plan any highway with transit!

Fran Tilse, a Highway Department employee, noted, "several citizens on the committee [what committee?] were worried about the environmental impact of a four lane freeway with a 46 foot median, which could be expanded into a six lane freeway."

October 28, 1969, letter from Bogart by Bell to State Director of Highways, Andrews attention Rinehart: "SCOPE OF PROJECT. The proposed systems from the Advance Planning Study, Interstate 5 to

Interstate 405, commence at NE 75th and Interstate 5, proceed in a generally northerly direction to Lake Forest Park, and then turn easterly to Bothell and Interstate 405 and SR 202."

October 31, 1969, to Bogart from Rinehart, "If, after this action [by the city of Bothell], District Management cannot assure that the municipal and county governments involved will not oppose the recommended corridor at the hearing—then the hearing will be canceled." [The County never approved; Councilman Ed Heavey said so at the hearing. The State had a letter from one DeSpain, a county employee (who was actually the King County Engineer), which they passed off as County approval.]

And finally, I found a wonderful writing by Prof. Earnest Barth, who had been appointed to a three-man committee of "consultants" on SR 522. His analysis of what should be done was absolutely accurate, but I never have found any trace of its use. "Six General Criteria that should be evaluated in realizing the impact of a freeway:

1. Define the level of integration of the local neighborhoods and families, the commitment of residents to one another, and the commitment of residents to neighborhood goals.
2. Define local community communication network and the effects of the freeway on it.
3. Examine the levels of anxiety in the community relative to the freeway, i.e., concerns over the danger to children, noise, etc.
4. Examine the impact on the scale of the neighborhood.
5. Define local involvement and the flexibility left to the people, land values taken into consideration, sense of contribution by the people.
6. Examine the effects on the local school system."

Preparation for the Hearing

The announcement of the corridor/route hearing on the north end of SR 522 was shocking because it confirmed our beliefs that the State Highway Commission intended the absolute minimum disclosure required by federal laws. When the newspapers announced the postponement of the hearing in late December, 1968, after our meeting at the Jane Addams school, they quoted District Engineer Wesley Bogart's statement about the postponement. "It was ... because of the many, many more objections to the project than we had anticipated. This is a clear signal that we must present better and more complete explanations of our planning to make it clear to residents we do not intend to ram through them or run roughshod over them." By December, 1969, the State had dallied along for a year, and, as far as we could find out, they had never met with any people. Furthermore, the project seemed to have been changed from the thirteen-mile connection between Interstates 405 and 5—it was now only a cut-off of the town of Bothell, and the State obviously was trying to limit the hearing and the comments to the proponents in Bothell.

We had not been allowed to inspect the Highway Department's materials relevant to the project and the hearing. The date had been set to discourage public participation—on a week night, one week before Christmas, in the middle of the winter. By law, the public was supposed to have ten days after the hearing in which to put comments on the record, but because of the holidays, we could have only five mailing days.

C.A.F. prepared this information sheet and tried to distribute it widely along with explanatory flyers:

"SR 522, the Corridor hearing at Bothell on December 17, at 7 P.M.

"The R.H. Thomson road is a fiction; it exists as an oddity crafted by a most peculiar funding fiasco. The Thomson is the middle of a road, its trifurcated tail being three roads—SR 900, SR 167, and SR 509, all due to become expressways, with its head curling around the north end of Lake Washington as SR 522. The Thomson became a named section of this road (although it is only the middle) because of the fact that the Thomson section of the road alone will be financed half from funds from the city of Seattle and half from funds arriving through the State; it has the questionable distinction, along with the Bay Freeway and the Connecticut Viaduct (the Cascade Freeway), of being a state road financed half by a city; City Engineer Morse says that he knows of no other state roads in the whole United States which are so funded. Seattle's share will be about $85 million. ... The State intends to get its half of the money from Federal road funds. ...

"The head of a worm or snake is after all the most important part—what happens to the head is bound to affect the middle portion. SR 522 then becomes the most important part of the road of which the Thomson is the middle, and as Wallace Foster, State Highways Design Engineer, said in September, 1968, 90% of the traffic arriving in Lake City on the proposed SR 522 will come from the area beyond Woodinville and North Bothell, and THEY DO NOT LIVE THERE YET.

"They still do not live there—drive out to see the contrast between the massive Woodinville interchange of SR 522 and Interstate 405 and the open country around it. Mr. Foster said also that the road would be full when finished, and the new SR 522 would pour four additional lanes of traffic into Bothell Way between Bothell and Kenmore. The Highway Department certainly anticipates this bottleneck and can be expected to continue with its plan to build MORE of SR 522, six lanes beginning at 80th NE in Bothell, eight lanes at NE 145th Street, the Seattle city limits. This traffic was originally supposed to go on to I-5, the present freeway, in a long access road between NE 95th and NE 75th [streets in Seattle], BUT, we all know the present freeway is full and that the Director of Highways has proposed metering traffic to keep it off I-5 in the north end.

"Six lanes of traffic, then, is SR 522 when it arrives at the middle section of the road, the R.H. Thomson, at NE 95th Street in lake City—the NEW road, plus four lanes of traffic on the existing Lake City Way. As someone from the Bothell City Council says, 'Six new traffic lanes, Seattle. What do you do with it?'

"The December 17, hearing on SR 522 at Bothell is all important to Seattle. Surely we must decide if we want the entire animal or if we can build up the Woodinville area with rapid transit using our newly proposed NE 145th Street rail line."

the problem:

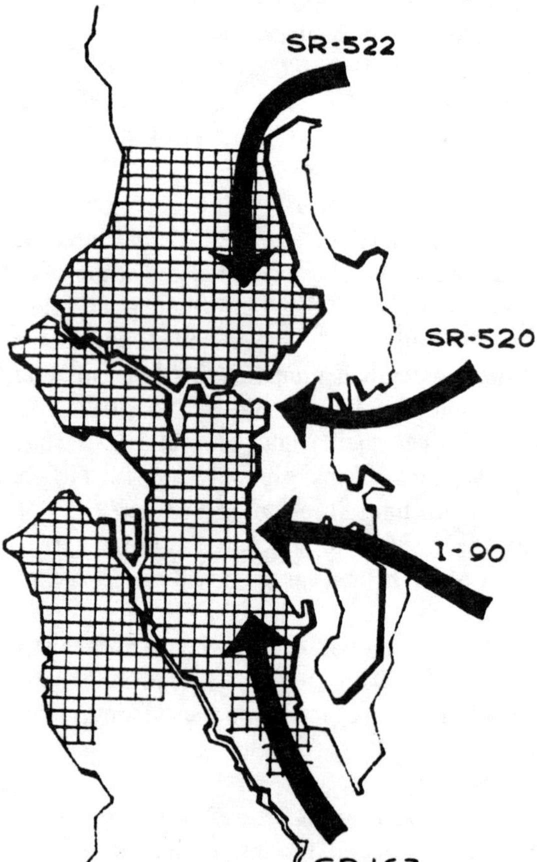

Seattle Citizens Against Freeways

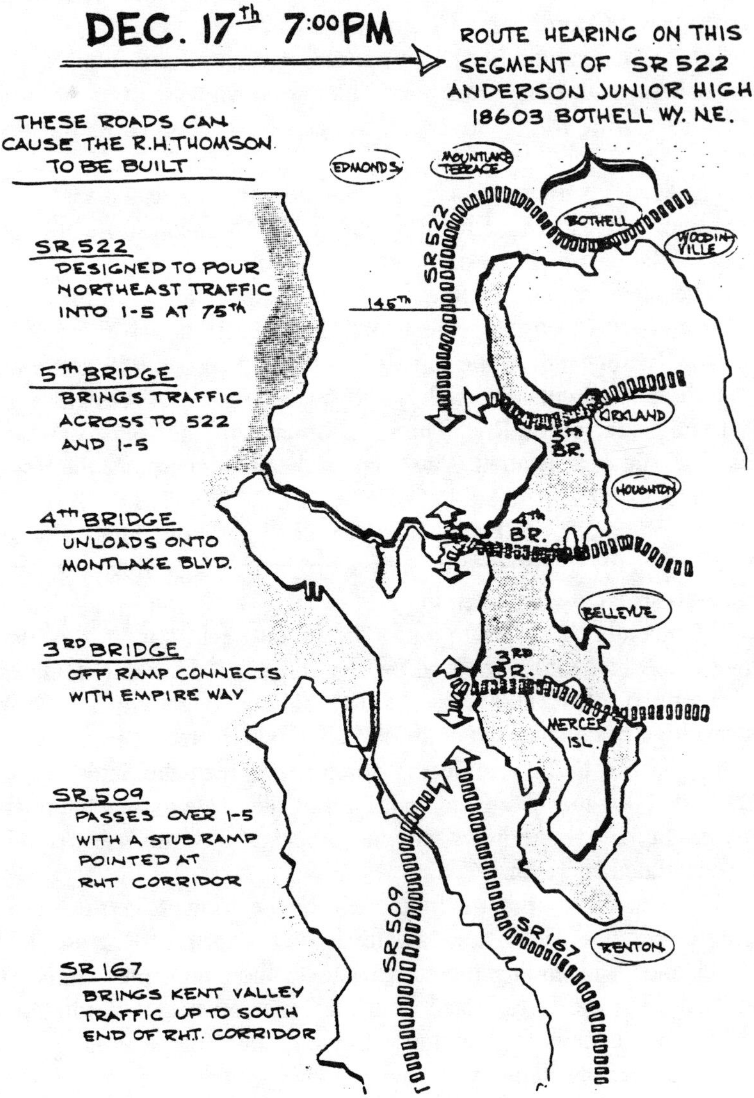

DEC. 17th 7:00PM
ROUTE HEARING ON THIS SEGMENT OF SR 522
ANDERSON JUNIOR HIGH
18603 BOTHELL WY. NE.
THESE ROADS CAN CAUSE THE R.H.THOMSON TO BE BUILT
SR 522
DESIGNED TO POUR NORTHEAST TRAFFIC INTO I-5 AT 75th
5th BRIDGE
BRINGS TRAFFIC ACROSS TO 522 AND I-5
4th BRIDGE
UNLOADS ONTO MONTLAKE BLVD.
3RD BRIDGE
OFF RAMP CONNECTS WITH EMPIRE WAY
SR 509
PASSES OVER I-5 WITH A STUB RAMP POINTED AT RHT CORRIDOR
SR 167
BRINGS KENT VALLEY TRAFFIC UP TO SOUTH END OF RHT. CORRIDOR
EDMONDS
MOUNTLAKE TERRACE
BOTHELL
WOODINVILLE
SR 522
145th
KIRKLAND
5th BR.
HOUGHTON
4th BR.
BELLEVUE
3RD BR.
MERCER ISL.
SR 509
SR 167
RENTON

I mailed this note to C.A.F. members and the members of the Transportation Coordinating Committee:

"From the secretary's desk, it appears that we all are going to have a real Charles Dickens Christmas with the enactment of the famous *Christmas Carol*, Mr. Bogart as Scrooge, the rest of us as the poor Cratchit family, and State Highway Director Andrews and assorted others as Marley's ghost and crew. In the next three weeks there will be three major moves toward building the R.H., Thomson in Seattle, and we will all be the unwilling participants in unrelished roles.

"The play has, so far, three acts. The first is the corridor public hearing on SR 522 on the evening of December 17 at *seven o'clock* at Anderson Junior High in the town of Bothell. Scrooge will argue that this is the Bothell cut-off which the town badly needs. We will argue that it is the start of the R.H. Thomson which will add four to six new lanes of traffic onto Bothell Way, forcing the construction of the rest of the Thomson. THE REST OF THE CAST OF THE PLAY MUST BE THERE—YOU CRATCHITS. The place will have five hundred seats, and we must fill them; sign a special list at the door if you want to speak—speakers will be taken in order of their signing in.

"Meanwhile, back at Olympia, the prelude will have taken place today, Dec. 15, with Mr. Andrew's request to the State Highway Commission for $120,000 for studies on how to get traffic off the fourth bridge [parallel to existing SR 522, the Evergreen Bridge], if the Thomson is not built. He seems not to have read the Tudor report which stated that the Thomson would not be adequate to take the traffic IF it were built. Mr. Andrews' announcement of this move seems to be more calculated coercion.

"On January 6, the next act will be performed in the design hearing on SR 509 across the Duwamish River (north of Boeing Field) over I-5 and dead ending there en route to the Thomson. Since I-5 cannot take the traffic expected, this road is another arrow pointed at the RHT. More about this hearing with your New Year's cards.

"TCC meeting January 5, see you in Bothell Dec. 17. Merry Christmas?"

On December 15, both Seattle papers published articles about the hearing. *The Seattle Post Intelligencer* published an article under the headline, "CLASH EXPECTED AT BOTHELL FREEWAY HEARING," reporting on an interview with C.A.F.'s David Lefebvre. "First, he sees the bypass as a stepping stone toward eventual construction of the Thomson because of the additional traffic it would dump into North Seattle.

"Second, he opposed all three proposed routes on grounds that building more highways in urban areas will use up land needed for other purposes and perhaps pre-empt future rapid transit system routes. He said, 'We can't have a highway system expanding and a rail transit system trying to be built because the two compete for the same rider. If the highway is built, it will preempt some of the best routes for rapid transit.'"

The *Seattle Times* article had the headline, "HEARING ON BOTHELL BYPASS LOOMS AS STORMY SESSION." The *Times* quoted Bogart's statements that the time of the hearing was set by Bothell's city officials, the Citizens Advisory Committee, and civic groups, while the records showed no such approval and only a single letter which objected to the hearings' conflicting with the annual Christmas concert. Bogart said, "This certainly is no plan to try to force construction of the R. H. Thomson Expressway, which is not a state highway, but a City of Seattle facility which may be abandoned by Seattle officials." But we had city records that showed the State and the city shared the costs of the Thomson, that the State's share would be paid from federal highway trust funds, and that the State had been spending large sums of money on property acquisition in the Thomson corridor in Montlake and Ravenna.

On December 15, the Seattle City Council passed a resolution, the mayor concurring, "That this Council urges the Washington State Highway Department to postpone any decisions on any segments of proposed State Route 522 until the mayor's study committee on eastern Seattle transportation needs completes its report." This was the elected officials only participation in the hearing, and it must have been the last time anyone pretended that the eastern corridor study had any value.

The SR 522 Hearing, December 17, 1969

It was dark and stormy—one of the darkest nights of the year. The hearing was supposed to start at 7 p.m., but it began a half hour late. It was recorded by a court reporter and run by District Engineer Wes Bogart, who infrequently spoke in whispers with a young man sitting beside him. We presumed he was seeking advice.

I wrote just after the hearing: "As we expected, the State paid little attention to the requirements for a federal corridor hearing; immediately afterwards I wrote these objections:

"The hearing was held at an inconvenient time, so close to Christmas that the 10-day time for submission of materials after the hearing was cut to five days because of legal post office holidays.

"We had been intimidated at the hearing by a State photographer who used a large camera and flash exposures at close range to photograph people who were expected to object to some part of the plan.

"The State divided the participants into three categories and took them in that order to speak: the officials in favor of the proposal; the people known to favor the proposal; the people who might object to the proposal, with those who lived along the RHT beyond the hearing segment called to speak last.

"At 10:30 p.m., I stood up to ask for this hearing to be adjourned and reconvened later. Mr. Bogart did not acknowledge my request. The hearing was closed at 1 a.m., December 18, when my name had been called and I was at the microphone. Many names of people who had left had been called. Many of us, still there, were not allowed to speak. The court stenographer was kept on his chair, with no relief at all, and he became terribly tired."

The *Seattle Post Intelligencer* published this article by Susan Hutchinson on December 19. "THE BOTHELL FREEWAY: A CONCRETE PISTOL,

"Staying up until 1 a.m. may be fun if you're with a beautiful blond, but it's quite another thing when sitting in a Highway Department hearing.

"Yet about 100 people did that Wednesday night to express their opinion...

"It was a highway hearing marked not only by controversy over the highway proposal itself, but also over the procedure of the meeting.

"It was a meeting that showed the Highway Department has learned a few lessons in its recent battles with angry citizens, but still displays some ignorance of human feelings.

..."The Highway Department went home thinking it had conducted a good hearing. A spokesman, Fran Tilse said: 'We think people will really look at this. Everyone got a chance to speak and they all got a lot of things off their chest...'

"Yet the people who did stay until 1 a.m. to testify were not happy about it. Ralph Morrison of Spare the Sammamish commented 'People have a right not only to be heard, but to be effectively heard. We were trying to present our case to the people of Bothell who are undecided. By the time we got to the mike at 12:20, many had left.' [Mr. Morrison had also said that the Department's preferred alternative, Route A., crossed the Sammamish River twice, taking Bothell City Park land to so do.]

... "Mrs. Madeline Shean, Bothell Councilwoman, was one of two who voted against the proposed route [and she was not called to speak until 11:20].

... "Morrison commented: 'We don't need to spend $8 million to relieve the traffic at one or two traffic lights.'

"Recognizing this, State Rep. Arthur Brown said, 'We are entitled to a statement from the Highway Commission itself as to their plans. Are they going to extend this into Seattle?'

"Many Bothell residents at the hearing who favored the proposal said a freeway through Bothell is Bothell's business. Yet when some people charged that the state hadn't cooperated adequately with King County in planning, officials later admitted it.

"They seemed to be admitting that one area can't plan in isolation from another anymore. Or, as Gary Ness, of Lake City put it 'We'd like to see Bothell solve its problems without pointing a concrete pistol at Lake City.' "

The *Seattle Times*, December 18, printed this article by Susan Schwartz under the headline: "FANS, FOES OF FREEWAY ABOUND BOTHELL IN NOISY MEETING.

"The State Highway Department says Bothell traffic jams alone make it worthwhile to build a freeway bypassing Bothell. But many Seattle people think the project would be a back-door way of building the controversial R.H. Thomson Way.

"That was the noisiest conflict at last night's five-hour hearing on turning State Highway 522 into a freeway south of Bothell.

..."Most of the opposition came from Seattle and Lake City residents, who feared the bypass would create bottlenecks, and thus revive the plans for a freeway through Lake City and R.H. Thomson Way—probably the most opposed freeway plan in Seattle's history. 'The bypass will dictate an extension of that freeway,' said First District State Representative Art Brown. 'Having failed to build the R.H. Thomson out of Seattle, the Highway Department now wants to build it in,' Brown said. 'My question is: Going back to where?'

"Two most important facts had been established when the Department answered specific questions: (1) there was no money for any promised ameliorative expenditures—highway funds could not be used for anything but the highway itself; (2) Ramesh Gangoli and Dr. David Rudo asked questions to establish the fact that the hearing segment was indeed part of the R.H.Thomson. The Findings record, "Mr. Andreas responded by stating that the traffic volumes were predicted on a complete system. He also said that traffic volumes would be less if the system is not built beyond the proposed segment, but a multilane facility would still be required."

Since the hearing was adjourned before I was allowed to speak, I thought that I should submit my statement to the State Highway Commission immediately. I wanted to be sure that the State would receive my comments for the record despite their being mailed during the Christmas post office rush. I wrote:

TO BE INCORPORATED IN THE RECORD OF THE HEARING ON SR 522 HELD BY THE FIRST DISTRICT, WASHINGTON STATE DEPARTMENT OF HIGHWAYS, DECEMBER 17, 1969, AT ANDERSON JUNIOR HIGH SCHOOL, BOTHELL, WASHINGTON.

"I. This statement is in support of the objections made at the time of the hearing as to its validity under the laws because of the following defects:

A. The public did not have adequate preparation for the hearing because the Highway Department did not allow the public to inspect the material in the record as required by the PPM after official notice is given.

B. The date and the time of the hearing was selected without regard to:

1. Significant community conflicts drawn to the attention of the Department well in advance of the hearing.

2. Consideration of the length of the Departments' presentation of the prepared statements in favor of the selected corridor which the Department knew would postpone participation by other citizens until a very late hour.

C. The Department failed to provide rules in advance for the conduct of the hearing in order that all participants could make rational plans and avoid the chaos resulting from procedure developed ad hoc by the highway officer presiding at the hearing.

D. The Department appointed a presiding officer who was known to be a protagonist of a selected corridor with a vested interest in building a road in that corridor, and this conflict of interest made it impossible for a fair and honest hearing to be held under that officer.

E. The hearing officer erred in denying an objection made by Mr. Beezer at the beginning of the hearing: that the Department present the proposal and adjourn the meeting until the citizens could study the proposal and in order that the citizens could speak before the hour became so late as to affect adversely their ability to make value judgments.

F. The hearing officer erred in denying the motion, made at about 10:30, to stop the hearing for the evening and to reschedule the remainder at a time more convenient for the persons left to speak.

G. The hearing officer erred in first hearing persons known to support his chosen proposal and in postponing statements and questions from persons not known to support his proposal. He erred in not allowing the Bothell minority to speak after the Bothell majority.

H. The hearing officer erred when he arbitrarily cut off the hearing in order to prevent questions which would have raised points of substantive objection to the proposal.

II. The hearing officer willfully refused to hear the following substantive points of objection:

- The elected officials of King and Snohomish Counties had not been consulted by the Department on plans for SR 522.
- There is no valid transportation plan for this area as required by the Federal Highway Act because the Puget Sound Regional Transportation Plan is limited by the financing to consideration of highway plans only.
- The rapid transit plans of Metro and of Snohomish County were not considered in the studies for these proposals.
- Corridors D and G are identical, the only difference being in the selection of the portion of the corridor which would be built first. The Department, in failing to tell the audience this fact, deliberately misled and concealed material facts essential to the hearing.
- The Department insisted upon limiting the hearing and the discussion

to a certain portion of SR 522, which put it in the posture of a Bothell city project, thus skewing the relevance of objections to the SR 522 highway system for which federal aid will be sought.

- The Department's statements varied fatally from the known requisites for federal funding of roads.

III. The hearing is invalid because of the absence of clearly-provided appeal procedure to test the validity of the rulings of a protagonist hearing officer; the hearing is invalid in that the clear intent of the Federal Rules that the procedure be valid was violated.

IV. And further, these objections must then be considered open-ended until such time as procedural rules are promulgated and the transcript is available."

On December 21, I wrote a letter to Washington State Highway Commissioner John Rupp, whom I had talked with several times and who was well known as an able attorney in Seattle. I wanted to tell him directly what I had learned about the two Highway Department hearings in North Bend and in Bothell, to give him first hand information that the department might not have told him. I summarized as follows:

"The losses at the hearings are these:

"AT NORTH BEND—The Department should have had a corridor public hearing, chosen a corridor, applied for federal approval, THEN sent out notices, etc., and had a design hearing on specific designs for the chosen corridor. The combined hearing didn't attempt to fulfill the requisites of the Federal government, the citizens knew that the Department of Highways in the State of Washington was committed to a specific corridor, and their rights to a fair and honest determination of one of several corridors was clearly gone. The design hearing was more of a mockery, for the corridor and one single design for it were presented, and the people could do little but plead for supposed ameliorative changes in the presented Chinese Wall, 20 feet high, 120 feet wide, a block or so south the main street dividing the town. If the Commission allows this defective hearing to stand without attempting to rectify it themselves, a great deal of time will be wasted in the ensuing objections being pursued. If the Commission now, of its own accord, would reschedule the corridor public hearing and hold it fairly, the Commission and the Department may regain some of the confidence of the public.

"AT BOTHELL—The citizens recognized that the Commission and the Department had no intention that their officials be fair, honest, or even polite. We are used to living in a democracy and to being governed by persons elected by the people and responsive to them. When I went to East Berlin I was prepared to be temporarily subjected to a discipline I did not, nor would not, have chosen. When I went to a hearing, held by the State of Washington, I expected it to be conducted as set out in the PPM [Policy Procedure Memorandum 20-8, the adopted Federal administrative rules for highway funding] and passed by our elected officials. The Bothell hearing, under Mr. Bogart, will long be remembered as a unifying force for all those who would question the procedures and decisions of those connected with the Highway Commission and the Highway Department of the State of Washington."

7. THE OMNIBUS HIGHWAY BUDGET BILL

It had long been obvious that the so-called "Omnibus Highway Budget Bill" was used to control the votes of the State Legislature. The bill was not brought out until the final hours of the very last day of the session, and it contained all the state's budgeted expenditures for roads. The procedure had been developed over the years by the Senate and House Transportation Committees (especially the Interim Committee chairmen and members), who ruled the Legislature by trading highways for votes and quashing highways in the districts of Legislators who refused to play the game. The Omnibus Highway Bill was a huge document of many hundreds of pages; in 1969, it contained seventy subjects, and when it appeared the last day of the session, there was no way a conscientious legislator could evaluate it.

On January 9, 1970, interested attorneys and environmental and community groups filed legal action asking the King County Superior

Court to rule that the State's Omnibus Highway Bill was unconstitutional because, among other things, it contained more than one subject. They said that the members of the Legislature were "not given the opportunity to consider the various subjects contained in the bill in separate bills so that each subject might stand or fall upon its own merits or demerits..."

The defendants were George Andrews, Director of Highways, the State Highway Commission, the Legislature Transportation Committees, and County and PSGC officials. The plaintiffs asked the court to prevent the state from taking further action under the Omnibus Highway Bill, in addition to declaring it null and void.

The Court ruled for the plaintiffs. But the highway proponent legislators still conducted their vote-trading schemes.

8. THE ZAHN OFFER, THE FICTITIOUS TRADE

On December 23, 1969, we were trying to write our submissions for the record of the SR 522 hearing—little did we know that powerful highway state legislators had managed to engineer another threat to Seattle, designed to take control of the city's highway construction projects. State Highway Commission Chairman George Zahn had written a letter to the new Seattle Mayor, Wes Uhlman, offering a trade involving both the Thomson and I-90, as well as other highways and projects in Seattle. Mayor Uhlman had already met with Chairman Zahn and had written a confirmation of his promise to arrange a meeting with proponents of the proposal and the City Council.

When the Joint Interim House and Senate Transportation and Ways and Means Committees scheduled a night meeting at Tacoma on January 19, 1970, we could not have predicted that this was the beginning of the story that may have been the most amazing machinations ever openly attempted by the highway builders.

I have named the sequence of records "the Zahn offer" because the written offers were sent by Chairman George Zahn, for the Washington State Highway Commission, to Mayor Uhlman.

The C.A.F. Steering Committee decided to go to the meeting, and members took hastily-prepared signs that they intended to use to lobby the elected officials. As we rode through that stormy night to Tacoma, we wondered why a night meeting with the Seattle officials had been set at a motel an hour's drive from Seattle.

We ran from the car through the rain, dripped into the motel, and went to the room scheduled for the meeting, but Legislature Transportation Committee Chairmen Representative Leland and Senator Guess recognized us and the two newspaper reporters present and announced that the meeting was closed to all of us. Then all of the officials were ushered into a meeting place that had been quickly made in the lobby by enclosing an area with wooden screens about seven feet high.

We were really angry. The Seattle Council members had used very poor judgment. The gathering had been set up by newly-elected Mayor Uhlman and Council President Charles Carroll—it was at a most unusual time and place for a meeting of committees of the State Legislature. The Council should have been most apprehensive about going all the way to Tacoma for a night meeting run by Rep. Leland. There was no available agenda for the meeting despite the fact that Major Uhlman and Council President Carroll had already signed a letter of intent to accept the Zahn offer.

The Council should have insisted that the meeting be open to the press and to the public because it was a meeting of committees of our State Legislature with the Seattle elected officials, and under the State Open Meetings Act, such meetings could not be closed. The Council members should have known that an open meeting would ensure fairness and protect them from improper influences. When Seattle elected officials did not object to the closed meeting, they agreed to procedures and presumptions that would seriously affect their duties and responsibilities to Seattle, and they should have known better.

So we few angry people stood outside as an amazing conglomeration of officials filed into the makeshift room behind the screens. And we found we could hear perfectly! Participants included:

— <u>State Highway Commissioners</u> [people appointed by the

Governor and confirmed by the Senate], who had complete control of the Highway Department, supposedly. Our State had no Department of Transportation as part of the Governor's administration; the Commission had been established to ensure that decision-making was completely separated from the Governor, the Legislature and politics. It was *supposed* to be absolutely autonomous, except that the Legislature still had to pass the final appropriations in the Omnibus Highway Bill. But when I began to go to all of the Commission's monthly meetings and read the minutes, I discovered that the Commissioners were merely rubber-stamping whatever the staff put before them. The Commissioners were not supposed to be making decisions, and they didn't make decisions. The Commission was merely a front, knowingly advancing the decisions made elsewhere.

— From the Legislature: Al Leland, Chairman of the House Transportation Committee, presiding; Senator Sam Guess, Chairman of the Senate Transportation Committee.

We were not popular with them. *Seattle Post Intelligencer* columnist Emmett Watson had written, "The Joint Interim Committee [of the Legislature] consists of such people as Rep. Leland, a real-estate man on the Eastside. It can be safely concluded that his interest in ten lanes of highway [on I-90] is not entirely neutral. Another is Sam Guess, who lives 300 miles away from all those homes that will be torn out. ...Another member is Brian Lewis, an engineer whose partner gets consulting fees from the Highway Department. ...Such examples are why the Interim Committee is commonly called a 'de facto arm of the highway lobby."

A quote from an article in the newspaper *Argus*, September 19, 1969, about a meeting of the Good Roads Association, "asphalt layers ... concrete pourers ... truckers from the Teamster's Union." ... "More fun, however, were the diatribes against 'them', those shadowy villains who would disrupt, for their own unspecified, nefarious reasons, the state's whole highway plan.

"Spokesmen against 'them' were chiefly Charles Prahl, who quit as state highway director under fire from the anti-freeway forces, and ne Kirkland master of illogic from the House Committee.

bile paled beside Leland's scorching which drew the biggest applause of them all. He presented an 'inventory' of seven Seattle area projects which the un*believer*s have blocked and then ticked off an impressive list of low-cost figures.

"Delays to the third Lake Washington Bridge, the R.H. Thompson [sic] Expressway, the Evergreen Point Bridge expansion, and the rest have cost $142 million already.

"$142 MILLION LOST?

"Yes, $142 million of precious resource badly needed to build important transportation facilities desperately needed by all of Washington State.

... "Leland ... put the onus for freeway stalling right on the Seattle council and other 'elected leadership.'

" 'The colored community,' he said, 'has been inflamed by the statements on the Thompson [sic]. 'But tell me,' he said, 'what single better hope exists for the thousands of these people to secure new homes, to get out of their ghetto housing and find their place in the sun?' "

— Seattle elected officials at the Tacoma motel meeting were: Mayor Wes Uhlman, whose term of office had just begun; Seattle City Council members including Charles Carroll, President, Wayne Larkin and Ted Best—all old timers; lawyers Tim Hill and Liem Tuai; Phyllis Lamphere; ex-state representative Sam Smith; Jeanette Williams; and newspaperman Don Wright. (And present were George Andrews, State Director of Highways, and Seattle City Engineer Roy Morse).

We stood close to the shutters, and we heard everything happening in the meeting.

We heard Rep. Leland outline the State's offer in magnanimous voice and terms. It was published in the January 20, 1970, *Seattle Times* by reporter David Suffia, headline:

"STATE WARNS CITY TO OK 3rd SPAN OR LOSE ROAD

AID.

"Mayor Wes Uhlman and the City Council got an ultimatum from the State Highway Commission last night—agree to plans for another major highway and rapid transit crossing of Lake Washington or see all major highway projects in Seattle and the domed stadium killed or delayed indefinitely.

"Councilmen said Al Leland, Republican State Representative from Redmond, was chairman of the meeting. Councilmen said the meeting was really an 'arm-twisting session' to get city approval of the major highway project that would cross on a third Lake Washington bridge next to the Mercer Island Bridge.

"Such a project, councilmen were told, could be eight or ten lanes wide. It could displace up to 230 families in the Mount Baker area, councilmen were told.

"[Councilman] Best said that Leland and Zahn said if the city doesn't come to agreement with them, the commission will refuse to put the Bay Freeway and Connecticut Street Viaduct on the state system.

"Councilmen said Zahn expressed frustration that the city has not cooperated in solving highway problems in Seattle for the past three years. Now he wants cooperation right away or Seattle will face great difficulty in getting state money for future highway needs."

The C.A.F. contingent behind the shutters heard the whole presentation, but then Sen. Guess came out and recognized us and had motel personnel usher us out. Our big regret was that we left so suddenly that we forgot to raise our sign above the wooden shutters; it read, "WE DIDN'T ELECT AL LELAND MAYOR OF SEATTLE."

The package struck me as absolutely incredible. The Zahn offer was presented as a quid-pro-quo trade in which Seattle was to get what Seattle already had under valid contracts with the State! The Bay Freeway was already on the state and federal-aid highway systems, and in 1967 the state had signed contracts with the city to share the costs of the Bay Freeway equally, with the state using federal funds for its share. City Engineer Roy Morse and the incumbent councilmen in

1967 surely knew about this contract. How could they allow the city to give up something in return for what the city already had?

I had found the 1967 Bay Freeway contract in the Seattle comptroller's files when I was trying to get information about the R.H. Thomson 1960 bond issue and found that the Bay Freeway was also a 1960 bond project. I had also discovered that the Connecticut Viaduct (which was planned to convey traffic from I-90 over the railroad tracks to a touchdown on Connecticut Street), was supposed to be the western terminus of I-90; it was so designated on state maps, and more than ninety percent of the Connecticut project should be funded as an essential part of the proposed Interstate-90 project.

When I began this history, I said that I was writing it because someone had to and no one had, but I had forgotten the writings I had done from time to time. I had read a series of Zahn offer-bargaining letters written from December 1969 to April 1970 between Mayor Uhlman or Councilman Carroll and Commissioner Zahn. I had assembled a 37-page review notebook about the offers and the relevant history and had it given to Seattle Council members. Although the Zahn offer was a pure fiction, we of C.A.F. were afraid that it might bind Seattle to political decisions on the Thomson and I-90 as well as to a proposed connection for an addition to the Evergreen Point Bridge (SR 520) over I-5 to Mercer Street.

Someone, not I, told Shelby Scates, the *Seattle Post Intelligencer* reporter, about my notebook. He telephoned to ask to see it. I gave him permission to use it, and he wrote an article which was published on the front page on April 4, 1970. He had used my notebook and his experience as a veteran Olympia newspaper man to write a digest of what happened after Seattle got the Zahn offer at the Tacoma motel. I had never met Scates and was greatly surprised that he even knew of my materials, but his article probably ended the possibilities that the city would even discuss the ridiculous Zahn offer.

The headline on Scates' story was: "FREEWAY PACKAGE ROBS CITY."

"The State Highway Commission, on behalf of present and future

Eastside commuters, is trying to take the City of Seattle to the cleaners.

"That's the conclusion one can draw from a carefully worded, laboriously researched investigation into the commission's proposed 'memorandum of understanding' with the city on highway construction.

"The study indicates it might be better labeled a 'memorandum of misunderstanding' as far as the public is concerned.

"The study was made by a Seattle housewife, Mrs. Margaret Tunks, a member of the League of Women voters and Citizens Against Freeways.

"It is an exhaustive look at the so-called 'package deal' of Highways—take them or leave them—offered by the Legislative Interim Committee on Highways to the mayor and City Council at a semi-secret meeting last January in Tacoma.

"The package has been formalized in an exchange of letters between Wes Uhlman and Highway Commission Chairman, George Zahn. It included the city's acceptance of the third Lake Washington Bridge for Interstate 90 (the final configuration still to be determined), further construction of Interstate 5 between Mercer and Roanoke Streets, a study of existing arterials with an eye to a fourth Lake Washington Bridge, ... and—depending on how you interpret Zahn's language—possible construction of the R.H. Thomson Expressway.

"In return, the city is supposed to get state financing for the Bay Freeway and Connecticut Street Interchanges that it considers critical to the construction of the new domed stadium at Seattle Center.

"The city hasn't signed this memorandum. Instead, officials signed a counter-offer, one that doesn't contemplate construction of the Thomson freeway and does contemplate a smaller-sized third Lake Washington Bridge.

"Quite apart from any conclusions one may draw from it, Mrs. Tunks' research uncovered these critical facts:

- There is in existence a contract between the city and the Highway Commission for construction of the Bay Freeway.

- The Connecticut Street Viaduct, far from being a purely city transportation need, is vitally necessary to handle traffic from I-90.

NEWS ITEM - STATE OFFERS TO HELP SEATTLE.

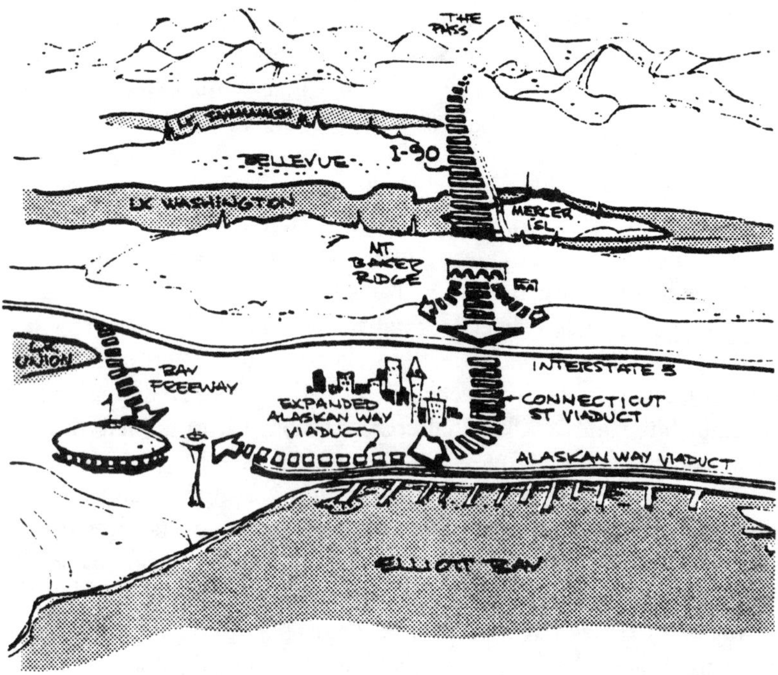

THE "BARGAIN"

THE STATE HELPS US BUILD THE CONNECTICUT ST. VIADUCT AND BAY FREEWAY - IF - WE ACCEPT THE WHOLE I-90 BRIDGE

THE PROBLEM

THE TRAFFIC WONT BE ABLE TO GET OFF ANY OF THESE ROADS UNTIL SEATTLE BUYS THE ADDITIONAL PARKING GARAGES AND NEW FREEWAYS THAT MUST GO WITH THEM.

Consequently, it could be built with state and federal funds, rather than state and city funds.

- Correction of the traffic weave between Mercer and Roanoke Streets on I-5 through further construction is an absolute necessity for handling traffic that might be coming off a fourth (correct, fourth) Lake Washington Bridge running parallel to the present Evergreen Point Bridge, if it is not the final justification for constructing the bridge."

[Note at the bottom of the Scates article on the front page:] "Seattle is being asked to accept a highway package that primarily benefits the east side of Lake Washington. Page 12." Turning to page 12, the headline reads:

"BAY ROUTE CONTRACT 'ALREADY REALITY'

"By Shelby Scates, PI Political Writer"

"The sum of research by Mrs. Margaret Tunks of Seattle shows Seattle is being asked to accept a highway package that primarily benefits the Eastside, in exchange for something it already has—a contact for the Bay Freeway.

"That contract, signed by former Mayor J.D. Braman for the city and W.E. McKibben, assistant director, for the highway department, calls for a 50-50 split of the costs. It was ratified by the City Council on December 11, 1967.

"It called for two, 40-foot wide roads of two lanes each running between I-5 at Mercer Street and Broad Street.

"According to Mrs. Tunks' study, the city's Capital Improvement Budget book of March 1969, showed that the city's half of the freeway would come from a 1960 bond issue and from urban arterial funds already allocated.

"Nevertheless, State Rep. Al Leland, Chairman of the House Transportation Committee and vice chairman of the Interim Highway Committee, told members of the City Council last January it would have to accept the total package of highways before the Interim Highway Committee would 'give its blessing' for state funding of the Bay Freeway and the Connecticut Street Viaduct by putting them on the state Highway system.

"Leland, an Eastside real estate dealer (Horizons East Inc., Riverscene, Ellarsee Investment Co., Leland Realty Co., and Reams-Goode and Associates) pointedly reminded the council that the Bay and Connecticut Street facilities were needed to make the domed stadium feasible.

"Highway Commissioner George Zahn's letters to Uhlman show him backing away from the Bay Freeway as an item of barter.

"On Jan. 21 he says, simply, the staff will support the Bay Freeway from I-5 to Aurora Avenue as part of the total package.

"In his letter of Feb. 11, however, Zahn acknowledges that a 'letter of understanding' already exists between the city and the state on the Bay Freeway and goes on to say: 'If we can reach a mutual understanding on several points (of the highway package) it is my understanding that the Joint Committee on Highways will be receptive to the State Highway Commission's placing the Connecticut Street Connection on the state highway system.'

"In short, somebody in City Hall must have remembered the Bay Freeway contract ('letter of understanding' is a mild phrase for a jointly signed, legally ordained, document), and Zahn backed away from it as a necessary part of the deal.

"Since the signing of the Bay Freeway contract, there has been a proposed design change. It would go from four lanes to six.

"Regardless, she [Tunks] argues against the additional lanes, if only because of the limited number of new parking places planned for the Seattle Center.

"The City's zeal for the Bay Freeway is based on the need to handle traffic coming from the north on I-5 to the center, and, presumably, the domed stadium.

"Equally necessary, the city feels, is a southern connection between I-5 and the Alaskan Viaduct. That would be the Connecticut Street Viaduct.

"I-90 cannot be built if Connecticut is not built also,' she [Tunks] says, citing a letter written by the [Federal] Bureau of Public Roads which says I-5 cannot handle the traffic coming off I-90.

"That being the case, she suggests the city should allow the state to shoulder the entire cost of the project. The state could then seek ninety percent federal financing for it as part of the interstate system.

"Item 3 in the Commission's package calls for an improvement of I-5 to eliminate the traffic weave between Mercer and Roanoke streets and to improve its capacity. Item 4 is the study, already funded, of the fourth Lake Washington Bridge, which would parallel the Evergreen Point Bridge.

"The Tudor Engineering Company's study of the fourth bridge, according to Mrs. Tunks, contained a warning that even if the R.H. Thomson Expressway is built, it couldn't handle the incoming traffic from the fourth bridge.

"Mrs. Tunks argues that little need exists for increasing I-5's north-south capacity, but that it must be enlarged from Roanoke to Mercer if more traffic is to enter the freeway from the east.

"Such an increase would make a fourth Lake Bridge feasible. Without it, the Bridge would have no place to dump its traffic and would be difficult to justify.

"Finally, Mrs. Tunks warns the Mayor and the Council that if they sign the Commission's memorandum they are locking the city into a transportation system without a complete awareness of its effects.

"Instead, she says the city must negotiate for a better deal for itself, one that might include termination of I-90 on the east side of the lake at I-405, and removal of the Thomson Expressway and the Fourth Bridge from any comprehensive plan."

The Seattle City Council and the Zahn Offer

I tried to follow the transportation decision-making processes of Seattle City Council members all through the next two decades. I have not yet been able to ascertain what they thought their duties and responsibilities were to the people of the city of Seattle.

By April, 1970, members of CARHT and C.A.F. were trying to get the Council to evaluate the Zahn proposals by finding out what

Seattle's transportation plans WERE and what Seattle's transportation plans SHOULD BE. We thought that the elected officials should first look at what had actually been built and the capacity of the system, then determine whether or not the existing highway plans were obsolete: for Seattle; for the four-county urban area of the Puget Sound Council of Governments; and for the state. Then our elected officials could decide what the city should do and how to do it.

Plain observation of what we already had was easy. All of the facilities mentioned in the Zahn offer involved already-gridlocked highways. We had a freeway network that did not work because there was no room for more vehicles in Seattle. But actions of city elected officials throughout the two-and-a-half decades after Zahn show clearly that they still did not pay any attention to the evidence before them—that Seattle is a double peninsula, a narrow corridor between Lake Washington and Puget Sound.

[All the projects the State wanted would reappear in the Memorandum of Agreement the Mayor signed for Seattle in 1976. In 1996 highway proponents are still trying to force construction of those same projects through the city.]

The Zahn offer was based on a principle that the only way to move people and goods was to make already-full streets and highways larger or to build new highways. Surely the Seattle elected officials could see that was impossible. I had sent them a copy of a letter from the Federal Bureau of Roads warning the state that traffic from the proposed SR 509 coming across the Duwamish could not be accommodated on Interstate 5, either going north or south; the traffic from this project would compete with traffic from the proposed SR 167 highway coming up from the south. The Tudor report had warned that even if the Thomson were built, expected traffic from the proposed new bridges across Lake Washington to Matthews Beach could not be accommodated in Seattle. The Zahn-proposed connection over I-5 from the Evergreen Bridge (the so-called "Mercer Weave Correction") and the Bay Freeway would feed more traffic into already gridlocked Mercer Street in the Seattle Center area. The present traffic from and to the Evergreen Bridge could not be accommodated in Seattle—any addition to the bridge was therefore impossible.

The most amazing part of Zahn negotiation correspondence is that no one—no one—mentioned the effects on Seattle of the construction and the use of the proposed highways. The Mayor and the Council all had seen the building of Interstate-5 through the city and its effects on the people in its corridor, but they did not seem to connect that trauma with the building of future highway capacity.

I wrote, in a letter to the Mayor and the Council, "Seattle has not planned transportation adequately ... we have only kept putting the same old roads on new maps. The road network of our Comprehensive Plan is practically identical to the roads planned by 1953, and the definitive transportation plan of the area, done by the Puget Sound Regional Governmental Conference, merely codified these roads—made them part of a regional system. Seattle has never determined what land use we want and how we can maintain the choices we make with transportation. We have never studied rapid transit, its effect on the City, and the alternative it might offer in transportation corridors.

"The citizens asked for a Seattle Comprehensive Transportation Study on April 1, 1969, a year ago. The Mayor appointed a task force which presented a proposal which was passed by resolution in August, 1969. At the hearing citizens were allowed to speak only on whether the study should be done or not, not its merits, and we were not consulted. Our disappointment to find that it was limited to the Eastern Corridor only was tempered by the discoveries that this limitation would not be sustained when the persons doing the study realized that Seattle is really only one corridor. Only one transportation study—parking—has been funded and begun by another agency, independent of any valid transportation studies.

"Seattle elected officials cannot enter into any agreements with the state concerning state roads within Seattle until a valid transportation study for Seattle is funded, completed, and policy decisions made.

"Certain stop gap measures must be taken. The Mayor and the Council must make their intent clear and immediately remove the R.H.

Thomson, [a new] SR 522, and the Fourth Bridge from both the Seattle and PSGC Comprehensive Plans. The Mayor and the Council must place all transportation planning (including parking) in a single unit of responsibility. The city must take a look at the system and decide how much of it needs, wants, and afford."

I did not get an answer to my letter.

The Zahn offer did not result in a contract, but the projects in it have been kept intact in the highway builders' plans which appear from time to time.

9. 1970 - IN RETROSPECT

In May, 1970, the second Forward Thrust Rail bond proposal failed. Unfortunately, the election took place at the beginning of what would be called "the Boeing slump," when people feared their jobs in the airplane construction industry of Seattle would be lost, but the people voted against it also for the same reasons they had voted in 1968: "There's nothing in it for us."

On May 20, 1970, CARHT wrote a letter to the Council and the Mayor requesting that the R.H. Thomson project be removed from Seattle's plan and map. On June 1, 1970, the Council so voted. But at the same meeting, they voted to build the Bay Freeway, another 1960 bond project!

[The reader of this history of the R.H. Thomson should remember that it was written as a record of the actions of the members of C.A.F., Citizens Against Freeways. The members of CARHT, the Citizens Against the R.H. Thomson, and the Montlake and Ravenna Community Clubs began their opposition before C.A.F. was organized, and Peggy Johnson's excellent publication, The Montlake Community and the R.H, Thomson, Case of a Successful Freeway Fight, is an excellent record available in the libraries. It was done for a class at Seattle University, and it should be read in conjunction with this history.]

By late spring in 1970, C.A.F. had carefully formulated outlines for action by the elected officials. As I read them now, I find that they were valid then and still are. We should have known who was controlling Seattle transportation decisions and where we could and could not make head way with our opposition to their decisions. If we had only been able to put together the facts we already knew, we could have avoided all the time spent on useless activities.

About the Legislature: We knew that the highway building legislators were working for their own special interests: to make money on highway construction (Example: Senator Sam Guess); to make money developing real estate with highways (Example: Representative Al Leland); to favor their own districts in order to maintain political power (Examples: Senator Al Henry: Representatives "Red" Beck and Len Sawyer). We knew that the influential pro-highway people had successfully opposed a Washington State Department of Transportation, and we knew that the State Highway Commission was a rubber stamping front for these people. We should have been able to predict that the Legislature would not make highway decisions on the merits and adverse effects of the projects.

About the mayor: Mayor Wes Uhlman had given good answers to our TCC candidate's questionnaire on transportation, but within a month of taking office he was promoting the Zahn offer. Our disappointment was continued all through his administration. Uhlman never acted for Seattle. He seemed to be motivated only by suburbia, real estate interests (especially in the Seattle Central Business District and Bellevue), and the desire to enrich the highway builders.

About the Seattle City Council: The Council had already reached the decision to avoid changing and would not change the process of transportation decision-making.

About Metro: Metro had moved into Seattle transportation by beginning to take over the moribund existing bus system, but we were very worried about the peculiar and potentially damaging Forward

Thrust process and its relationship to Metro. In 1968, Jim Ellis had led the campaign to get King County voters to approve the sale of bonds for $380 million to be used to match Federal funds to build a $1.155 billion rail transit system. We did not know of any preliminary planning of the rail transit system by any of the jurisdictions, and there had been no attempt to consider the relationship of public mass transit alternatives to the planned highway system. In fact, Mr. Ellis said he thought a ten lane I-90, the second Evergreen addition, and the R.H. Thomson Expressway were necessary. The rail bond proposition had not received the required number of votes in 1968, nor did the $440 million bond issue for the $1.321 billion system on the ballot in 1970. We feared that Metro might continue this peculiar, closed process.

About the federal agencies: We had found that Congress had passed some excellent laws designed to control the spending of federal funds for land use and transportation planning, to preserve parklands and clean air, to ensure that the social, economic, and environmental consequences were known to the decision-makers, and to ensure fair processes for those decisions. We had learned that these laws would not be enforced by the controlling federal administrative agencies. The Puget Sound Governmental Council (PSCG) had engaged in a land use and transportation study of the four-county Puget Sound urban area, but the study was funded mainly by state and federal highway trust funds, restricted to planning highways. There was no evidence to show that elected officials set policies in the study. We had found that the Federal Bureau of Public Roads had rubber-stamped the federally funded activities of the State—our appeals to them about the unfair SR 522 hearing had not been recognized, and they had approved the State's hearing procedures and decisions, never considering our deliberate and well-founded objections.

Our problem was that we had no political power, that we were incredibly uninformed. We presumed that the elected officials would make their decisions for the people of Seattle, but we learned that they were working for suburbia.

We thought that elected officials would read what we were writing and hear what we were saying and begin to make value judgments on the merits of the issues. But it was obvious that the real decisions were being made in secret, the process was closed to the electorate, and that the real decisions were not being made to maintain Seattle as a livable city.

10. FIGHTING FIERCELY AND WINNING SOMETIMES

1970, Fighting Fiercely

The city bureaucrats and Council members who confirmed and signed the 1967 contract with the state must have known that the Zahn offer on the Bay Freeway was a farce. By the time the Scates' articles were printed in the *Seattle Post Intelligencer*, the Council and Mayor must have realized that our objections were based on facts.

By the end of April, 1970, elected officials should have known the following several pertinent facts. By personal observation, they should have seen that both Mercer Street and Interstate 5 were in capacity gridlock and could not take traffic from the designed six-lane Bay Freeway. Valid attacks had been made on the proposal, and our opposition appeared to be basing its objections on the history of the project and on alleged illegalities in the decision-making process. We protesters had read the contracts, the records of previous hearings and decisions, and the election information used in the 1960 bond issue vote. We had tried to write and talk to elected officials about what we had learned. We were raising important issues which could subject the city to lawsuits.

The minutes of the Transportation Coordinating Committee for the first half of 1970 show its great concern over the failure of Washington elected officials to plan transportation. Two University of Washington professors, Dr. Jerry Schneider and Dr. Ed Horwood, spoke at the March 23, 1970, TCC meeting. The TCC minutes said, "Statements made were: The demand for roads is created by the expenditure of gas tax money obtained by the use of the same type of facilities; the only method for future planning will involve either the increase of residents in Seattle, the decrease in employment in the Seattle CBD, or the increase in jobs on the Eastside. A fantastically small amount has been spent for transportation planning as opposed to highway planning. We are getting into transportation systems which involve land use plans we did not choose; we have not asked the questions—is this trip necessary and for whom?"

The Mercer Street-to-Roanoke Overpass

The C.A.F. *Interchange* published an article I wrote about the March 23, 1970, meeting where the City Council recorded its vote for an item called, "the Mercer-Roanoke weave correction and increase in I-5 capacity improvement." I said, "It was part of the Zahn proposal and was accepted with nary a qualm by all the City Council who, as of March 23, did not know what and where it was—the Bay Freeway! It was funded for the 1969-70 biennium (now), and involved $1.5 million for right-of-way with the total cost to be $5 million and the length to be 1.43 miles. City Engineer Morse said that it would have to go over existing I-5 which was already three layers at that point. He said that details of this 'structure' should be part of the Bay Freeway materials for inspection, but it is not. [This project is essential to the addition of lanes to the Evergreen Point Bridge (SR 520), and the City Council does not even know that in voting for it they are approving an additional Evergreen Point Bridge.]

Suggestions made: that we work to get the R.H. Thomson off the Comprehensive Plan of Seattle; [City Planner] John Spaeth said on March 23 that it was off for all intents and purposes."

The Bay Freeway Hearing, April 18 & 19, 1970

I submitted six pages of materials for the record of the Bay Freeway Hearing. Summarized the points were:

"The notice was defective under both state and federal laws. It stated that the hearing would be held according to State Law RCS

47.52 and listed federal laws and administrative rules. However, the notice said that it would be a Seattle City Council hearing, and that "those appearing will be mailed a copy of the findings of the Council," but the City of Seattle had neither the jurisdiction nor the authority to make findings in state limited access or federal corridor/design hearings!

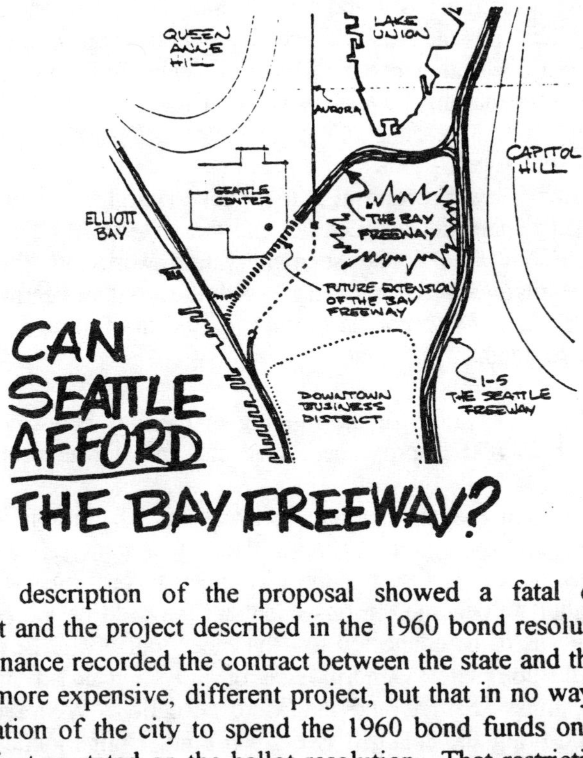

"The description of the proposal showed a fatal difference between it and the project described in the 1960 bond resolution. The 1967 ordinance recorded the contract between the state and the city for a larger, more expensive, different project, but that in no way changed the obligation of the city to spend the 1960 bond funds only for the 1960 project as stated on the ballot resolution. That restriction on the use of the 1960 bond funds could not now be changed by this hearing.

"While City Engineer Morse repeated that "we" and "I" did not know there were any federal dollars in the project, the 1967 contract ordinance stated: "WHEREAS, the State has approved the allocation and expenditure of 50% matching Federal Aid Urban funds in the acquisition of right of way and the construction costs of the project." Therefore it had to meet federal-aid laws.

"Inspection of materials before the hearing was repeatedly denied.

"The findings were incomplete and the citizens' questions unanswered. The findings were confined to a four-lane project beginning at I-5 and ending at Broad Street, and the city consistently refused to answer questions about provisions for traffic on and off the project (effects on the rest of the highway system), although the transcript records statements by Morse, Buswell and Braman, all city employees, said that the Bay Freeway is an integral part of the 'limited access loop around the entire Central Business District.' [This is the 1963 "Noose," page 16.]

"The Bay Freeway proposal at this public hearing constitutes a little over one-half of the link between I-5 and the waterfront. There was no information about HOW the segment would work into this system. There were many objections before and during the hearing that no information was not given at the hearing nor did the findings record that it was not provided."

I got the information for the funding of the Bay Freeway from the City's 1970 Capital Improvement Budgets and those proposed for 1971.

The new total cost for the Bay Freeway—$27.8 million in 1971—was a shocker, and it is no wonder that city employees and elected officials tried not to disclose it in the Bay Freeway hearing. If they had, people might have become curious about what would be the cost of the highways it was to be connected to—the other half of the Bay Freeway which would complete the north side of the Ring Road around the Central Business District, and the Mercer-Roanoke Weave correction which would bring the enlarged Evergreen Point Bridge traffic from the east to connect with this section of the Bay Freeway. People would be been extremely interested in knowing how all of these tie-ins were to be paid for.

Amateur Politicking

When the City voted on June 1, 1970, to stop action on the R.H. Thomson project and to continue to build the Bay Freeway, city engineers who had been working full-time on the R.H. Thomson began to work on the Bay. The period between then and the autumn of 1971 was marked by our amateur attempts to educate members of the City Council to get them interested in the material facts essential to good decision-making on the Bay Freeway project. We thought that if they had the facts, they would make decisions on the merits. Here are two examples of my attempts: my meeting with Councilman Liem Tuai; and my October 1, 1970, letter to Councilwoman Phyllis Lamphere.

Councilman Tuai appeared to have swallowed the Zahn offer and to have approved giving the Leland crowd the right to plan transportation for the city. He was a lawyer of good repute, later to be a Superior Court Judge, and I thought I could get him to look at the facts by meticulously reviewing the legal evidence on the Bay Freeway with him. He agreed to meet me. I had prepared two sets of materials, and I sat opposite him at his desk. We turned over the items, simultaneously, and I told him why each was valid and important. I proved that the spending of the 1960 bond funds for the different and more costly Bay Project was illegal, and he should have realized that we had the evidence for a lawsuit against the City which we would win. What happened? Absolutely nothing. Mr. Tuai was going to make (had made?) his judgments on the issue with no attention to the facts or merits involved.

Councilwoman Lamphere had read the Zahn offer and had written a counteroffer, which showed that she knew some of the facts but not all of them. She was known as the expert on finances on the Council, and I wrote this letter to her on October 1, 1970.

"The most important citizen's responsibility in our government is surely our duty to ensure the carrying out of the processes of that government according to the standards we have set. When the processes are not performed openly, the citizens must insist on full disclosure of all acts performed before their desired standards can be used for evaluation of the process.

"The Bay Freeway procedures are like the croquet game played by poor Alice in Wonderland, with hedgehogs for balls and long-necked birds for mallets, and—what bothered Alice the most—the rules changing every minute."

To show the duplicities of the Zahn offer, I pointed out that they were still refusing to admit that there was federal funding of the project. If they had, they would have admitted that their offer was phony because it was a trade by which Seattle got nothing, and they would have had to admit that their procedures had to conform to federal laws. Here I cited the federal-aid funding language in the state/city 1967 Contract, the fact that the route or corridor had been federally approved, the fact that laws requiring hearings on federal-aid highway projects and the adopted administrative rules required that "the State highway department shall describe the State-Federal relationship in the Federal-aid highway program by an appropriate brochure, pamphlet, or statement, or by other means.

I concluded, "The case of the Bay Freeway gets curiouser and curiouser until my head spins. It's indeed like a game which we must win but for which there are no rules, and we are prevented by blindfolds from seeing the ball." Unfortunately, this is what was going to happen in all the major highway decisions through the 1970's. Mrs. Lamphere never acknowledged my letter.

The Bay Freeway Lawsuit

In November, 1970, the City had approved the 1970 Bay Freeway design and project, and City employees were working on it when the Council voted to remove the Thomson from the Seattle Comprehensive Plan. At the end of the next summer, CARHT and C.A.F. reviewed the status of our opposition to the Bay and decided that we had made no progress at all. Not a single elected official had responded to us. We looked at all the materials we had on hand (the same materials I had shown Councilman Tuai—to no avail). We had the 1960 and 1970 ordinances, the drawings and descriptions of the 1970 project. We reviewed Attorney Al Schweppe's warning to the Seattle public advising them not to vote for the 1960 bond funds because the bond funds might be misused. We decided to sue the City of Seattle to stop the Bay Freeway project. CARHT and C.A.F. agreed to share the costs. We asked an attorney, John Phillips, to represent us in court, and, after we had laid all our evidence before him, he agreed to take the case.

On October 29, 1971, the *Seattle Post Intelligencer* published this story written about the trial by Bill McClave:

"BAY FREEWAY HALT URGED.

"The city should be enjoined from building the proposed $28 million, six lane Bay Freeway between Interstate-5 and Aurora Avenue without first resubmitting the entire freeway proposal to the voters, an attorney for a citizens' group argued in Superior Court today.

"John E. Phillips ... said the planned freeway as approved by the City Council last November is substantially different in design and cost from the proposal submitted to the voters who authorized the issuance of bonds for the project.

"He argued that the changes constitute major deviations from the original proposal and that the council thus did not have the power to approve the 1970 plan.

"When voters approved the issuance of $1.9 million bonds for the freeway in 1960, the estimated cost of the whole project was $4 million.

"A plan released in 1960 ... showed a two-deck, three lane freeway. The $28 million plan approved last year calls for a single deck, six lane freeway and other changes.

" 'We feel the proposal is null and void as long as they're using city bond money,' Phillips said.

" 'Because of the changes,' he said, 'the bond money authorized by the voters should be withdrawn from the project.'

"Phillips said the new design includes changes in length, location, and number of interchanges, in addition to the change in the number of lanes.

"He said the original cost estimate included $700,000 for right-of-way requirements, whereas the new plan includes $11 million for right-of-way.

" 'This certainly indicates they don't plan to go the same way,' he said."

Judge Solie Ringold handed down his oral decision on the Bay Freeway case on November 3, 1971; his written decision is dated December 13, 1971. He said,

IT IS HEREBY ORDERED, ADJUDGED AND DECREED:

"1. That the City of Seattle, its Mayor and City Council, are enjoined and prohibited from using any of the bond funds approved on March 8, 1960 by the voters whatsoever for the Bay Freeway in a manner substantially different from the plan approved in 1960 (Ex. 6) and which is substantially more expensive than $4,000,000.

"2. That the City of Seattle, its Mayor and City Council are hereby prohibited from using any of the 1960 bond funds whatsoever, for the acquisition of land and/or construction of the Bay Freeway as now approved by the City of Seattle, pursuant to Ordinance No. 99377.

"3. That all ordinances of the City authorizing the expenditure of 1960 Bond Funds for the Bay Freeway as approved by the City in 1970, Ordinance No. 99377, are illegal and void; except for Ordinances providing for the expenditure of the City's funds for Phase One of the Bay Freeway.

"4. That the City of Seattle, its Mayor and City Council may use the Bond Funds approved by the voters in 1960 for a purpose substantially different and a major deviation from that approved by the voters in 1960, provided the matter is submitted to the voters for their approval and provided the voters approve the deviation or deviations at an election held pursuant to the laws of Washington and the City of Seattle.

"5. That the City of Seattle is hereby ordered to pay plaintiffs for their costs and disbursements incurred therein."

[We plaintiffs never received anything.]

The Demise of the R.H. Thomson and Bay Freeways

The Seattle Council and Mayor decided to take Judge Ringold's advice to let the people vote on the Bay Freeway and R.H. Thomson 1960 bond funds. The ballot for the special election on February 8, 1972 was confusing. It had two parts:

"Referendum No. 1: Should the city construct Bay Freeway and Interchanges?"

"Referendum No. 2: Should the City terminate the R.H. Thomson and other specified projects and revote the bond funds for specified Seattle bridges and street repairs?"

The task of clarifying the ballot for voters was really difficult. I was in Olympia for the Legislative Session, and I didn't really participate in the campaign. But a campaign flyer shows how effectively the "stop freeway campaign" was fought.

> "STOP $15,000,000 IN NEW CITY TAXES."
>
> "Referendum No. 1: 'VOTE NO BAY FREEWAY."
>
> "Referendum No. 2: 'VOTE YES TERMINATE THE R.H. THOMSON."

The city engineering department entered the campaign, probably spending city funds illegally to so do. A four-page flyer titled, BAY FREEWAY: REPORT TO PATRONS OF SEATTLE CENTER, with "City of Seattle Department of Engineering" printed on the back, was given to everyone attending functions at the City Center. The flyer was printed on very attractive paper with both a drawing of the project and six pictures. These statements show what their arguments were:

"The Bay Freeway will lift much of the present and projected traffic off the surface streets—separate local traffic from thru [sic] traffic, enabling the total roadway system to carry the expected traffic volume" [I would have asked, "Carry it to where on what?"]

"The need for the Bay Freeway was visualized long before Seattle Center. While part of the total freeway system—it is a local facility, and, as such, will provide much improved access to Seattle Center and to the entire area between Lake Union and Elliott Bay."

On February 8, 1972, the voters of Seattle effectively wiped out the R.H. Thomson and Bay Freeways by voting to use those 1960 bond funds for other streets and bridges (described specifically in the bond referendum) to save the city's having to find some $15 million to repair and rebuild them.

The savings could have been far greater if the Mayor and City Council had paid some attention to freeway opponents:

- If they had wanted to find out what the Thomson and Bay projects really were;
- If they had tried to evaluate these projects by weighing the benefits against the adverse consequences;
- If they had planned transportation in Seattle.

I do not have a final figure for the funds Seattle misspent from the 1960 bond issue on the Thomson and the Bay projects up to the election in 1972, but I do have the State's figures dated July 31, 1970: The total cost of the Thomson was $2,279,953.59. The State had paid $1,124,660.42 from federal funds, and the city paid $1,601,343.71 and owed $426,683.20 (presumably funds advanced by and to be paid back to the State).

The July 31, 1970, costs of the Bay Freeway were $904,777.67, all "due from the city," and in the March, 1970, bargaining between Zahn and Uhlman, the State promised to spend $42 million on the Bay; in 1971-72—I have no record of how much of that was spent by the time of the 1972 election.

Obviously the city was stuck with replacing all 1960 bond funds illegally spent on the Thomson and the Bay projects, including all the Federal funds the State had spent. All of the 1960 bond funds should have been repaid from the general funds of the city; the property acquired for the Thomson was sold for that purpose. As far as I know, the property acquired for the Bay Freeway was not sold. City laws provide that the department which will use the bond funds takes full possession of the money when the bonds are sold and the department gets to keep the interest money received from the investment of them. But the property bought for the Bay was not sold to pay back the bond funds, and the invested funds plus the interest were not returned. The acquired property has become very valuable and is part of the proposed Lake Union area project.

Meanwhile, through the years, the engineering department "planners" have renamed that area the "Mercer Mess." and they constantly come up with still other enormous and expensive road plans that won't work there for the same reason the Bay Freeway project wouldn't. There's no place for the additional traffic to go!

Several years ago I went to a meeting in Montlake where a new project was being discussed "to cure the Mercer Mess." I asked the speaker from the engineering department how much capacity Interstate-5 had for additional vehicles from Mercer during commuter peaks, and he answered, "We think that there is capacity for 65 more vehicles an hour." Now, years later, there's NO additional capacity available on Interstate-5 in either direction, but the city still has not been able to see that the Mercer Street problem is caused by the traffic gridlocks on both ends and that no amount of enlarging it will move more vehicles. The city still is moving vehicle bottlenecks around instead of planning transportation that will work.

We should not forget the hearing testimony of three city employees that the Bay Freeway project was an essential part of the Central Business District's Ring Road, "the Noose". We must never forget the 1968 Tudor report and the fact that there are always plans to add lanes to the Evergreen Point Bridge and to bring that traffic into the Lake Union area. Since there is no capacity for more vehicles there, the plans must still exist for the building of the Ring Road with its parking garages on all four corners.

As the planning of the area south of Lake Union develops, we can tell ourselves that we, the opposing citizens, take credit for the fact that the Bay Freeway, with its elevated six lanes, was not built, and that there is still a Lake Union shore to develop.

But how we wish the elected officials of Seattle would adopt the maxim so well evident on Mercer Island, "If we are not for ourselves, then who will be for us?"

PART II
THE WASHINGTON STATE LEGISLATURE, 1991 - 1978
THE CITIZENS' ROLE

(How a citizens' lobbying group originated and how it functioned)

The history of our group activities at the Washington State Legislature begins in 1971, and I have thousands of pages of relevant materials, too numerous to print here. These contemporary items are better than any digest I might make of them, so to the extent possible, I will make copies of the most interesting and/or informative writings we used during the decade. The basic materials are bound as the *Washington Coalition for Sensible Transportation Newsletter*, with my analyses of the important bills in each session, and all the printed handouts we used in our lobbying, along with some copies of newspaper articles. I hope the University of Washington Archives will save other materials about the Legislature in the 1970's.

1. BASIC HOMEWORK

As the opposition to the R.H. Thomson and Bay Freeways began to coalesce, we started to search for better means for promoting sensible transportation decisions—surely there were better procedures than last minute grassroots fights against specific freeway projects, long years after the first decisions had been made. By late fall of 1970 we had begun to think about what could be done by citizens working through the State legislature—to look back to examine our original goals, to make plans to carry them out, and to begin procedures to get what we wanted.

When I decided to oppose the planned freeway through Lake City in 1968, I justified my decision by writing two pages on transportation planning and goals for Seattle and the area affecting it. After Citizens Against Freeways (C.A.F.) and Citizens Against the R.H. Thomson (CARHT) were organized, the members spent many hours writing broad analyses of the existing transportation plans in the area, both the applicable statures and the resultant decisions, and the existing elements of the transportation systems: streets; roads; highways; freeways; ferries; trains; public transportation; and buses. These writings are the most important account of the anti-freeway effort because they were always our guidelines; they are the reliable record of what we were trying to do.

We began to read the city and county ordinances and the state and federal laws for information about the transportation planning and funding processes. We found that we had to begin with this agenda:

- Read and evaluate all local ordinances, and state and federal laws that applied to transportation processes;

- Record and evaluate the results of these processes and use these results to divide the processes into two categories, those we would not need to change and those which we must try to change on a schedule that matched our priorities.

- Set a schedule for action depending upon the need for the changes, usually determined by activities of the local jurisdictions and of the Legislature.

Looking back on all the years, I find that we worked:

- To prevent increases in the state fuel tax which would be used only for highway purposes;
- To change the laws to allow highway trust funds to be used for any transportation purpose;
- To change the mandatory priority programming criteria and six-year planning processes that all local jurisdictions and the State were forced to use;
- To repeal the urban arterial funding laws based on those processes;
- To establish a cabinet-level Department of Transportation with the secretary selected and appointed by the governor and under the governor's administration like all the other departments of the state government.

We found that there were no state or local laws that required comprehensive transportation planning, as opposed to planning only for highways and ferries. We found that state laws locked in a thoroughly obsolete planning process through the six-year plans that required the state and local jurisdictions to categorize all streets and road by specific criteria, and to rate their projects according to "needs" based on these criteria. Three of the five criteria were intended to increase the vehicle capacity of streets and highways; the other two criteria were intended to prevent motor-vehicle accidents, but the entire process was clearly intended to promote spending on highway construction.

There was no process in the existing laws for planning multimodal transportation systems. At the state level, tax funds collected from the sale of motor vehicle fuels paid for planning of highways only, because the 14th Amendment of the State Constitution restricted their use to highway purposes only. The planners could not consider other forms of transportation. (The state ferry system was considered part of the state highway system). Federal fuel taxes were similarly restricted.

The planning process at the state, county, and city levels was carried out by traffic engineers. trained to control existing traffic and to provide additional capacity for vehicles. Neither the state nor Seattle had a transportation department or transportation planners. Neither the state nor the local jurisdictions had any process for planning public transportation, even as a complement, a supplement, an alternative, or a substitute to highways.

By law the Highway Commission had complete control of all the highway planning and construction processes. The Highway Commission consisted of five people, appointed by the governor and confirmed by the Senate. This system had been instituted to "take the politics out of highway spending," but the Commission was merely a rubber stamp for decisions made elsewhere. I began to attend their monthly meetings in the early seventies, and I was present at most of them during that decade. When I could not attend, I read the minutes, which were very accurate. In all this time, I seldom saw or heard them discuss any of the important decisions which were made. They merely acquiesced to items as presented by the Highway Department, and I could find no way to determine where the major decisions had originated and who had developed them.

The budgeting that provided for the spending of the highway trust funds was a process that was completely closed to the public. The result was a huge pile of paper called "The Omnibus Highway Bill" that was introduced the very last moment in the last day of legislative sessions. The reason for the delay was obnoxiously obvious: the hidden hands who made up the budget used it continually throughout the session to control legislators by threatening to withhold a promised highway project unless the legislator voted as they instructed. In 1970, several young Seattle attorneys and citizens' organizations challenged the Omnibus Budget Bill on the grounds that it illegally contained more than one subject, and they won.

This suit helped, but the technique of identifying each highway expenditure with a particular legislator's district and then threatening to withhold that project from the budget remained a constant factor used to control the legislature all through the decade, and it is still prevalent. In 1977, Representative Bill Burns, from the Montlake area in Seattle, had the votes to prevent the funding of a study to extend SR 520 farther east of 148th Street in Bellevue. He thought that this extension would build up the areas east of Redmond and Woodinville with auto-oriented suburbanites who would demand additions to the Evergreen Point Bridge through Montlake. He had the votes until the Representatives who had promised him their votes came around, one by one, to tell him they had been threatened that if they so voted, the highway projects in their districts would be deleted from the Budget Bill. I can well remember the utter disappointment on Bill's face as his friends explained why they had to change their votes.

In 1970, we began to realize what the entire system was and how it was so closely and secretly controlled. We began to see that in our state, transportation decisions were made by people whose goals were political power and personal enrichment. They were able to maintain their power because they were supported and instructed by the highway construction industry and land development interests, and they were well rewarded for their efforts.

When I review the decade, I find that we really worked to get an open, fair and sensible process for the planning of transportation (which meant the establishing of a department of transportation as part of the state government with a secretary appointed by the governor) and to change the restrictions on spending of transportation funds so that we could begin to have sensible transportation.

2. THE CITIZENS' LEGISLATIVE PROGRAM FOR 1971

In the fall of 1970 some of the Transportation Coordinating Committee members drafted the first citizens' statement for action in the 1971 session, and it was adopted by several organizations. They listed three categories:

"LEGISLATION WE WILL INTRODUCE:

Repeal of the 18th amendment of the Constitution
3 Cent Reduction in the State Gas Tax
Add Federal Hearing Procedures to State Highway Hearings

"LEGISLATION WE WILL SUPPORT:

The State Department of Transportation
Public Park Enabling Legislation
Elimination of the Earmarking of the 10-Mill County Property Road Tax

"LEGISLATION WE WILL OPPOSE:

New Gas Taxes for Urban Arterials
The Highway Finance Board Bill"

In October, 1970, Virginia Gunby and I began to consider the state of public transportation in Seattle and in the urban area. We collected the information we needed, we wrote what we called a "white paper," and we sent it to the Seattle and King County elected officials on November 4, 1970. We said that Congress had voted Urban Mass Transit funds to match each local dollar two for one. We said that the State of Washington through House Bill 641 would remit auto excise funds for transit on a two-for-one matching basis, so one local dollar would be the equivalent of four dollars for transit. But there was no qualifying agency!

Under "Current Activities," we wrote, "Seattle has no current plans nor does it have the authority to run transit beyond the city limits. Metro has made no transit plans since the failure of the May 13, 1970, bond issue. King County has indicated an interest in transit, but Norman Erbe, the Regional Director of Department 10 of the U.S. Department of Transportation, said last week that he did not know of any group that was considering the undertaking of bus transit for the commuter area. E.I. Roberts, District Engineer, stated on October 26th that the State has been unable to begin plans to fulfill the new federal requirements for bus facilities for commuters because there is no agency to plan with the State Highway Department and to run the transit system after the bus facilities were built."

In "Alternative Transit Model," we said, ... "The commuter shed is not the same as now served by Metro; transportation is more than a public service and must be considered one of the most important tools to implement comprehensive plans. Metro is not legally able to perform transportation functions; any agency should have the authority to tax for maintenance and operations, and this would limit Metro's consideration [being considered] unless changes were made in its enabling legislation." We pointed out, "King County already has a Department of Public Works, Utilities, and Transportation and, as a general purpose government, it has broad taxing powers and plans for area-wide land-use."

Under "Conclusions," we wrote that local governments should act immediately and, "We interpret the passage of the [Seattle] Transit Charter Amendment to mean that people do not want a separation of the transit function from a responsible and responsive government."

Under "Recommendations," we wrote:

"1. An Intergovernmental Transportation Task Force should begin immediately to consider alternative agencies which could effectively administer urban transportation services." We added,

"2. The Task Force must be completed before the 1971 legislative Session.

"3. Consideration of the administrative agency should *not* be limited to the Municipality of Metropolitan Seattle [Metro]. A general purpose government should be considered as the logical structure to administer and finance transit."

We never saw any evidence of any effect our "white paper" had on the elected officials or of any public discussion of the transit problem, but I can't say that we were surprised Metro went to the 1971 Session of the Legislature, requested and got all the authority they needed to run a commuter area bus transit system, and in 1972 Seattle voters transferred the Seattle Transit System to Metro.

Metro remained a special purpose agency completely divorced from planning transportation to implement land use decisions.

3. ORGANIZED CITIZENS BEGIN TO ACT

The history of the 1970's battle over the gas tax began in 1967 when the Legislature passed an additional 2 cents a gallon fuel tax and authorized bond sales for $400 million of highway construction, $200 million to be spent on state highways and $200 million to be used for a new category of large city and county projects, called the urban arterials. The end of these funds was in sight by 1971 (although the bonds would not be paid off for decades), and the highway builders came back to the Legislature for more money to continue their program of highway building. They pointed with pride to their funded projects and viewed with alarm the tremendous future "needs" to be funded: highways for business, for industrial and residential development, and for reducing urban highway bottlenecks by increasing capacity. We found that the state's planning process required all the counties and cities to prepare lists of projects by priority. Seattle's list included everything imaginable [and it still does in 1996], from widening a few hundred feet of a street to "improving" a single intersection, to building huge projects like the R.H. Thomson and the Bay Freeways.

Throughout my years of lobbying the legislature, I often contrasted the enormous lists of highway "needs" with the incomplete information available for "needs" for funds for health, education, and welfare.

Initiative 274, Cut the Gas Tax Three Cents

By 1971, many people in our state had been immediately and adversely affected by highways already built and those planned for the future. They banded together, first as neighbors to fight a particular project, and then as organizations to try to get some attention paid to the damaging effects of highway projects. They alleged that the state highway planning and funding laws were based solely on the benefits to highway users. They claimed that the laws did not provide for any consideration of the costs of the damage caused by the construction and traffic on the people in the immediate vicinity of the projects and on the surrounding area. They said that highway decisions were foreclosing the land use and energy decisions of the future.

It *would* have been sensible if the Legislature had been able to listen to the two factions and had examined the relevant state and federal laws to see if any changes were needed in the basic highway priority planning programming and funding criteria. But the people in the Highway Department and the Legislature liked the status quo and repeatedly stonewalled a review of the process. Our favorite panacea, a department of transportation organized as part of the state's administrative branch under the governor, became a political symbol of what the governor did *NOT* get out of each session of the Legislature.

If the controversy had been over anything but highway funds, there would have been an automatic review of program planning and funding in the usual legislative biennial budget review, but the spending of highway trust funds has always been a unique and separate process in our state, far removed from any legislative budget review oversight. Earmarked highway use funds are budgeted in a highly political process in some hidden arena, under the cover of an incomprehensible prioritization system.

Seattle Citizens Against Freeways

PULL THE PLUG ON THE
PAVING MACHINE
SPOKANE
SEATTLE
PASCO
TACOMA
WALLA WALLA
RICHLAND
SAVE MONEY AND SAVE THE STATE'S
CITIES FROM DESTRUCTION
CUT 3¢ FROM OUR 9¢ GAS TAX
BY SIGNING INITIATIVE 274

Our priorities were set by proposed legislation to pass additional fuel taxes for the highway purposes of state and local jurisdictions and for urban arterials. A few of us decided that the best way to attack obsolete highway funding laws was to try to make less money available for the highway trust fund. Since we had found the Legislature to be completely unresponsive, we decided to take our cause to the people, and with very little knowledge of the initiative process, we filed Initiative 274, Cut the State Gas Tax 3 Cents.

The initiative turned out to be a time-wasting mistake. We had too little knowledge of the tremendous work involved in obtaining over 100,000 signatures statewide, and we had no organization at all at the beginning. We had not thought about what would happen if we got the issue on the ballot. If we had paid any attention to the politics of obtaining votes for an initiative, we would have realized that we would be wiped out by the high-spending highway lobby. There was a long record of citizens' efforts being defeated at the polls by opponents who had the money and expertise to get votes. Actually, we were spared that obviously futile task by failing to get enough signatures to put the initiative on the ballot.

House Bill 812, Repeal the Urban Arterial Laws

One immediately effective action to change the process for building urban highways was to repeal the state urban arterial laws, to wipe out the whole process. I convinced my representative, Paul Kraabel, that such a bill should be written, and in January, 1972, he submitted House Bill 812, which would repeal the urban arterial statutes and delete all reference to them in other laws. I had to leave Olympia immediately because of family illness, and when I returned two months later, I found that the bill was completely dead and buried. Nevertheless, I believe that the urban arterial process must be entirely repealed, and I have worked and worked on the issue.

The illustration here is from a flyer, "Rest in Peace Urban Arterial Board, 1968—1973" that we had used in lobbying for House Bill 812 in 1972.

Our message was clear:
"REPEAL THE URBAN ARTERIAL LAW! HERE'S WHY:

(1) It maintains a completely separate highway planning process which is independent of all other transportation planning.

(2) It maintains a system for special purpose funding—a completely separate process for funding only one category of transportation—the biggest urban-area highways.

(3) It maintains a process for continual and effective lobbying by the cities and counties so that they will be able to get these additional funds from new vehicle taxes—to raise gas taxes for this special purpose."

"This complete repeal is the only possible way to put highway planning and funding under an enlarged and complete transportation system, but the people who want to continue the process are numerous and powerful, acting in their own self interests. The concrete lobby wants to build more and bigger projects. The people who draft, examine, and sell bonds want more work.

"The cities and the counties have been trained to believe that this process is essential to their obtaining fuel-tax funds. They have been duped. They chose to get urban arterial funds for specific large projects instead of annual gas tax funds; and the city of Seattle's share of the 1968 urban arterial funds was equal to what Seattle would have

"WE'LL HAVE ONE MORE ROUND OF HIGHWAYS, AND GIVE THE BILL TO MY YOUNG FRIEND HERE"

received in only five years—Seattle got nothing from the new gas taxes after that. Furthermore, the gas tax funds could have been used for any highway purpose—pot holes, repaving, bridge repair, etc.—which the city cannot now fund. The traffic engineers set the lobbying policies for the Associations of Washington Cities and Counties, and they are annually promised more money for big projects if the Legislature passes additional fuel taxes. They come to Olympia as a very strong lobbying force.

"Our state cannot get the sensible transportation solutions we want by continuing the life of a separate agency supported by special-purpose highway funds."

4. THE WASHINGTON COALITION FOR SENSIBLE TRANSPORTATION (WCST)

WASHINGTON
COALITION FOR
SENSIBLE
TRANSPORTATION

The state of Washington is divided by the Cascade mountain range, and the people on the west side and the people on the east of the state had been exchanging information and meeting together on transportation problems for several years. In August, 1972, Cuba O'Neill in Spokane and I began to plan a statewide meeting, and we set it for the last weekend in September. I described it in the first *Newsletter* in October:

"THE WASHINGTON COALITION FOR SENSIBLE TRANSPORTATION"

"The first state-wide brainstorming meeting of the anti-freeway groups in the state was held at Sun Lakes park on the weekend of September 30. The agenda was not set, but the course of the meeting had been set by the invitation:

" 'Much can be accomplished for all of us in the next session of the legislature if we work together. We need an understanding of each other's problems, ideas, and plans for action.'

"The meetings resulted in unanimous agreement between the participants: they wanted to meet again; they did not want to organize into a group which might supersede their own organizations. They decided to form a new purely liaison group, the Washington Coalition for Sensible Transportation (the WCST). Activities planned are a rally in Olympia for lobbying the Legislature on January 20 and the printing of a newsletter for exchanging information."

The history of WCST is recorded in the *NEWSLETTERS*, which are available as a separate volume as well as inserts in the files for each year 1972 to 1979 in the University of Washington archives.

By 1975, the WCST coalition was made up of 42 organizations; we met annually in October, we had gone to Olympia on the train to speak at a hearing, and we had a very effective telephone tree to alert the entire membership for lobbying on particular bills. In March of each year, when most of the bills had been submitted to the Legislature, we evaluated them, wrote, and circulated a special *Newsletter* to all the legislators.

5. THE CITIZEN LOBBYIST

I think it was Mr. Justice Holmes who wrote, "The life of the law is not logic but experience," and that was what I learned as an unpaid citizen lobbying the legislature during most of their sessions for ten years.

The "unpaid" part of the description is important because it meant that the lobbyist not only did not get paid but that the job cost a lot in time, travel expenses, awful food, telephone and copying costs. The "unpaid" part of the description also points out the main benefit of that kind of lobbying, for it meant that the lobbyist had to gain the support of a constituency by presenting convincing facts and planning effective assistance—and on an almost day-to-day basis because there were no instructions from any ruling body.

I soon learned that some activities were essential. I had to get to certain committee meetings, and to do so I had to go to the Bill Room every day for the meeting schedule, new bills, and the status sheets of the old bills. Then I had to find somewhere to sit quietly to read everything, decide what action I might want to take that day, and prepare to make a statement at a committee meeting held in the morning before the session or in the afternoon or evening after the last session of the day. In between the session and the committee meetings I would try to lobby and, since it was usually difficult to make an appointment, I would nab the legislator as he or she (almost always he) left for the office or the Capitol. I would give a breathy four-minute capsule of what I wanted, while we walked across the street, rain, snow, slush, or sunshine.

WCST built up a very efficient telephone tree, and I could call on them to alert members to contact elected officials when particular issues were before the legislature.

The Mail Room distributed the cartoons Dave Lefebvre had drawn for us to the legislators, their assistants and their secretaries, and especially to the press. The cartoons explained the issues better than any words we could use, and they made our work so much easier.

I liked my fellow lobbyists and the newspaper reporters, the legislators who would listen to me and their secretaries. I managed to find a table outside one of the House offices where I kept a large cardboard carton of my files—a big help. I enjoyed sitting up in the galleries, watching and waiting for something to happen. I liked to sit on the old leather sofas in the Gulch, the lobbyists' hangout, complete with always-available telephone operators. In the early 1970's, we parked on the street six or seven blocks from the government campus, and we walked past people's houses and under their trees, which showered us with Japanese cherry blossoms in the spring.

I finally managed to smooth out relationships with some of the more rigid legislators—with humor. Representative Red Beck was a most powerful pro-highway legislator, and he always used to leave the room whenever I stood to speak. I decided on a strategy, and it worked. The next time I was called, I went to the podium so fast that he did not have time to escape, and then I just stood there, relaxed, and said, "I am waiting for Representative Beck to leave the room before I speak." Senator Sam Guess, the most influential person on the Senate Transportation Committee, would sit at hearings completely occupied by writing and writing, so that we would know that he did not intend to pay any attention to us. My strategy with him was to go to the podium and just stand there and say, "I am waiting to give Senator Guess time to finish his writing." It worked; he stopped. I can also remember standing in the back of the hearing room listening entranced to Senator Guess' thirty-minute revelation that his studies of asphalt had led to the findings that no one knew what it was made of—he didn't seem to notice that the hearing was going on and that he must have been bothering the audience.

The most interesting altercation was with Senator Al Henry (when he was Chairman of the Transportation Committee), and it was carried on through the newspapers' reports. Senator Henry had held four meetings at which highway department employees spoke about the highway budget. We had waited around for an opportunity for us to speak at the budget hearing, but he never scheduled or held it , and the minutes proved we were right. I wrote in the *Newsletter* that the bill had been passed out of committee without a hearing, and the press picked up the story. Senator Henry announced to the press that Margaret Tunks had lied and that she was not going to be allowed to speak before his committee ever again unless she apologized. The press sought an answer from me, but the whole thing was too silly to discuss, and the reporters knew it.

6. CITIZENS' ACTION IN THE LEGISLATURE, 1975 - 1977, Sensible Transportation Lost

Looking back on all those years, I can remember only a few of our efforts which were really successful operations. I will review only two: our helping the Governor to sustain his gas tax veto in 1975; and my amendments to the Department of Transportation bill in 1977. I will write about two bills I wrote to try to put sensible transportation planning into the state statutes; one funded a study for changes in functional highway criteria—it passed (but was emasculated), and one which was defeated. I will give short shrift to what I call the "silly" bills because they were not enforceable—the State Legislature had tried to set up processes for receiving federal funds for highways without meeting the federal law requirements for so doing. I will write about our disappointment in our failure to pass bills which would expedite planning and funding of public transportation and our defeat at trying to affect the laws which continued proliferation of highways for urban travel.

The Defeat of the Bus Transit Bill

In 1971, I copied a new federal law which allowed spending of federal highway trust funds for ferries and for mass transit facilities. My bill, SB 510, duplicated the provisions in the Federal Highway Act Section 142 except that the federal statute is permissive, and my bill made this funding of transit mandatory where the transit system would not cost more, would accommodate the same number of persons, and where a transit authority had capability to operate the system. My bill would have really promoted sensible transportation by setting up a process for the consideration of transit in addition to highways.

The day the bill amendment was to be voted on, I saw James Ellis, the founder of and counsel of Metro, and others at lunch time in the Capitol Building restaurant. I thought they were there because of my bill amendment, so I went over to tell them how much I would appreciate their support. Mr. Ellis turned white as a sheet. [I later learned that he was in a period of suffering from stomach ulcers.] None of the men at the table said anything to me then, and as the years have gone by, I learned that we could not count on the people who controlled Metro to act for transit. [It's interesting to note that in 1975, Aubrey Davis was Chairman of the Metro Transit Committee, the Urban Arterial Board, the PSGC Transportation Policy Commission, and the King County Sub Regional Transportation Policy Committee—and now, in 1996, Aubrey Davis is on the State Transportation Commission (the name having been changed from "Highway Commission"), which still operates under all the ancient state statutory and political limitations to multi-modal transportation systems.]

My amendment died when a motion to table it was passed, but nineteen Senators did <u>not</u> vote to table it—in effect, they *voted for* the bill, and I felt that we all had learned something about highway and transit decision-making.

The Failure of the Priority Planning Study

I wanted to try to change the state's priority programming criteria for the expenditure of all state and local jurisdictions' highway funds—a system erroneously called "functional classification." Three of the criteria were based on increasing traffic capacity by requiring all jurisdictions to examine and rate each segment of the jurisdiction road/street/highway system to find:

(a) Its structural capacity to carry the loads imposed upon it;

(b) Its capacity to move traffic at reasonable speeds without undue congestion;

(c) Its adequacy of alignment and related geometrics;

(d) Its accident experience; and
(e) Its fatal accident experience.

These ratings became "needs" and the highest rated gained first priority for funding.

I was impressed by new federal laws that required classification of streets, roads, and highways by purpose, a real functional classification process, and I drafted a bill for a study to classify trips by the percentage of each kind of trip:

Home-to-work (commuter) trips;
Commodities movement (including farm-to-market) trips;
Mandatory trips—defense, emergency;
Essential trips—mail, school bus;
Recreational trips.

My bill passed with $30,000 funding for an interim study, which was given to a Bellevue firm, VTN. The study was a complete disaster—the Interim Transportation Committee people supervising the study wanted to wipe out the new federal criteria-based system law, even though the states were required to adopt it as a condition precedent to obtaining federal transportation funds. The VTN study approved the existing obsolete state criteria and recommended funding for the existing system and an expanded sixteen member Urban Arterial Board! Fortunately nothing came of that, but I had been exceedingly stupid to set up a mechanism for VTN to collect $30,000 for doing worse than nothing, and I began to learn that when our state refused to pass laws incorporating federal laws, our state did not intend to comply with those federal laws!

7. THE SILLY BILLS

Two of the bills we opposed must be categorized as the silly bills because they were attempts to repeal the federal laws which required the local jurisdictions to meet certain requirements in land use and transportation planning processes as a condition precedent to federal funding of capital projects. I thought that these bills were incredibly ridiculous because the legislators who proposed and voted for them were actually announcing that they, the legislators of the State of Washington, could evade federal laws at will—and if Washington could so do, any state in the union could at any time pass laws which could supersede any provisions of federal laws that controlled federal funding of all highways (or anything else?). If, I reasoned, the legislators were right and they could write laws to cancel these federal laws, then why were Congress and the President taking the trouble to pass federal legislation? Or, why are we paying them if the laws they pass have no lasting validity?

I thought that the introduction of the silly bills was proof of the failure of the legislators to try to find out what the federal laws meant, but I was totally wrong. The silly bills could be effective because federal administrative agencies did not enforce the conditions required for federal highway funding in the state of Washington. By 1976 at least three different Washington state court judges had ruled in three different cases that the state law superseded the applicable federal laws.

In our state, the elected officials of all the jurisdictions are entitled to seek and obtain advice and guidance from the office of the elected attorney general, who also assigns competent lawyers to each individual department in the state government. A lawyer from the Federal Highway Administration is supposed to be constantly monitoring and working with our Highway Commissioners (to see that the requirements of federal laws were met?), but the closest FHWA lawyer was in Portland, Oregon. In my experience, the commissioners and many legislators either did not get any legal advice (because they did not want it?) or they paid no attention to legal advice—the horrible example being the nine-year delay in the I-90 project due to the failure of the State to meet federal law requirements as mandated by the federal court judges in the I-90 case.

I thought that no intelligent lawyer would ever write such silly bills. The silly bill, HB 1141, set up a time schedule for the various steps in the completion of I-90 by substituting the Legislators' laws for the requirements of the federal highway funding laws. HB 1141 was a mechanism to preserve the 1971 Mercer Island design of the project in 1975 by taking away the rights of the adjacent corridor jurisdictions and the people to consider the adoption of any other design or any alternative—the bill was intended to prevent the consideration of any of the alternatives which had already been provided for in amendments to Section 103 (e) of the Federal Highway Act, that allowed local jurisdictions along the I-90 corridor and the governor to withdraw any or all of the I-90 federal funds so that they could also be used for highways and public transportation outside the Mercer Island corridor.

HB 803, the other silly bill, was supposed to abolish the Puget Sound Governmental Conference outright. Forty-one Legislators had signed it shortly after it was introduced. I wrote an entire page on it for the March 4, 1975, *Newsletter*, and I quote from it here:

"The PSGC exists (as far as transportation statutes are concerned) as a highway and public transportation planning body under two sets of laws attached to federal-aid: The Federal Highway Act and The Urban Mass Transportation Act. Both acts require a comprehensive, continuing, cooperative planning process to be carried out by the local governmental bodies in the urbanized areas of over 50,000 population. PSGC has been planning transportation since 1962." [The members of the PSGC are elected officials chosen by their local governments, and their votes are weighted by the percentage of their population in the four-county area which they represent.]

"Federal agencies require the PSGC to adopt a regional development plan, but they extended the deadline from Jan. 1, 1975, to July 1, 1976. New federal regulations will require an adopted transportation plan for both highways and transit with a long-range plan (20 to 30 years), a medium range plan (3 to 5 years), and a biennial and annual element. No project can receive federal funds unless it is part of the plan." [And I added,] "and that's why the pro-highway Legislators decided to throw out the PSGC."

In the March 4, 1975, *Newsletter*, I wrote under the title 'THE SAGA OF THE PUGET SOUND GOVERNMENTAL CONFERENCE (as a transportation planning agency):

"HB 803 abolishes the Puget Sound Governmental Conference outright. It makes no substitutions for the PSGC, and the framer of the bill, Rep. Rick Bender, says that he believes the other state departments, of transportation, natural resources, and ecology, and other agencies can take over the functions of the PSGC. [Rep. Bender had apparently not noticed that our state did not have a department of transportation.]

"HB 803 is only the last of a long line of symptoms which prove that many people did not understand the federally-required transportation and land-use planning processes, people who should know. For instance:

"Last year the State Highway Commission withdrew $87,000 [matching] highway funds from the PSGC despite the fact that they had passed the budget containing these funds earlier. Commissioner Walsh said that the Commission did this, 'to show our displeasure'.

"Under new Chairman Spellman, PSGC has begun a reorganization which will minimize regional in favor of county-level planning—the main reason for so doing is generally given as "saving the Conference.

"State Highway Commissioner Baker Ferguson said last month, 'We don't want any more groups like the PSGC,' and the Commission cut the PSGC budget by $100,000."

I was totally wrong about HB 803—it passed, and its intent was perpetuated as a threatening device used by critics of PSGC to cancel the effectiveness of PSGC Transportation Planning Department, especially the work on I-90.

Both laws were very effective—see how they were used by Judge Scholfield in his decision on the I-90, Initiative #21 [page 255].

8. THE DEFEAT OF THE VARIABLE GAS TAX BILL

The Legislature had raised the state tax on motor vehicle fuels in 1967 and authorized the sale of $400 million in bonds—$200 million for state highways and $200 million for urban arterials. By 1970, the highway lobby was trying every year to raise funds for highways by raising taxes on motor vehicle fuels.

The long session of the 1975 Legislature was devoted to three main bills all in one trade-off package, which actually was pure and simple blackmail: if there were not enough votes on the bill to raise taxes for highway trust funds, Governor Evans' bills establishing a state department of transportation and providing funds for education would not be passed.

Our lobbying in 1975 is well-documented by the WCST writings in that year. Two items were especially effective: my discovery that the highway department had added pork-barrel projects in certain influential legislators' districts to push the tax raise; and my Alice-in-Wonderland spoof of the 1975 session.

The pork-barrel project story was picked up by reporter Shelby Scates and appeared in the May 15, 1975, *Seattle Post Intelligencer.*

"OLYMPIA—House speaker Len Sawyer and highway booster, Sen. C.W. (Red) Beck, got two of the largest slices of pork in the House-approved versions of the 1975-77 budget.

"An analysis of the budget by Margaret Tunks of the Washington Coalition for Sensible Transportation shows that 76 percent of the projects added by the House fell in six districts.

"Sawyer takes the plum, four miles of what's ultimately to be a four-lane limited access highway that runs parallel and only a few miles away from Lake Tapps.

"The Lake Tapps real estate development, which once offered choice lots at low, low prices to selected Pierce County officials, is represented by Sawyer, not only in the House, but as its legal counsel.

"Curiously, the Highway Department describes this project to members of the Transportation Committee as being in three legislative districts — the 11th, the 30th, and the 25th.

"It isn't. An examination of the district lines show that it's all in the 25th district represented by Sawyer.

"The project is scheduled to spend $3 million in the next biennium and to cost a total of $9 million when completed.

"Additional money is in the House version of the budget total $20.9 million. Money for these projects is contingent on passage of a gasoline tax increase.

"The other winners include the 26th district of Pierce and Kitsap Counties, represented by Beck, a leading fighter for highways. About $4.6 million of the additional $20.9 million goes to his district." ...

With apologies to Lewis Carroll, who wrote *Alice in Wonderland*, and to Shelby Scates, I wrote this in May, 1975, and had the Mail Room send it around to the press, the legislators, and their staff members. It still sums up the session.

"ALICE, THE MAD HATTER, AND THE 1975 LEGISLATURE

The Mad Hatter sat down beside Alice and poured himself a huge cup of tea. "I don't understand it," he said, "My calendar has gone wrong. I just came back from Olympia, and the legislators are still there so it must be April."

"No," said Alice, "It's May all right. And they call it the 135th day of the session. They are breaking all records," she said with pride. "What did you do in Olympia?"

"Well," said the Hatter, "I went to the Senate to hear them raise the highway budget to meet the variable gas tax, and I went to the House to hear them raise the gas tax to meet the highway budget. Even without the projects they added for Governor to veto, they will need 27% more gas tax."

Alice's voice trembled, "But I thought the Legislature promised this year not to raise taxes. Didn't they promise?"

The Mad Hatter had no trouble with that one. "The promises they made do not apply to highways—just to every day things like schools. You see they need more money for new construction on new alignments."

"For new what on where?" asked Alice, trying to understand.

"For new highways on new routes," said the Hatter. "They have a list of sixteen projects which will cost $47.4 million. They say that if the Legislature does not pass a construction budget of $355 million, these projects might be deferred. That sounded as if it would be real bad."

Alice knows the value of money, never having had more than a few pennies of pocket money at a time. "But didn't anyone object to the $47.4 million? Or the 27% raise in the gas tax?"

"Not really," the Hatter reported. "Everyone liked the gas taxes and their highways—the cities, the bus companies, and the construction people all thought they would get lots of both highway and gas tax money. Only one fat lady objected. She said that it was too much of a raise and it looked as if there was pork barreling because the powerful legislators would get the sixteen projects."

Alice was absolutely fascinated. "And were they pork barreling? Did you see them pork barreling? Is it a game like croquet?"

The Hatter was aghast. "Of course not. Pork barreling is not a spectator sport. Besides, the fat lady was wrong. Eleven of the projects would not have been deferred because they were to be paid partly with federal funds. So it wasn't real pork barreling, but I am not sure if the legislators knew it was really just a pretend game."

"Curiouser and curiouser," said Alice. "but why wasn't everyone allowed to play, anyhow?"

"No one objected," said the Hatter. "The leaders were playing a game, and everyone in Olympia is used to following the leaders, and besides, the people who never get to play and never get any roads are used to not getting any roads. They weren't even bothered when they didn't get anything for their votes for transit or the department of transportation. but I did wonder how those Legislators were going to explain it to their voters when they have to pay 40 cents more for a tankful of gas for other people's roads."

Alice was truly intrigued. She put on her hat with the ribbons hanging down her back and was off to Olympia.

"I'm going down to see the trade-offs and the pork barreling games. They sound like fun!"

We will never know what part our organization played in the governor's decision to veto the variable gas tax bill. The highway lobby had placed him (and, in fact, the whole Legislature) in an extremely unsavory position. All through the long session, they had opposed the funding of schools and the Governor's department of transportation because he was opposing the gas tax bill. By the time the gas tax bill had passed both houses, the Governor surely must have been ready to object to the whole procedure by his veto. WCST wrote to him that if he did veto, we would do everything we could to sustain it.

When he did veto the bill, we immediately notified our WCST telephone tree, which then consisted of forty-two organizations across the state, and they began to contact their legislators. As the Legislature wound to an unproductive close the last day, the last item was the vote to override the Governor's veto. I sat alone up in the gallery overlooking the floor of the House, and all of the professional highway lobbyists were nowhere in sight. The visible portion of the House has curtained-concealed walkways on either side, and no one is supposed to have access to them unless summoned by a house member; but I was the only lobbyist sitting up in the gallery, and it was obvious that all of the missing lobbyists were busily working behind the curtains.

Finally, all at once, the lobbyists came to sit down in the gallery, all of them [and I thought at the time that there were 96, but I now don't see how that was possible]. They did not have enough votes, the Governor's veto was intact, and although the legislature held a special session in September to pass the gas tax bill, they never got enough votes for it!

9. THE STATE DEPARTMENT OF TRANSPORTATION

Dan Evans was governor of the state of Washington for three terms—twelve years—and throughout all that time one of his primary objects was to establish a state department of transportation which would be like all other departments of state government—part of the governor's administration, with a secretary chosen and appointed by the governor. For twelve long years, the highway lobby kept this legislation hostage (often along with important school funding bills) trying to force the governor to agree to raises in gas taxes. As a smoke screen, highway backers devised their own DOT bill, which merely perpetuated the old completely closed machinations of the highway lobby. Their bill (SB 164 in 1975) enlarged the highway commission from five to seven members to be appointed by the governor and to have all the policy-making power in the department. Obviously they intended to continue the system of using the highway commission members as figureheads, who would merely nod from time to time to acquiesce to the decisions that had already been made. In their bill, the secretary was to be appointed by the governor from a list of three persons submitted by the commission, and the secretary was to have no term of office, unless forced out of the job by proof of wrongdoing.

The highway lobbyists' bills perpetuated all of the old practices by which the spending of funds was controlled. The department still would be funded with state highway trust funds limited by our constitution to being used only for ferry and road purposes, so that the transportation planning processes could not be comprehensive and multimodal. The highway budget would continue to be controlled, used to coerce legislators to vote at the threat of losing their highway projects and kept undercover to prevent any worthwhile legislative review.

In 1977, we knew that new Governor Dixy Lee Ray would immediately be presented with the highway proponents' department of transportation bill, and it was predictable that her action on it would show the course of her entire administration on transportation decisions. And so it did. I got an appointment with ex-newsman Lou Guzzo in her office to tell him why I really needed to talk to the Governor about transportation. He listened carefully, said I should talk to her, and that he would set up an appointment—but I never got to see her. She turned out to be a vituperative spokesperson for the highway lobby, swallowing their orders without any attention to facts.

"SHADDUP AN GET YOUR OWN PONY- THIS'NS MINE"

The bill she signed gave us the obsolete and useless department of transportation we still have. But when I stood in her office in May, 1977, and watched her sign the bill, little did she know what I had done to improve it. Representative Robert Perry was Chairman of the House Transportation Committee, and just before the bill was to be passed out of his committee, he allowed me to stand up and read three pages of amendments which I had typed out in a hurry. The Committee adopted all of them! The bill passed through both the House and Senate with my amendments almost intact. As I read them now, I find that a second draft would have improved them, but I didn't have time. I will write them here as they were printed in the bill when it was passed by both houses and signed by the Governor.

"*New Section*, Sec. 7. There is to be added to chapter 13, laws of 1961, and chapter 47.01 RCW a new section be read as follows:

"The transportation commission shall have the following functions, powers, and duties:

(1) To propose policies to be adopted by the legislature designed to ensure the development and maintenance of a comprehensive and balanced state-wide transportation system which will meet the needs of the people of this state for safe and efficient transportation services. [They added, "Whenever appropriate,"] "the policies shall provide for the use of integrated intermodal transportation systems to implement the social, economic, and environmental policies, goals, and objectives of the people of the state, and especially to conserve nonrenewable natural resources including land and energy. To this end the commission shall,

(a) Develop transportation policies which are based on the policies, goals, and objectives expressed and inherent in present state laws;

(b) Inventory the adopted policies, goals, and objectives of the local and area-wide governmental bodies of the state, regional, and local governments in determining transportation policies, in transportation planning, and in implementing the state transportation plan;

(c) Propose a transportation policy for the state, and after notice and public hearings, submit a proposal to the legislative transportation committee and the senate and house transportation committees by January 1, 1978, for consideration in the next legislative session.

(d) Establish a procedure for the review and revision of the state transportation policy and for the submission of proposed changes to the legislature.

(2) To establish the policy of the department to be followed by the secretary on each of the following items:

(a) To provide for the effective coordination of state transportation planning with national transportation policy, state and local policies, and local and regional transportation plans and policies and programs;

(b) To provide for public involvement in transportation, designed to elicit the public's views both with respect to adequate transportation service and appropriate means of minimizing adverse social, economic, environmental and energy impact of transportation programs;

(c) To direct the secretary to prepare and submit to the commission a comprehensive and balanced state-wide transportation plan which shall be based on the transportation policy adopted by the legislature and applicable state and federal laws. After public notice and hearing, the commission shall adopt the plan and submit it to the legislative transportation committee and to the house and senate standing committees on transportation before January 1, 1980 [they made the date a year later] for consideration in the next legislative session. The plan shall be reviewed and revised in the next regular session of the legislature and biennially thereafter. A preliminary plan shall be submitted to such committees by January 1, 1979 [a year later than I proposed]."

My amendments added essential procedures, but in no way cured the basic defect. <u>In 1996, the State of Washington still does not have a real Department of Transportation</u>.

"Create a Department of Transportation by changing the name of the Highway Department? They gotta be kidding!

10. INITIATIVE 348, REPEAL THE VARIABLE GAS TAX

In 1977, the highway lobby was going all out to get an increase in the fuel tax, and the outcome was certain because they knew Governor Ray would sign the bill. After all, they had the votes in 1975, but Governor Evans had refused to sign a bill which allowed variable fuel taxes.

In April, two polls were taken that showed that the public was strongly opposed to additional gas tax taxes:

GMA Research Corp. in Bellevue, a well-respected polling company, telephoned a statistical sample of King County residents to ask this question: "The State Legislature has considered a bill to increase the tax on gasoline to finance highway construction. The bill calls for an increase of 2 cents a gallon on July 1 for a total tax of 11 cents a gallon. The bill also allows for a possible eventual increase to 12 cents a gallon. Would you say you strongly favor, somewhat favor, somewhat oppose, or strongly oppose such an increase in gasoline taxes?" The answers were: Strongly favor, 2.5%; somewhat favor, 11.8%; somewhat oppose, 25.5%; strongly oppose, 55.4%; don't know, 4.8%

The Automobile Club of Washington's members voted by paper ballot on this question: "The present state gas tax of 9 cents per gallon was adopted in 1967. Since then, inflation and a reduced rate of growth in the sale of gasoline has contributed to a reduction in expenditures for highway purposes (which include the State Patrol and certain public transit facilities) in constant dollar terms. The Legislature approved an increase in the gas tax in 1975, but it was vetoed by the Governor. Do you favor or oppose an increase in the state gas tax to counter the downward trend in expenditures for highway maintenance and construction?" Despite this obviously loaded question, the results were: Favor, 31%; oppose, 65%; no reply, 4%.

When Initiative 348 was filed, it was given this simple ballot title: "Shall the new variable motor vehicle fuel tax law be repealed and the previous tax and distribution formula be reinstated?" But there is little doubt that the polls would have been any different if the real title question had been asked—the electorate did NOT want additional gas taxes.

The history of the initiative is well documented in the microfilmed newspaper articles and advertising. Somehow an odd coalition appeared. King County Assessor Harley Hoppe was leading a group of service station operators and members of his anti-tax group in a last-minute drive to put an initiative on the ballot to repeal the variable gas tax, and we immediately joined them in a last-minute effort to get more than 130,000 signatures on the petitions. The *Post Intelligencer* published a cartoon and article about "The Odd Couple," with Hoppe and Tunks as Jack and Jill trying to go up the hill to get Initiative 348 on the ballot. To this day, I have never met Mr. Hoppe, and I never discussed the initiative with him, but he certainly provided the technique. He paid to have the petitions printed in the major newspapers in the state, the complete petitions to be returned to certain gasoline service stations. The signatures were in Olympia by the July 8 deadline.

But our opponents "SAY NO 348" began an unfair campaign by violating the state laws limiting the amount which could be spent. I wrote: "VARIABLE GAS TAX GOES TO THE POLLS"

"We find that were in a very difficult battle—on October 29, the *Seattle Times* reported that we had $35,867 in contributions while our opponents had already spent $141,295.74, and had an additional $200,000 available for last minute campaigning. [If anyone wants to know what the highway lobby is made up of, their list of contributors will tell you: the highway builders, the cities and counties (after more urban arterial funds), the labor organizations, the real estate developers, and such unlikely contributors as the banks.]

"If the *Times* was correct, the anti-initiative group, "SAY NO 348" had some $341,295 to spend—far over their statutory limit of 15 cents per voter in the last presidential election."

On October 30, I sent a complaint of violations of the State Code to the Public Disclosure Commission in Olympia requesting, "the

Commission to begin immediately all statutory procedures and administrative actions which are designed to remedy this wrongful act, to stop the receipt and expenditures of illegal funds, and to bring sanctions against those who have violated this code.

"The violations are as follows:

"(1) The Public Disclosure Commission had prepared a document which was signed by the Washington Citizens Against 348 and in which they promised to abide by the voluntary limitations of 15 cents per Washington voter in the last presidential election, $237,688 ...

"(2) The Washington Citizens Against 348 had, as of October 26, accepted more than $259,000 in campaign contributions. As of October 26, this group had knowingly accepted more than $11,000 over the known limitation on their campaign receipts.

"(3) In all probability, further violations occurred since October 26.

"I urge the commission to proceed immediately to impose all possible sanctions against the Washington Citizens Against 348 in order that the proponents of Initiative 348 will not further suffer further damage cause by this unfair practice."

The Commission never acted on my complaint, and after the election had been lost by a mere 884 votes out of 941,178 votes cast, less than one percent, we discovered that a group of Senate employees, working on October 18 and November 1, had used state offices and telephones to poll three legislative districts (where candidates were battling for vacant Senate seats) to conduct telephone polls on Initiative 348. We learned later that the results of these polls were published in the *Aberdeen Daily* on November 3, the day before the election.

We filed another complaint alleging other violations; it was signed John Barber as chairman and William Dawson as treasurer of our REPEAL THE NEW GAS TAX Committee and by me as president of CARHT. The Commission had already had a hearing on the issue on December 20, and we were urging them to immediately make these recommendations and findings:

— The people who did the polling had misrepresented the ballot issue: they asked, "Initiative 348 would repeal the recent 2 cent increase in the gas tax. How do you feel about this one?" (The ballot issue was "Shall the new variable gas motor vehicle fuel tax law be repealed and the previous tax and distribution formula be reinstated?") We objected to their leaving out the fact that it was a *variable* gas tax, and the State could raise it—we expected it to be raised beyond 2 cents in the biennium.

— The facilities of state public officers were illegally used by persons who were either elected officials and/or their employees, and/or persons appointed to office, and/or employees of public offices or agencies for the purpose of assisting the campaign against Initiative 348."

The Public Disclosure Commission finally held a long hearing on January 17, after which the members voted 3-to-1 that there was no evidence that the polls violated the state's public disclosure laws, but they also decided to refer the matter to the Senate Board of Ethics and to the state auditor, requesting the state auditor to conduct a special audit of the Senate to see whether some other law had been violated. Nothing came of that, either. It is important to remember that the Public Disclosure Commission is funded by the Legislature, which put it in a rather difficult position when it was asked to rule against the Senate leadership.

ME FIRST- ME, ME, ME-- ME!!
CAN'T YOU SEE- I'M STARVING TO DEATH?

11. 1977, THE END OF AN ERA

For twelve long years, Governor Evans had been the great equalizer between the controlling highway-building legislators and sensible transportation. When Dixy Lee Ray became governor in 1977 and began to wildly repeat the promptings for the highway lobby, we knew that it would be a long time before the state of Washington achieved sensible transportation planning and funding. When she advocated and signed the Variable Gas Tax and the State Department of Transportation Bills that Governor Evans opposed for a decade, we knew that all the important decisions in transportation would be made outside any rational decision-making process. So the year of 1977 was the end of the era, and the focus now should be to try to get something rational out of the enormous amount of money which would be spent on I-90. That history is in Part III: Interstate 90, The Mercer Island Scam.

PART III
INTERSTATE 90, SEATTLE, 1970-1980

This history is the report of how the small town of Mercer Island was able to design the entire 1.56 billion dollar Interstate-90 project — the seven-miles from Interstate-405 in Bellevue to Interstate-5 in Seattle. It is a record of how the proponents of the plan worked together through nine long years to protect the Mercer Island 1971 design by evading the controlling federal laws. It is a record of the failure of the electials of Seattle to protect the city and its residents from the I-90 project and how the entire urban area lost the real alternative to the 1971 highway project.

When it was finished in 1990, the Bellevue/Seattle section of I-90 was the most expensive (per mile) road project ever built in the United States. Nine years elapsed between the filing of the I-90 lawsuit and the final approval of the project, but the politics of the era and the media blackout of the period leave little evidence of the causes of the delay.

The proponents' attacks through the years revealed their strategy. It was summarized in Governor Dixy Lee Ray's speech to the Good Roads Association report in the *Seattle Post Intelligencer* on September 16, 1977, under the headline:

"DIXY BLAMES I-90 BLOCKERS FOR DEATHS

... "Referring to the 'few individuals' who have taken every advantage of the technicality of the law to stop completion of I-90,"

On September 22, 1977, the *Post Intelligencer* published an interview with John Stephenson, who had been the project engineer for I-90 since 1967. "He blames six or eight people for the exceptionally long delay in the completion of I-90" ... "Fighting freeways is an obsession with this handful of people. They are obsessed with the glory and grandstanding. Their minds are closed to the facts."

Sixteen years later, the *Mercer Island Reporter* editor Peggy Reynolds wrote a history of I-90 for the September 9, 1993,

Seattle Times, where she repeated this statement originally made in 1977: "Gov. Dixy Lee Ray called [Margaret] Tunks 'the one person who alone has been responsible for the 20-year delay in completing I-90.'"

I am a grandmother whose opposition to I-90 was my studying the applicable laws, writing analyses, and infrequently speaking on the issues. How could I alone have delayed the project? The complaining proponents did it themselves! And on purpose!

I began to write this history after carefully re-reading all of the papers in the 14 cartons of material I had kept from 96 cartons I had stored. I selected the information which I could use to prove what really happened to I-90: how the project was deliberately delayed while proponents built up enough political power to get exactly what they wanted; how proponents were able to completely ignore the federal laws and the courts' mandates enforcing them.

January 1970, marked the beginning of a long decade of transportation decisions to Seattle. When the activities are listed in chronological order, we see how project decisions were made separately and how they overlapped. Everything seemed to be happening at once in 1970:

In January: The State began I-90 design meetings, held separately in Seattle and on Mercer Island, described as for "citizens' participation."

January 19: The Washington State House and Senate Interim Transportation Committees called a meeting with the Seattle City Council and Mayor to unveil the Zahn offer which included I-90.

January 27: The federal corridor/design hearing on the Seattle segment of I-90 was held in Seattle.

February 13: King County voters rejected the Forward Thrust bond issue for public rail transportation.

April 17: The combined federal corridor/design and state hearing on the Bay Freeway was held in Seattle.

May 5: Seattle citizens living in the I-90 corridor filed a lawsuit in the U.S. Court for the District of Western Washington against the State and the Secretary of the U.S. Department of Transportation. The case became known by the name of the lead plaintiffs as the "*Lathan*" case. Citizens' organizations filed as intervenors, and since Citizens Against Freeways was listed first, the court decisions group all of those plaintiffs in the category, "Citizens".

June 1: The Seattle City Council voted to stop work on the R.H. Thomson project and to build the Bay Freeway.

November 19: U.S. Court for the District of Western Washington Judge Beeks ruled for the *Lathan* defendants; plaintiffs' requests for an injunction and new hearing were denied. Plaintiffs appealed to the U.S. Court of Appeals for the Ninth Circuit.

My active participation in the I-90 opposition began on January 19, 1970, with the announcement of the Zahn offer to the City of Seattle. I was interested because the offer involved I-90, the R.H. Thomson proposed freeway, an addition to the Evergreen Point Bridge Highway (SR 520) (including an overpass to bring that bridge traffic over I-5), and the building of the Connecticut and Bay Freeway as parts of the 1963 proposed Seattle Ring Road. The offer even had provisions for the future of SR 522, the Bothell highway which was to connect to the Thomson Expressway.

I had moved to Seattle in late 1963, and I did not know anything about the I-90 project until the late 1960's when the State Highway Department was purchasing property in two corridors in Seattle: the I-90 corridor; and the proposed corridor for the R.H.Thomson Expressway, a project we were opposing because it would go through the Lake City community. These routes were marked by the continuing devastation of houses and property the State bought for the freeways.

Until 1970, my knowledge of the I-90 project had consisted of a Citizens Planning Council picture showing a horrendous interchange between the proposed Thomson Expressway and I-90.

1. THE 1970 I-90 CORRIDOR/DESIGN HEARING IN SEATTLE

In their preparation for the Seattle January 27, 1970, federal corridor/design hearing, the State showed a great propensity for ignoring the federal procedures required to obtain federal funding for I-90. I had prepared for the corridor/design hearing by studying and becoming familiar with the hearings laws in Section 128 of United States Code 23, the Federal Highway Act, and in the administrative regulations promulgated under them. I learned that I had the right to inspect the materials the district highway office had prepared for the hearing on the design of the Seattle part of I-90, and I went there to get information about the I-90 corridor hearing held in 1963 in Seattle. I wanted to compare the 1970 proposed corridor with the corridor the federal Secretary of Transportation had approved in 1963. I found that the

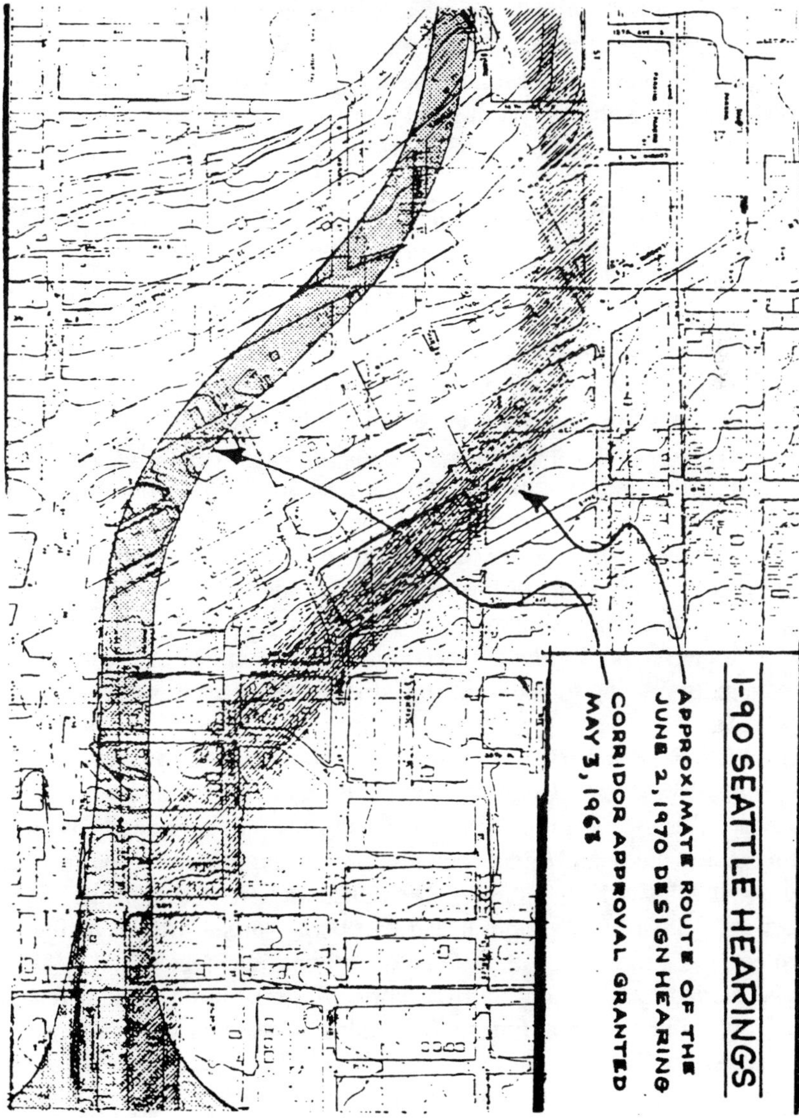

I-90 SEATTLE HEARINGS
APPROXIMATE ROUTE OF THE JUNE 2, 1970 DESIGN HEARING
CORRIDOR APPROVAL GRANTED MAY 3, 1963

district office had virtually no records; they had no copy of *any* 1963 Federal approval of the corridor/design and only a pencil outline of the I-90 corridor which they said had been approved in 1963—I traced it to obtain a copy (with their permission).

When I compared the 1963 approved corridor to the corridor to be presented at the design hearing, I discovered that the two corridors were very different. The map the State would use for the design hearing showed a new corridor curving north of the 1963 route, the deviation beginning at 23rd Avenue and proceeding to the already-built connections to I-5. The 1970 corridor would take far more property than the 1963 version and would leave an island between the old and the new highways. I asked my friend Dave Lefebvre to draw both corridors on a flyer that we printed and handed out at the hearing. The drawing was self-explanatory, and it must have influenced the decision—the State Highway Commissioners submitted the old 1963 corridor for federal approval!

The citizens had not been aware of the most important defect in the process—the 7-mile project had been divided into a Mercer Island segment and a Seattle segment, and the I-90 process was proceeding through the required federal procedures as two entities. Mercer Island was rapidly moving to determine the size of I-90 in Seattle.

2. THE FORWARD THRUST RAIL BOND PROPOSAL

In 1966, Metro Counsel James Ellis and others had organized Forward Thrust, a group of some 200 people appointed by the Governor to study and select capital improvement projects to be funded by bonds sales in King County. The transportation section of the 1968 Forward Thrust bond proposal had two parts: urban arterial highway projects to be matched with state urban arterial funds; and a rail system to be funded by $380 million from Forward Thrust bond sales matched by $740 million Federal funds. Two railroad lines had been proposed: an east/west line to be built on the I-90 project across Lake Washington; and a north/south line through the Seattle business district to 95th Street NW in Ballard.

I went to several public information meetings on the rail proposal where people said that it did not seem to be part of an areawide, multimodal transportation plan—none of the governments in any of the local jurisdictions had participated in any rail plan. People said that they didn't know if it were to be a supplement, a complement, or an alternative to, or substitute for, parts of the existing and planned highway system. They kept saying, "It doesn't do anything for us." The bond issue failed to get the required 60% vote.

The Forward Thrust rail bond issue was put on the ballot again in a special election in May, 1970. The plan had been changed in the two years since the bond issue failed in 1968. A line had been added on the SR 522 corridor to 92nd Street in the Lake City area, and an auxiliary bus system had been designed to connect with all the rail lines. The Okomoto/Liskamm firm again acted in a dual role of both designing the system (with Deleuw/Cather) and promoting it in public meetings. The plan still had the original defects the people had objected to; it still did not seem to be a part of an area-wide, multimodal transportation plan. I spoke at several meetings to present the projects to the people and to get them to vote for it, but the people kept repeating the objection they had in 1968, "It doesn't do anything for us."

In May, 1970, the rail bonds were again rejected by the voters. The voters may have been affected by the state of the local economy because the election was at the beginning of the Boeing Airplane Company's "slump" (as it was called in Seattle). Thousands of people lost their jobs with Boeing and the companies who supplied Boeing, and in May, 1970, people were apprehensive about being taxed for the rail system when so many jobs were being lost.

3. AN OVERVIEW OF THE I-90 LAWSUITS

[I will review the various steps in the I-90 Court case now as they fit into the rest of the history of the 1970-74 period. My writing, the *Critique of the I-90 Environmental Impact and 4(f) Statements*, [the *Critique*], contains some 330 pages of available information, and it can be found at the Seattle Public Library and the University of Washington Library.

The I-90 lawsuit was filed on May 28, 1970. The State obviously had intended to ignore all the federal environmental laws which applied to the project—the requirements of NEPA (the National Environmental Protection Act), the Federal Highway Act, and the Clean Air Act. The State also was ignoring the federal laws that required fair treatment in the relocation of the people whose property had been acquired and the "4(f)" laws which protected parklands.

The State's early and continued decisions to withhold all possible information from corridor residents and other concerned citizens in Seattle became the basis for the lawsuit; the case was named *the Lathan v. Volpe* case after the lead plaintiffs and the lead defendant, the Secretary of the U.S. Department of Transportation—[the name of the case changed when a new Secretary was appointed]; the Washington State Highway Commission [called the State in this history] was the other defendant.

The plaintiffs sued to obtain an injunction from the court to stop all property acquisition and construction of the I-90 project until the defendants met the requirements of the federal laws. The National Environmental Protection Act (NEPA) had become federal law on January 1, 1970, and the plaintiffs asked the court to order the State to prepare the adequate 4(f) and Environmental Impact Statements required to record the social, economic and environmental effects of a federally-funded project. They asked the court to order a new corridor hearing to be held <u>after</u> the requested materials were available for elected officials and people to read <u>before</u> any decisions were made on the project.

In 1970, the case was tried before Judge Beeks in the U.S. District Court for Western Washington. The defendants submitted a "sales" type pamphlet for an environmental impact statement, Judge Beeks found it to be adequate, and he said all other requirements of federal laws were met. The plaintiffs lost their case on every issue. The judge did not grant an injunction or a new hearing.

The plaintiffs appealed to the U.S. Court of Appeals for the Ninth Circuit. In 1971 a three-judge panel heard the case, and they found for the plaintiffs, reversing Judge Beeks' 1970 decision. They ordered the requested injunction on the I-90 project and remanded the case back to the Federal District Court. Defendants were told to prepare a new and adequate Environmental Impact Statement, to provide adequate information as required by Clean Air, 4(f) Parkland Protection, and Relocation Laws, and to hold a new hearing based on them. The district court judge was then to evaluate the information and to lift the injunction if it were adequate. 455 F. 2d 1117 (1971),

The defendants ignored the Circuit Court's opinion—they merely re-submitted all the materials they had given to Judge Beeks in 1970, including the pamphlet 16 page Draft Environment Impact Statement. On August 8, 1972, he wrote that the 4(f) and Environmental Impact Statements and the other information was inadequate, but that a new hearing was not necessary. Judge Beeks' reaction to the defendants is explained in a very few words. "The impact statement submitted in this case fails to meet minimum legal standards. ... By seriously underestimating their duty, defendants have caused yet another costly delay in this project." 350 F. Supp. 265 (1972)

The plaintiffs returned to the Court of Appeals requesting a reversal of that part of the opinion which said that new hearing was not needed. The defendants returned to the Court requesting a reversal of the ruling that the submitted statements were inadequate.

In 1973, in their decision on the second appeal, a three-judge panel from the U.S. Court of Appeals for the Ninth Circuit reversed the 1972 Beeks decision and ruled that a new hearing was required. However another panel of the Ninth Circuit Court of Appeals ruled in a very similar California case that a new hearing was not required. In 1974, the cases were combined and heard by the entire Court of Appeals which confirmed the 1973 I-90 *Lathan* opinion and remanded both cases to the Federal District Courts.

When Judge Beeks wrote in his 1972 opinion that the defendants had caused yet another costly delay in the project, the date of his decision marked the beginning of the real delay of the I-90 project, the delay that would last until the State submitted the court-mandated materials to a Federal District Court judge assigned to the case and that judge determined that the State's submissions were adequate. Until the decision of Judge Thompson in 1979!

4. THE MERCER ISLAND DECISION AND HOW IT WAS MADE; THE FOUNDATION FOR THE PLAN

The I-90 project activities continued throughout the nine long years of opposition and litigation, but I did not learn how and when the I-90 decisions had been made until 1994—when I was sorting out papers our attorney had given me and found the deposition of Aubrey Davis for the 1979 *Lathan* case trial. His sworn statement was the real history of the I-90 project, the Mercer Island Plan.

In 1970, the State had set up meetings with the people in Seattle and with the people on Mercer Island—the State said that the meetings were to determine the design of I-90 through their cities. This division of the short I-90 section, (slightly over seven miles), into two segments was a clever device used to prevent any consideration of the design of the complete project.

These meetings in Seattle and on Mercer Island were held separately, but they were certainly not equal!

The Seattle meetings were structured to be ineffective. State employees conducted the meetings and ignored anything people wanted to say. They said that they had already designed the I-90 project in Seattle—they were not going to change it. They presented drawings of possible structures and landscaping to ameliorate neighborhood damage caused by I-90, but when they were asked, they said that the State would not pay for any of this work—they had just been showing the people of Seattle what they could do with their own funds! The people in the audience were angry.

[And for the next eight years, whenever the difference between the designs of the Mercer Island and Seattle portions of the project were questioned, the proponents of the I-90 project said that the Seattle people did not want to cooperate in the design of I-90 in Seattle!]

When they were not allowed to participate, the audience decided that the State's meetings were a complete waste of time; they rebelled, decided to structure their own meetings, and they met for eight months on their own agendas. In August of 1970, the Mayor appointed a "Mayor's I-90 Design Advisory Committee"—and these local residents and community leaders worked long hours for six months to give the Mayor their excellent and complete *Citizens' Report on I-90 in 1971.* The Mayor did not publicize the *Report* or respond in any way to the members of the Committee.

A member of the Committee, Mt. Baker architect Seth Jackson, was surprised one day by a phone call from Councilman Tim Hill, who asked him if he knew that the Mayor was holding a press conference on the *Report* the next day at 11 A.M.—the Council would be present and would have speaking time from 11:30 until noon, when they had to leave for a previously scheduled meeting. Seth immediately notified the committee members, and they went to hear the Mayor's biased presentation of their *Report* and the Council's reaction because they had not had an opportunity to study it. Then Ike Ikeda, a community leader who is usually a quiet man, rose up in anger to protest. He said that the *Citizens' Report* had deliberately been withheld. He asked the Council to hold their own hearing on the report. They did, and, as Seth Jackson said, "They acted favorably."

I was working at the legislature in the 1970's, and I am still trying to put together exactly what happened to the design of I-90 in Seattle. Seth Jackson says that in 1971 the city approved the *Citizens' Report* 3-2T-3 plan, (three lanes in each direction with two transit lanes in the center), but it was changed by the efforts of Councilman Kraabel to 3-2TCP-3 (three lanes in each direction with two lanes in the middle for transit <u>and carpools</u>), but in 1979, State Secretary of Transportation Bill Bulley had said, in his sworn deposition for the 1979 District Court trial on I-90 that I-90 Chief Engineer John Stephenson came before the Mediation group in 1976 to show drawings to prove that the 3-2-3 design for I-90 was wide enough to be restripped for 4-2-4. Seth Jackson points out that the highway in the old tunnel through Mt. Baker is only forty-four feet wide and can accommodate only three lanes of traffic if the federal standards are met. [It would be safer for four lanes than the old tunnel because the lanes would be in one direction, not reversible.] However, all throughout the nine years before the final decision on I-90, the State refused to tell what the actual width of the project in Seattle was—they would only give its width in lanes.

Meanwhile, the State held 54 meetings in 1970 and 1971 on Mercer Island, the people were promised everything they wanted in the I-90 project at no cost to them, and costs were never discussed.

On June 13, 1971, a federal hearing was held that portion of I-90 from the west shore of Mercer Island to the end at I-405 in Bellevue. The limitation of the hearing to the Mercer Island segment was to prevent any consideration or discussion of the whole project. Seattle was being locked into Mercer Island's decision on the size of the whole project, whether or not it should incorporate rail, and the decision that no alternatives to it were available.

The I-90 project was set in concrete by the autumn of 1971, state and federally approved, never to be changed. The Mercer Island Plan had begun, and it would run its merry course until late 1979—but I never really put the whole picture together until I had finished this history in 1996.

In 1994, I learned about the 1970 start of the Mercer Island Plan process when I read that Aubrey Davis, the Mercer Island leader of the I-90 proponents, was sworn and answered questions requested by the plaintiffs recorded in a 1979 deposition for the Federal District Court trial on the I-90 *Lathan* case. [A deposition substitutes for the opportunity to swear in and question a witness in court.] Most of the questions were asked by the plaintiffs' lawyer, Roger Leed; some questions were asked and statements made by the defendants' attorneys, Secrest and Rutledge.

Mr. Davis first said that he was a member of the City Council of Mercer Island from 1968 to August 30, 1978, and Chairman of the Metro Transit Committee from August, 1971, to August 30, 1978, when he was appointed director of District 10 of the Federal Department of Transportation, effective September 1, 1978.

Mr. Davis was a member of the Mercer Island I-90 Committee, established in the spring of 1970, and Chairman of that Committee while he was mayor. He said that they had worked with a State Highway Department consultant on the design of I-90 to be built across Mercer Island. He said, "...The consultant ... essentially started from scratch in meeting with citizens, finding out what their concerns were, producing data for discussion and evaluation by the citizens."

"...And out of that mutual process—it was quite a lot of give and take—evolved what was later to become known as the 4-2-4 design." [Four lanes west, four lanes east, and two lanes in the middle.]

Here Attorney Rutledge asked Mr. Davis a question intended to try to conceal the difference between the process of consulting citizens on Mercer Island and in Seattle. He asked, "Other communities did this as well. Were you aware of that?" Mr. Davis answered, "Yes, Seattle had an ongoing process about that time, I believe."

Mr. Davis described the design process on Mercer Island, beginning with a description of a 1970 proposal for ten new highway lanes in addition to the existing [Lake Washington] bridge four lanes. "And it was a rather substantial, a very large—and we felt such a substantial effect on the Island—that we requested that it be redesigned, that it be buried, that it incorporate environmental amenities: berms; sound barriers; and so forth; that be [sic] involved in the design team a number of consultants beyond engineering, such as sound consultants, lighting consultants, landscaping consultants—all of whom were to be involved in the process."

Continuing with the questioning, our attorney asked, "As a result of the whole process that you described, the representatives of Mercer

Island and the representatives of the State Highway Department reached an agreement on the design; is that not true?" Davis answered, "Yes."

Mr. Davis continued, "And there was a final agreement reached that involved coming around First Hill at a substantial savings over a tunnel but having a lid, since that is a residential community on both sides."

ON PAGE 10, LINE 16, MR. DAVIS SAID THAT COSTS HAD NEVER BEEN DISCUSSED! (Emphasis added.) Mr. Leed asked, "At any rate, it took some convincing to persuade the State to pay for a lid, even though it was cheaper than a tunnel; is that not right?" Davis answered, "Our dealings at that time were with the design team, and they proposed that as one of the alternatives, and whether they had a problem of convincing or not, I do not know. We did not have any substantial discussions or arguments about it. That was the proposal that they came up with."

Mercer Islanders had wanted the design for their three-mile segment of I-90 to include what they called "amenities." Mr. Davis had been quoted as saying, "It's a cliché on Mercer Island that we don't want to see, hear, or smell I-90," and the parts of the design that produced these results were apparently classed as amenities. My small dictionary defines amenities as, "(1) courtesies or civilities; (2) pleasantness or agreeableness." I have never been able to find the word used in the official specifications defining what state and/or federal highway trust funds could be used for, but apparently Mercer Islanders got everything they wanted in the 1971 design: the total destruction of the old highway to leave land for development of a new Mercer Island business district; and their chosen design for the new highway with all the amenities—the long lids over it and the protecting architectural additions.

[In 1972, the very next year, the State refused to consider the lidding of I-90 in Seattle from where the freeway would come out of the west side of the tunnel through a residential area and a park, and immediately adjacent to a school. In all of the 54 meetings on Mercer Island, the State had NEVER discussed any of the costs of the project on Mercer Island—everything Mercer Island wanted was funded without objection. In 1977, various Federal employees wrote about I-90 alternatives that would be less costly: They said the Mercer Island Project would need more than fifty percent of the total funds, the high costs being due to the "amenities."]

Mr. Davis was asked (See page 11), "What were the other amenities that you got?" He answered, "We paid a lot of attention to step-by-step stages across the Island to make sure residential communities nearby were protected by berms and sound barriers. We spent some time with landscape architectural consultants."

On page 12, Mr. Davis was asked, "How did the design to which Mercer Island ultimately agreed also provide some better access for Mercer Island traffic to the facility?" The answer was: "Let us be clear about this in terms of time sequence. The redesign started in the fall of 1970. It was underway in the fall, winter and spring of 1971. The design was largely agreed upon in the late spring or early summer of 1971. Hearings were held I believe maybe in August or September of '71 for the first design hearing."

Mr. Davis continued, "I became Chairman of the Metro Transit Committee in August. We started our study that year, August of '71. We started our planning in the fall of 1971—November, December. We got finished with that planning process in about May of 1972. So the transit decision-making followed on after the decision-making was largely complete on that stage of the freeway design." [But only across Mercer Island.]

Mr. Davis continued (See page 12), "I played a major role in persuading the transit, persuading the I-90 committee on Mercer Island to in effect turn it, exchange with the State the use of the four lanes which had been in their former plan for a lane each way on the new one, new bridge. The plan was Mercer Island would use the present four lanes and the other highway would come through, and it seemed to me if we were going to shrink this thing down in size, which most of us wanted to do—in width particularly—and because the lanes which we were offered on the old bridge didn't really go any place, ending at

Dearborn Street—and, we found also, we were going to share truck traffic for trucks that happened to get out in the Rainier Valley. It was to our interest to have a lane each way. And a lane was just about equal to the amount of traffic projected for 1990 originating on Mercer Island."

(Mr. Davis continued on page 13), "It was to our interest to settle for a lane on the new facility instead of the old bridge so we could use the old bridge for one of the directions and therefore narrow the project appreciably."

This answer was not complete because he talked only about Mercer Island lanes on the NEW bridge. He did not mention the complete abandoning of the old four lane highway, so that the land could be used for the Mercer Island business section, and the addition of four lanes to the new highway across the island. An important part of the plaintiffs' arguments before the judge in the final I-90 trial would be that the defendants had not considered alternatives, and the plaintiffs could prove that there was no evidence that the defendants had considered the great cost when they refused to continue to use the old highway . The City of Mercer Island had been a strip city, built after and around the old highway, and the undesired social, economic and environmental effects of it had already been taken care of, but the costs of abandoning the old highway and adding four lanes to the new highway were never discussed.

Mercer Islanders wanted and got the abandoning and destruction of the EXISTING I-90 highway on Mercer Island, and four replacement lanes were added to the new highway.

Mr. Davis continued, "So settling for one lane was a trade-off to make the whole thing smaller than it had been before. That was the trade-off we agreed upon. It had to start on Mercer Island, as the present bridge does. So settling for one lane was a trade-off to make the whole thing smaller than it had been before."

1971 and 1978 designs are identical

The 1971 Design

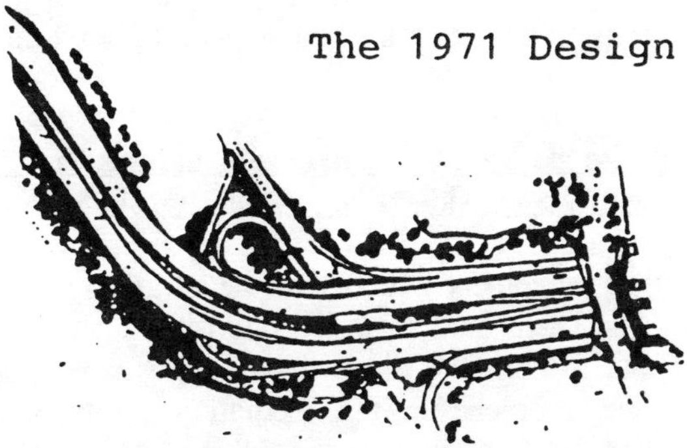

. Department for massive Interstate 90 as it runs through the Central District.

The 1978 Design

Final vol I EIS Pg.115

THUS, THE 1971 DESIGN BECAME:

- The final design of I-90 through the Mercer Island segment.
- The 1971 size of the whole seven-mile project federally approved in 1971 and never changed.
- The plan for the Seattle segment in the drawing in the environmental impact statement.

<u>Seattle was stuck with the Mercer Island design and the width of the 4-2-4 lane freeway with no consideration of rail transit and/or other highway alternatives.</u>

The 1976 mediation agreement stated that the original project had been made smaller [Mr. Davis said so in his deposition, and the State also so maintained], but the original planned width was never changed, and the mediators and everyone in the mediation group knew it. William Bulley, then Secretary of the State Department of Transportation, had made a sworn statement in his deposition for the *Lathan* case in 1979: He said that the Chief Engineer of the I-90 project, John Stephenson, had presented drawings to the mediation group to show how the 3-2-3 project could easily be converted to the old 1971 4-2-4 design. When Mr. Davis was asked about it in his deposition, he answered that they had never told him this, but he did not say that he did not know it.

And on page 24 of the deposition, Mr. Davis made this important statement about rail on I-90 when he said, "It occurred just by looking at the geometrics, but the fact that the lanes, that the rail would take less space than the middle lanes were now taking because, lacking cars, they would not need shoulders, and by moving barriers it would be possible to get another lane for carpools and Mercer Island, however, they wanted to adjust it." Nevertheless, the essential rail line in I-90 has never been seriously considered.

One important factor deserves special emphasis. The Davis deposition shows clearly the intention that the 1971 size and design of I-90 on Mercer Island would never be changed, but he was Chairman of the Metro Transportation Committee, supposedly working for public transportation. When the Federal Highway Act was amended in 1973, 1975, and 1976 to allow the withdrawal of Federal highway I-90 trust funds from the 1971 project for any substitute mix of public transit and highway purposes in the Mercer Island corridor and in the entire urban area, Mr. Davis should have led Metro to explore thoroughly all possible alternatives. He was faced with a severe conflict of interest, and the deposition shows clearly that he decided to act for Mercer Island at the expense of better Metro transit—that he was able to prevent any scrutiny of the I-90 design which might have resulted in decisions to use the old highway and to shift some of the Mercer Island "amenities" funds to benefit public transportation in the whole urban area.

Aubrey Davis was interviewed for an article published May 31, 1971, in the *Seattle Times* entitled, "MERCER ISLAND DEFENDS INTERSTATE 90 PLAN." David Suffia reported, "Mercer Island Mayor Aubrey Davis, Jr. is concerned that fighting freeways such as Interstate 90 in the name of pollution abatement is the wrong approach to the problem because it won't halt auto pollution, but it will hurt the general welfare of the area."

He quoted Mr. Davis, "We have to do something about pollution, but Federal muscle on manufacturers is the answer, not forcing people to change their way of life and take away their freedom of movement."

Mr. Suffia continued, " 'It's a cliché on Mercer Island that we don't want to see, hear or smell the new I-90'," Davis says.

"Working with the Islanders, the State Highway Department agreed to underground much of the freeway and provide what Davis thinks will be very good landscaping so I-90 won't become an environmentally disturbing factor.

"On the other hand, he sees I-90 as a chance to renovate the stagnate Mercer Island business district. He says studies show only 25 percent of the potential retail trade stays on the Island. The rest flees to communities that have more to offer.

"Clearing the land for the freeway using the old freeway land could be an opportunity to upgrade the Island's commercial area and keep customers home. [emphasis added]

" 'That in turn could mean a larger tax base and thus more income for the city and schools.' Davis says that he is sold on his Island as a place to live because it provides good schools and a pleasant tree-studded environment. 'We've sought to control I-90 through Mercer Island, not fight it.' "

In 1978, the new Deputy Mayor of Seattle, Bob Royer, accurately evaluated the chosen project when he said that the I-90 project was "a $500 million urban renewal project for Mercer Island".

5. THE I-90 DECISION, THE FINAL PLAN CAST IN CONCRETE, 1971

In the fall of 1971, Chairman Aubrey Davis said, the duly assembled Mercer Island I-90 Committee had made the final decisions on the I-90 project which set: the size (capacity) of the entire seven mile project (from I-405 in Bellevue to I-5 in Seattle); AND the design of the Mercer Island section. The size of the highway was not described in measured width, but by lanes to be striped: 4-2-4 lanes (4-west, 2-middle and 4-east highway lanes). The abandoning and destruction of the old highway and the additions to the new highway called "amenities" had raised the cost of the Mercer Island segment to almost fifty percent of the total funds available—a much higher cost than was necessary for that virtually level section less than three miles long. The remaining fifty percent of the I-90 funds was to pay for an additional 6-lane bridge between Mercer Island and Seattle, an enormous tunnel in Seattle, and high-elevated construction over Rainier Avenue to connect with I-5 in Seattle.

The Mercer Island decisions were hurried right along. In the autumn of 1971, a hearing was held on Mercer Island, and nothing was ever changed. Not ever! The State applied for Federal approval. The

I-90 project planned by Mercer Island was the I-90 highway which was built.

[Please see my *Critique*, pages 134—135, and 161—162 for a more complete review of the relevant EIS materials on these issues.]

Even now, 25 years later, I find that it's almost impossible to believe that in the summer of 1971, the State announced both the completion of the designs of both the Mercer Island and Seattle sections of I-90 and said that the State intended to hold the necessary hearings and complete the essential legal processes immediately. It was true that the State had completed the design of the Mercer Island section exactly as Mercer Islanders wanted it, without even discussing the huge added costs of the so-called "amenities", but it was not true that the State had completed the design of the Seattle segment—as far as the Seattle officials and residents knew, the State had only a very small scale drawing and a table model of the project with nothing to show its width, the essential elevations, termini, ramps, rights-of-way and land-taking, especially west of 23rd Avenue, and nothing had been done to design anything for transit. [The table model was used again in the 1976 hearing, and a clever observer pointed out that it was the old 1971 version except that they had painted the brown vegetation green.]

It should have been obvious to all of us (including our attorney) that the defendants could not segment the seven-mile project—Bellevue I-405 to Seattle I-5—into two parts. The Seattle segment was only 3.2 miles long; and since the eastern end of the so-called Seattle segment was on the west shore of Mercer Island, this clever segmentation enabled the State to foster and allow Mercer Island to set the size of the project, with Seattle having no chance to participate in the decision. On July 19, 1973, the Regional Office of the Federal Department of Health, Education and Welfare sent a letter which summed up the effects of segmentation on the plaintiffs. [The letter is printed in Volume II of the FEIS on page 13.] HEW said that segmentation prevents environmental review and that the major inadequacies of the defendants' process were:

(1) Failure to identify and discuss the ultimate goal of the project.
(2) Failure to examine seriously alternate courses of actions which don't accept as inevitable or desirable an increase in auto traffic across Lake Washington.
(3) Failure to examine in detail the social problems and environmental effects of the project.
(4) Failure to consider major secondary impacts and constraints.

On January 1, 1970, the National Environmental Protection Act became effective, and court decisions were setting the parameters for meeting the Act's provisions. In 1971, a three-judge panel of the U.S. Court of Appeals for the Ninth Circuit was working on Judge Beeks' decision that the defendants had met federal law requirements and need not submit any further statement. It was certain that the court would reverse the Beeks decision, and they did. Judge Duniway wrote the Court's opinion on November 15, 1971. He said that the I-90 project EIS did not give enough information about the project that it could be used in the I-90 decision-making, and he specified what was wrong with it.

Nevertheless, the State hurried to approve the project and submit it for Federal approval in November, 1971, and in December proceeded with the state-required Board of Review process—with information the Federal courts had found repeatedly was fatally inadequate.

6. THE BOARD OF REVIEW

State law RCW 47.52.13 was intended to preserve the rights of local jurisdictions to prevent the state's closing needed local streets by the construction of state highways. . It is called the Board of Review process.

The state law reads, "The state is to submit...to the city officials a report...Conferences shall be held on the merits of this state report and plan, and any proposed modification or alternative proposal of the...city in order to attempt to reach an agreement between the state highway commission and the ... city officials. As a result of the conference, the proposed plan, together with any modifications thereof, shall be prepared by the state highway commission and presented to the ... city for inspection and study."

On June 19, 1971, the State held a federal/state hearing on the Seattle section of I-90 and published findings although it was still not designed. In December, Seattle filed a disapproval of the project with ten objections to the proposal, and the state Board of Review process was set in motion.

When the State and the city disagree, the law required the establishing of a Board of Review, to be made up of two persons appointed by the mayor and two appointed by the State, with those four appointing a fifth person. The process is frequently called an arbitration, but it is a completely different process. The Board begins ab initio; it collects its own facts and makes its own decisions. The law requires the Board to begin and to finish its review within set time limits, but the State did not meet them—choosing instead to begin meeting privately with pro-I-90 Seattle Mayor Uhlman. And there were no public records of any Seattle elected official "conferences" on the State's plans for I-90 in Seattle before the Board of Review process.

When the Board of Review process was being delayed, 25 of us signed a letter with our objections that the statutory limits for the Board of Review process were not being met. We said, "There is no room for the off-the-record dickering now being undertaken by the Mayor and the Highway Commission." When the Board of Review was finally openly convened, Seattle's ten items of objection to the design had been reduced to two, and the process had been delayed for an entire year beyond the time limit set by the law.

Seattle had two main objections to the State's design:

(1) The State had refused to agree to the relocation replacement of Colman school, which was immediately adjacent to the project and subject to all the disruption caused by the construction of the freeway and its subsequent traffic;

(2) The State had refused to "lid" the freeway from the west tunnel entrance to 23rd Avenue, although the project would go through

a residential area, taking land from Mt. Virgin Church and school and Judkins Park.

The minutes of a meeting of the State Highway Commissioners record that they had discussed Seattle's requests and had decided that Seattle could not be given both the lidding of I-90 to 23rd and the replacement of Colman school on a new location, and they so instructed the Director of Highways, George Andrews. His statements were published in the March 6, 1973 *Seattle Times* and were really unbelievable, especially when the items that Seattle requested are compared to what Mercer Island actually got. Andrews said: "If the freeway north of the school is not lidded, the noise may be so bad that the department that can justify using fuel tax funds to purchase the property and relocate the school, including complete reconstruction; but if the freeway is lidded adjacent to the school, the noise will be reduced, and then the State cannot pay for the relocation and rebuilding of the school."

Mr. Davis had said, in his sworn deposition, that costs were never discussed in the meetings to design the Mercer Island segment of I-90—so Andrew's statement was absolutely untrue. Funding had been approved from both the state and federal highway trust funds for all of the Mercer Island design which included items so unimportant that they were called "amenities"—the protections which Seattle wanted in the design were *needs*.

The minutes of the State Highway Commission meeting also record that Andrews had said that the city had accused the State of not furnishing necessary information for the city's case before the Board of Review, but he said that "overriding social factors made the furnishing of cost of the lid on Mercer Island not pertinent to the city's case." (Quoting *The Times* again). Andrews said that, "The city has no use for data on the lidding of the freeway on Mercer Island." The costs of the Mercer Island part of the project were never publicly disclosed or recorded in the EIS. Andrews was not anxious to reveal that the Mercer Island section was to use fifty percent of the I-90 funds.

The Board of Review findings and order were handed down in March, 1973. The Seattle city attorneys and some of the Seattle Council members, particularly Jeanette Williams, had worked extremely hard. The decision was in their favor—the I-90 freeway in Seattle would be lidded west of the tunnel (the 23rd Avenue bridge making the lid still longer), *contingent upon* Mercer Island's also getting their lids! And Colman school would be moved.

We in Seattle never did get any information about the proposed projects' actual widths, elevations, ramps, right-of-way, termini for both the Interstate highway and transit, the Connecticut Viaduct connection, etc.—Secretary Adams initially wrote letters to the State demanding the design of these connections and of the project west of 23rd Avenue before he would approve I-90, but in his final approval letter in 1978, he reneged and approved the project although the State still had not shown a design for the project in Seattle.

7. DEFENDING THE 1971 I-90 DESIGN: THE DEFENDANTS' CRISIS, 1976, 1977

In 1976, the supposedly inviolable 1971 Mercer Island I-90 project was under severe attack.

- The Federal Court decisions of 1972, 1973 and 1974 had proved that: the State had not met the requirements of federal laws—the Federal Highway Act, the Clean Air Act, and NEPA (the National Environmental Policy Act); the defendants must prepare adequate statements to be used by the elected officials and the public, and then a new corridor-design hearing must be held. All work on the project had been stopped in 1971 by the Courts' injunction.
- In 1976, the plaintiffs were proving that the court-mandated Draft Environmental Impact Statement (submitted as a draft EIS in late 1975), the 4(f), and other required statements were inadequate and had not been submitted in time for the elected officials and the public to read them before the 1976 January/February corridor/design hearing. The defendants had not tried to meet the

I-90 process requirements as set out by the Ninth Circuit Court of Appeals on August 18, 1974.
- The plaintiffs were proving that the State had deliberately refused to consider the Interstate withdraw/substitution funding options available under amendments to the Federal Highway Act.

The Federal Court Mandates: 1973, 1973, 1974

SHOOTOUT AT THE 9th CIRCUIT CORRAL.........

Judge Duniway summed up the earlier Federal Court opinions on I-90 in his opinion *Lathan v. Brinegar*, U.S. Court of Appeals, Ninth Circuit, August 27, 1974: *"We cannot ignore, as judges, what we know as citizens. The knowledge and attitudes of the public, of the Congress, and of State and local governments about the environmental and social consequences of freeway building have been drastically changed in the last decade. With knowledge has come concern, and that concern is reflected in the 1968 and 1971 amendments to [Federal Highway Act] section 128(a) and in NEPA. The proposed segment of I-90 is to be built in the future, and decisions about it are to be governed by the law as it reads now, not as it read in 1963.*

In short, we hold under the facts here that ... NEPA and section 128(a) must be construed together and that section 128(a) provides a public forum at which, among other things, the NEPA required EIS will be the basis for the hearing.

In so holding, we have the support of our own and prior decisions and those of other circuits. ... With respect to ongoing projects, section 128(a) and the regulations which implement it must be interpreted and administered to the fullest extent possible, in accordance with the policies of NEPA. In appropriate cases, this may mean total reassessment of the project in light of its potential environmental impact, i.e. the consideration of its wholesale alteration or abandonment." [emphasis added]

Further on, Judge Duniway said, *"We stress that the hearing under section 128(a) must take into account the factors that are now outlined in that section and in NEPA. It will not be merely a new "corridor" or "location" or "design" hearing, although of course what was considered at those hearings can now be considered. The major focus must be on the total impact of the project as a whole, including whether it should be built at all, as well as whether, if it is to be built, it should be built where and as previously planned."*

Judge Duniway had written the first *Lathan* case opinion in 1971 and strengthened the language in his 1973 and 1974 opinions. Surely any reader of these opinions could follow his analysis of the laws and reach the conclusion that the State should immediately begin to follow his instructions.

The project design was not finished enough that people could tell what it was going to be and what the effects of construction and use of it would be. People said that there was no answer to their questions regarding width of right-of-way, transit (both in and out of the corridor), air and noise pollution, provisions to protect owners whose property would be acquired, and provisions to protect adjacent and area residents from the damage caused by the freeway construction and use.

An unfinished project design could not be used for the essential comparison of alternatives to it, and the State had not considered alternatives.

After the January, 1976, hearings on the I-90 project, interested people had submitted many oral and written comments for the State's records, and I had collated them in a 25-page writing I called, *THE I-90 DECISION, THE MOMENT OF TRUTH.* I mailed it on May 11, 1976, to the Seattle elected officials and the federal Secretary of Transportation. I said (page 3), "The comments led straight to a simple conclusion: the Highway Commission, its staff and attorneys had simply not changed the process to meet Federal and common-sense requirements for modern transportation planning, for the wise allocation of limited transportation funds, and for the determination of social, economic and environmental effects."

The Withdraw/Substitution Amendments to the Federal Highway Act

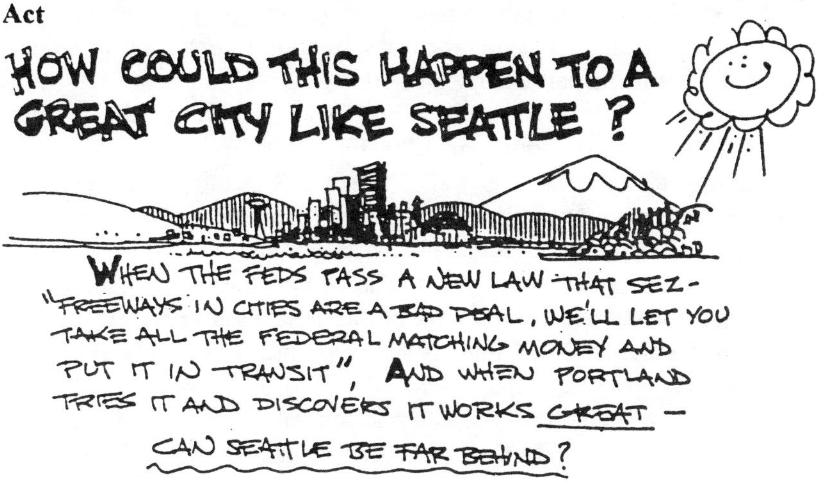

HOW COULD THIS HAPPEN TO A GREAT CITY LIKE SEATTLE ?
WHEN THE FEDS PASS A NEW LAW THAT SEZ- "FREEWAYS IN CITIES ARE A BAD DEAL, WE'LL LET YOU TAKE ALL THE FEDERAL MATCHING MONEY AND PUT IT IN TRANSIT", AND WHEN PORTLAND TRIES IT AND DISCOVERS IT WORKS GREAT - CAN SEATTLE BE FAR BEHIND?

By December, 1975, the State highway department officials and the Commissioners knew that Congress was going to pass an amendment to Section 103 of the Federal Highway Act which would put great pressure on them to reconsider the 1971, I-90 projects by examining alternatives—the new amendment would allow the withdrawal of the Federal funds already allocated for non-essential interstate projects and the funding for substitution of any type of transportation project, in the corridor and in the whole urban area. The I-90 project had been classified non-essential—not necessary—so the ninety percent federal share of the project was available for alternatives.

At the same time, we realized that there was no newspaper record of consideration of the existing, pre-1976 withdraw/substitution alternatives to the project—we didn't yet know that the Highway Act was going to be amended again, but previous amendments had given us many options to consider.

Most of the media in Seattle supported the highway proponents—the newspapers had not published and the television and radio stations had not broadcast any information about the I-90 options. Exceptions were *The Weekly*, published by its editor, and the *Seattle Sun*, published by young people—both papers printed some good, fair and true articles; KING TV had some transportation information programs which did not focus particularly on I-90.

We decided that we must publish some record of the options available for the spending of I-90 funds. The basic reason for considering alternatives was well known; the Seattle area is unique because of its geographical phenomena—its topography. The planning of sensible transportation should have been simple:

— There was a single north/south traffic corridor between Puget Sound on the west and Lake Washington on the east because Seattle was so narrow. Highway 99 and Interstate 5 were already carrying traffic in that corridor.

— There was a single traffic corridor across Lake Washington served by both the Evergreen Bridge [SR 520], and Interstate 90, which were less than 4 miles apart.

The Seattle area was exactly right for commuter-rail transit alternatives. Further area growth could no longer be based on proliferation of more automobiles. Further growth should be directed and accommodated by north/south rail systems on both sides of Lake Washington and across the Lake.

The Federal Highway Act and the National Environmental Policy Act required the consideration of these alternatives as a condition to the dispensing of I-90 funds, but we could find no public record that the elected officials (who should be considering and making the decisions on those options) paid any attention to alternatives.

We decided that we must leave some history of what should have and did not happen, and we prepared a newspaper advertisement to record that the withdraw/substitution option had existed in early 1976. Our ad was a map of a possible rail transit system all the way around and across the Lake to show one available alternative to the spending of all the I-90 funds on the freeway in the seven-mile long route across

SHOULD WE SPEND $600 MILLION FOR 6 MORE LANES ON I-90?

NO, it's too big and harmful and old-fashioned.

WHAT ELSE IS THERE TO DO?

We should build a sensible size I-90 (two new lanes for transit/carpool, transit stations, safety features), then spend the rest of the money for a network of transit/carpool lanes in the other commuter trouble spots. The cost is the same as the big I-90.

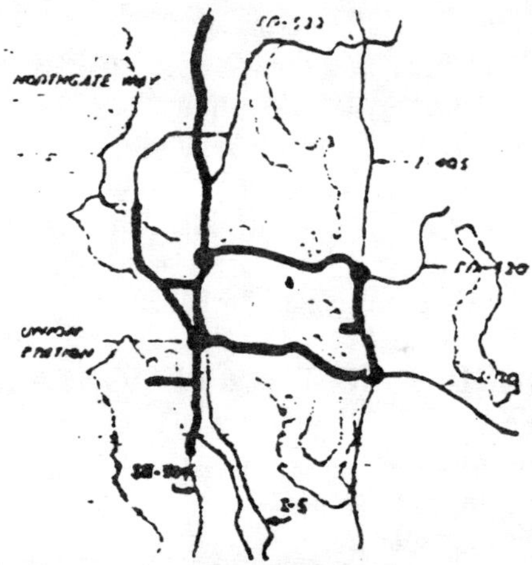

IS IT REALLY POSSIBLE?

YES, new federal laws allow all or part of the I-90 money to be spent on regional transit, and some transit facilities can be shared with carpools. Portland, Oregon and many other cities are using these legal options now. We can do it here, too.

PUT TRANSIT ACROSS, Seth Jackson, Chairman,
3431 Cascadia Ave. So., Seattle, Wa. 98144.

Mercer Island. The ad was published in the January 13, 1976, *Seattle Post Intelligencer*. And there it is on microfilm to this day.

[Two years ago, I read through microfilms of Portland newspapers to study the press coverage of the meetings on withdraw/substitution on the Mt. Hood Interstate freeway/Banfield rail project. I found that 43 newspaper articles had been published in 15 months! The Banfield alternative rail, built adjacent to the new highway, was chosen, and the Banfield rail line opened in Portland in 1986.]

The proponents of the I-90 project were fond of stating that the no State was using withdraw/substitution process, but that falsehood is contradicted by data on the withdraw/substitution projects in the entire United States during the period when our State should have been considering the I-90 alternatives. From 1972 to 1983, 35 interstate projects had been withdrawn, costing $5,897.4 billion, in these areas: Boston, Philadelphia, Washington, D.C., Hartford-New Britain, Tucson, Chicago, Denver, Albany, Sacramento, San Francisco, New York City, Duluth, Indianapolis, Baltimore, and Waterloo, Iowa. And it seems most unlikely that our opponents did not know that Oregon had withdrawn Interstate funds and used them for substitute projects in Portland in 1976 and Salem in 1977.

8. DEFENDING THE I-90 DESIGN: THE DEFENDANTS' DEFENSE

All through the 1970 decade, the I-90 proponents continued a massive campaign to defend the 1971 Mercer Island I-90 project—to keep their Plan intact.

The Downtown Seattle Bus Tunnel

In December, 1974, a few of us were invited to the Mayor's office for an afternoon meeting which we thought was to discuss I-90 alternatives—we had prepared an oral presentation and a series of charts for illustration. To our great surprise, the meeting agenda was devoted to the presentation of a Seattle downtown bus tunnel project!

A bus tunnel option as part of the 1968 and 1970 Forward Thrust Rail Proposal had been rejected, and the results were clearly presented in the records we all had. Nevertheless, in 1974, most unexpectedly, the concept was being revived. The tunnel was obviously a clever red herring, devised to prevent any consideration of I-90 rail alternatives.

When the tunnel presentation was made in the Mayor's office that afternoon, we just sat there aghast, dumfounded, non-plussed, and bewildered—thoroughly.

We thought that the bus concept had been dead since 1968, when Forward Thrust wrote in its committee rationale (the whole report signed Mr. Ellis): "The bus-subways in Systems IB and II were estimated to be 35% more costly than a rail subway in System III because of the added need for ventilation ducts, emergency exits, fan equipment, lighting, and the platooning stations at the north and south ends of the bus-subway", and yet here the tunnel was revived, fully formed, in 1974! It was to be another of those decisions made secretly and never really questioned.

An I-90 Concept

Bold Subway Plan

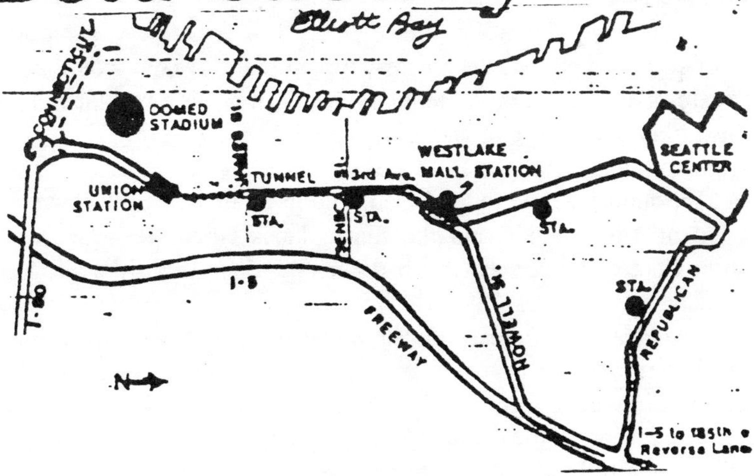

The newspapers called it the Uhlman/Adams proposal, but it had been prepared by engineer Victor Gray and James Ellis, the very influential originator of both Metro and Forward Thrust and the General Legal Counsel of Metro from 1954 to 1976. Early in 1975, a group of officials went to Washington, D.C., where they had lunch with William Coleman, the appointed Federal Secretary of Transportation, whose appointment was to be confirmed by Senator Magnuson's committee that afternoon. The officials were: Governor Evans; King County Executive Spellman; Seattle Mayor Uhlman; Aubrey Davis, the Mercer Island Councilman who was Chairman of the Metro Transit Committee; Representative Al Leland, Chairman of the House Transportation Committee; Senator Walgren, the chairman of the Senate Transportation Committee; and representatives of the State Highway Department. Washington's influential Senior Senator Magnuson and Junior Senator Jackson were present. The group had been sent to present the tunnel proposal to the new Secretary and to secure assurances that federal funds would be available to pay for a downtown bus tunnel in Seattle—a major step to prevent any opposition to it.

On February 21, 1975, the *Seattle Post Intelligencer* reported: "Unveiled in December, the Evans-Uhlman plan for I-90 would reduce the scale of the seven-mile Bellevue-Seattle link highway lanes to six highway lanes and <u>extend two exclusive I-90 transit lanes through the downtown tunnel</u>. [emphasis added]

"The tunnel would extend from Union Station through downtown via 3rd or 4th Avenue, and the transit lanes would resurface at the Seattle Center to connect with Interstate 5 at the Mercer Street Interchange.

"The idea is to increase transit connections to downtown from the Eastside and Mercer Island in order to reduce auto demand on I-90, which in turn would allow a reduction from eight to six highway lanes.

"In addition, <u>the exclusive transit lanes and bus tunnel would be readily convertible to rail rapid transit if the region voted in the future to build a rail system</u>." [emphasis added]

I decided to try to get an appointment with Senator Magnuson to discuss I-90 and the bus tunnel, and I went to see Norm Dicks, who was then in Senator Magnuson's office in Seattle, to try to get an appointment with the Senator. Norm heard me out and then said, "Why don't you go to Jim Ellis? He's the one who sent them all to Washington." So I made an appointment with Mr. Ellis at his office, and three of us went off to talk with him—an architect, an attorney new to Seattle, and I.

It was a most peculiar meeting. Before we could do anything but introduce ourselves, Mr. Ellis talked for forty-five minutes! We then did get to tell him that we wanted to discuss the available withdraw/substitution I-90 alternatives, whereupon he sadly related the highway accident deaths of his daughter and her unborn child due to unsafe highway conditions. I wanted to discuss the continuing accidents on the present I-90 and the State's refusal to try to make it more safe, but I felt it was futile to raise the issue. Finally we proposed a consideration of available withdraw/substitution alternatives to the I-90 project including transit. Mr. Ellis said, "IT'S AN UNWORKABLE, UNTHINKABLE SCHEME."

We left Mr. Ellis, went down in the elevator, and just sat in the lobby in some kind of shock. We couldn't reconcile Mr. Ellis' work for a rail transit system in the Forward Thrust campaign with his refusal to consider rail transit alternatives to the Mercer Island I-90 project.

Well, the bus tunnel was built—it's 1.2 miles long under Third Avenue in Seattle, which was torn up for years during the construction. It cost almost $500 million. The 282 Italian dual mode buses—powered by electricity when they are in the tunnel and diesel fueled outside of it—cost $360,000 each (the replacement buses now cost $800,000 each and are so heavy that they exceed the state's weight standards). The total cost of the bus tunnel and the buses was over $1 billion. It was funded by Urban Mass Transit federal funds, by Metro bonds, and by the city of Seattle, City Light, and the property-owners along the tunnel.

The story of the bus tunnel ends with the unbelievable failure of Metro to try to comply with federal laws and with their original promise that the tunnel was being built to connect to the I-90 project. Secretary Adams kept warning Metro that he would approve the I-90 project only when the State and Metro gave him the design of the transit connections from the tunnel to I-90 as well as all the other transit termini in both Seattle and Bellevue and the Connecticut Viaduct connection at I-5 and I-90. Secretary Adams wrote several letters to say that he would not approve the I-90 project until these connections were designed, but in 1978 he reneged and approved the project anyway, with the condition that he would not take final step to approve the P.S.&E. (plans, specifications and estimates) until the transit connection were completed.

Secretary Adams' approval of the still-undesigned I-90 project in Seattle took away the legal rights of the people of Seattle to know about and participate in the decisions for the part of the I-90 project west of 23rd Avenue—to seek to diminish the damage caused by the enormous project by changing the design, adding necessary protection for the area, and restoring damaged areas.

The bus tunnel was opened in 1990. Third Street above the tunnel is not closed, and traffic has increased. In 1995 the elected officials of Seattle laid the tombstone on the Seattle bus tunnel which portends its future: they have voted to issue $100 million councilman bonds to fund a downtown parking garage, right above the bus tunnel in the vicinity of Third Avenue and Pine Street! Seattle must be the only city in the United States that is bringing more vehicle traffic into the downtown section.

1975: Can State Laws Supersede Federal Laws? The Silly Bills

Two "silly bills" were introduced in the 1975 session of the State Legislature: House Bill 803 and Senate Bill 1141. I read the bills, and decided that they both were illegal because the Legislature was trying pass state laws to supersede federal laws—the Legislature was trying to evade the requirements of federal laws relating to the withdraw/substitution decision of I-90. I did talk at a meeting in Olympia one evening about the bills, but I didn't lobby actively against them because they were so obviously illegal. I considered them to be more of the worthless threats that our opponents so often publicized.

SB 1141 set up deadlines for federally-required procedures which made it impossible to consider and withdraw the I-90 funds. The federal law had deliberately excluded any legislature's participation in making decisions, no voting procedures were required by that law, and no time limits were set.

But these deadlines were set in this bill:

— The studies to withdraw I-90 interstate funds had to be completed by November 1, 1975. [The draft EIS was not available until January, 1976—a deliberate evasion of the National Environmental Policy Act and of the mandates of all of the judges, who had ruled in the I-90 appeals that the EIS was prepared for the use of the people who were to make decisions on the projects and that the EIS must be available for their use <u>before</u> they made their decisions.]

— The vote on the withdrawal of the Federal funds on I-90 had to be taken by January 15, 1976, with all jurisdictions having equal voting power. Three of the four jurisdictions had to vote for the withdrawal: Mercer Island had a population of 20,000; Bellevue, 66,000; King County, about a million; and Seattle, about 500,000. [It is interesting to note a letter from a Federal Department of Transportation official in 1977 that predicted that if Seattle alone did not want the project, it would probably not be built.]

— The new corridor design hearing must be held by February 1, 1976—the State did hold the hearing before then, but it was not legal because the draft EIS had not been prepared in time for either the officials or the public to use it before the hearing, as mandated by the federal courts.

— The final EIS was to be filed with the Federal agencies by May 1, <u>1976</u>. [In <u>1977</u>, the defendants had not filed the final EIS, so the Legislature passed another silly bill, SB 2385, which provided that no new state limited access hearing was necessary if the local jurisdictions have agreed on a design. The 1976 Memorandum of Agreement is supposed to be such an agreement, and the project proponents believed that this law would protect the Mercer Island Plan. SB 1141 became RCW 47.20.645. and it was the basis of I-90 Superior Court decisions for the defendants. I shall always wonder what Judge Duniway, who wrote the *Lathan* opinions for United States Court of Appeal for the Ninth Circuit, would think of this interpretation of the laws; *the Ninth Circuit Court's* instructions were written in the clearest possible language—it was inconceivable that a state could act as if federal funds could be used for a project even if the court orders were deliberately ignored.

Silly Bill HB 803 required any withdraw decision to be approved by the Puget Sound Governmental Conference, PSGC, the metropolitan planning agency responsible under Federal laws for area-wide planning. This was a most remarkable condition—the Legislature itself already abolished the PSGC!

I wrote for the March 4, 1975, Washington Coalition for *Sensible Transportation Newsletter*:

"The PSGC exists (as far as transportation statutes are concerned) as a highway and public transportation planning body under two sets of laws attached to Federal-aid: The Federal Highway Act and the Urban Mass Transportation Act. Both Acts require a comprehensive, continuing, cooperative planning process to be carried out by the local governmental bodies in the urbanized areas of over 50,000 population. PSGC has been planning transportation since 1962." ... [The members of the PSGC are elected officials chosen by their local governments, and their votes are weighted by the percentage of the population of the four county area which they represent.]

"Federal agencies require the PSCG to adopt a regional development plan, but they extended the deadline from Jan. 1, 1975, to July 1, 1976. New Federal regulations will require an adopted transportation plan for both highways and transit with a long-range (20 to 30 years), medium range (3 to 5 years), a biennial, and annual element. No project will receive Federal funds unless it is part of the plan." I added, "and that's why the pro-highway Legislators decided to throw out the PSGC."

On March 4, 1975, I wrote under the title, "THE SAGA OF THE PUGET SOUND GOVERNMENTAL CONFERENCE (as a transportation planning agency):

"The Puget Sound Governmental Conference was abolished outright by HB 803. The bill makes no substitutions for the PSGC, and framer of the bill, Rep. Rick Bender, says that he believes the other state departments of transportation, natural resources, ecology, and other agencies can take over the functions of the PSGC! [Note: The State Department of Transportation did not exist until 1978.]

"HB 803 is only the last of a long line of symptoms which prove that many people are trying to avoid the Federally-required transportation and land-use planning processes. For instance:

"Last year the State Highway Commission withdrew $87,000 [matching] highway funds from the PSGC despite the fact that they had passed the budget containing these funds earlier. Commissioner Walsh said that the Commission did this, 'to show our displeasure'.

"Under new Chairman Spellman, PSGC has begun a reorganization which will minimize regional in favor of county level planning—the main reason for so doing is generally given as 'saving the Conference'.

"Commissioner Baker Ferguson said last month, 'We don't want any more groups like the PSGC,' and the Commission cut the PSGC budget by $100,000."

I was totally wrong about HB 803—it passed. The complete history of PSGC is thoroughly entangled with the history of the I-90 decisions because the information being produced by the PSGC's professional transportation planners was eroding the 1971 I-90 project decision. In their study of alternatives they had found that a "no-build" solution, a transit line only, could supply all the capacity of proposed project! They had finished the first phase of a study, and Metro was trying to stop any further work on a second phase.

Meanwhile, the PSGC's name had been changed to PSCOG, the Puget Sound Council of Governments, and it was being dismantled by its own members. On September 11, 1976, I wrote: "Faced with a Federal mandate to complete a land use plan (and a transportation plan based on it), PSCOG president Spellman [the King County Executive] began a restructuring of the already fatally-weak organization designed to prevent the PSCOG from being effective for years. It worked beautifully. Seven of the eight top transportation planners resigned, those who stayed had salaries drastically cut. Three years after the Federal mandate the PSCOG is still not a functioning body."

On October 2, 1975, CARHT and C.A.F. circulated this press release:

"The building of Federal-aid highway projects in the four county Puget Sound region has come to a screeching halt! But don't blame us!

"While we yelled and screamed and waved the Federal laws in the air, the elected officials of three counties have destroyed the area-wide Federally-required planning process (and the Federal agencies have stopped funding highway projects and other capital projects) because they are required to withhold funds until valid regional plans are made.

"The Federal processes are designed to ensure wise and careful spending of the taxpayers' money. Federal-aid projects must be part of a plan adopted by the governmental agencies in the area. The area must first adopt plans and *then* decide how to use projects to carry out those plans.

"The Puget Sound planning agency, the Puget Sound of Council of Governments, PSCOG, has been knowingly and deliberately destroyed by those county elected officials who have wanted to prevent coordinated and cooperative planning in an open forum. The difficulties began two years ago after the Federal agencies listed planning deficiencies, and PSCOG began a curative process. Then Pierce County's plans to develop farm land were questioned, and that county resigned. Last year King County started a reorganization

NOW GENTLEMEN- LET'S DECIDE WHAT TO DO WITH I-90

designed to cripple the process. When the Federal agencies insisted on PSCOG's conforming to the Federal laws and decertified it, Snohomish County resigned immediately, and King County resigned effective December 31 of this year.

Apparently [King County] Executive John Spellman then thought that he should complete his memorable year as Chairman of PSCOG—he appointed Aubrey Davis to be Chairman of the Transportation Policy Committee, an "interim" appointment. This appointment is clearly illegal because Davis as Chairman of the Transportation Policy Committee obviously cannot fairly evaluate and review his decisions made on transit plans and funding as Chairman of the Metro Transit Committee and his decisions on allocation of urban highway trust funds (between highways and transit) made as Chairman of the Urban Systems Board for King County.

"The appointment of Davis is also dangerous and improper because Davis will use his new committee chairmanship (and has already used it) to prevent or demolish the completion of the full study of the transit substitution on the I-90 highway—Aubrey Davis has consistently opposed ... area wide transit, and we believe he will continue to do everything in his power to build the highway. The fact that he now holds three transportation policy committee chairmanships proves that he lacks the ability to avoid conflicts of interest."

[I add in 1996: It also proves that he was acting for and was backed by great political power that was able to obtain the Federal Secretary's final approval of the 1971 Mercer Island I-90 project without the essential transit parts being designed.]

"CARHT and C.A.F. stand by to pick up the pieces—just as we always have. We predict that there will be a short interval while the elected officials finally read the Federal laws and administrative procedures to see what they must do. Then they will look at their losses of Federal Funds while project costs escalate. Then they will decide whether they want to develop and adopt a regional development plan and a transportation plan based on it. We predict it will be a long, hard winter, but don't blame us." Signed by David Lefebvre, President of C.A.F. and Bill McCord, President of CARHT

The Draft Environmental and 4(f) Statements

I will not write about the validity of the Draft Environmental Impact Statement (DEIS) because in 1976 I wrote a 250 page evaluation of its contents. I called it the *Critique of the 4(f) and the Draft Environmental Impact Statements of I-90 (the Critique).* It should be shelved with this writing, and it is included in the discussion of the Final Environmental Impact Statement. The FEIS did not even mention the 1976 Highway Act Withdraw/Substitution amendments, let alone discuss any of the available alternatives available. The FEIS did not have any design for the Seattle section—no actual width, no elevations, no record of property taken, especially of parklands taken. Since there is no design, there is no valid report of the effects of the construction and use of the project and how adverse effects will be ameliorated.

The Attacks on the Plaintiffs

The open attack on the I-90 opponents was carried out mainly in the newspaper reports that the plaintiffs were causing the accidents on I-90 by delaying the proposed project—although the writers obviously knew that the delay was due to an injunction imposed by the federal courts because the defendants had not met the federal law requirements to qualify for federal funds. The newspapers' publishing of the continuing attack on the I-90 opponents was part of the defendants' deliberately-planned campaign to prevent the publishing of the truth and to support the Mercer Island Plan.

Then individual people were attacked—and I became the frequent victim. For example, they wrote that one person was said to be delaying I-90 and causing the deaths by accidents. Soon Margaret Tunks was named, and ridiculous statements were made about my having delayed the project and my having "blood on my head". When Governor Dixy Lee Ray took office, she kept repeating the old attacks although she had no accurate information and she had refused to take her adviser Lou Guzzo's recommendations that she meet with me—she obviously was a funnel for misinformation originating in the highway proponents. On July 22, 1977, the *Tacoma News Tribune* reported that the governor said she is angered by obstructionist groups "whose only purpose is to stop something"... "We have many examples of important developments being delayed or stopped by an insignificant minority of irresponsible, vocal people. ... Highway I-90 in Seattle has been held up nearly 15 years by the action of one person—I won't identify her, but she's well known. How many lives have been lost on the Lake Washington Bridge because of too heavy traffic on an inadequate structure just because this person was able to block a project that needed completion?"

This attack was still being used in *1993*, in the *Seattle Times* September 19 article, a history of the I-90 project. It was written by Peggy Reynolds, of the *Mercer Island Reporter*. She said, (as she had said several times before), "Gov. Dixy Lee Ray called Tunks 'the one person who alone has been responsible for the 20-year delay in completing I-90'." [I had been living in New Jersey in 1957, and I did not know anything about the existence of the I-90 project until 1970, only seven years before Ray's statements.]

The Reynolds' 1993 article did not include any of the information about the *Lathan case* lawsuit federal court decisions. The suit had been filed in 1970, and the seven-year delay in completing I-90 began in 1971 when the U.S. Court of Appeals for the Ninth Circuit had ruled that the State and Federal Department of Transportaion must stop all work on I-90 until they submitted the adequate environmental impact and other reuqired statements and held a hearing based on them. I wrote to ask the *Times* if they would publish this all-important history; they did not answer my letter

I still cannot think of anything I did which actually delayed I-90. I have re-read everything in my files and written this history of I-90. I find that I have made a valid analysis of the opposition's attacks.

My opposition to the project began with the State's starting land acquisition devastation in the I-90 corridor and in the R.H. Thomson freeway corridor through Montlake. As the State continued their heavy-handed activities, I began to think that there must be a better process for preventing damage to Seattle and insuring the best spending of freeway funds, and I began trying to find out what *should* be done. I read the relevant federal laws, cases, administrative rules and definitive writings. I began to find out what the State was *not* doing, especially as outlined in the U.S. Court of Appeals for the Ninth Circuit's opinions that gave the reasons for imposing the injunction on I-90 in 1971 and continuing in 1972, 1973 and 1974. My opposition to the project began to consist mainly of fact-finding and record writing. When the State finally submitted the draft environmental statement for the 1976 hearing, the I-90 plaintiffs' attorney suggested that I digest the DEIS. I did, and my 1977 *Critique of the 4(f) and Environmental Impact Statements of I-90* is accurate still. I continued to find facts and write about them—and that's how I continued to oppose the I-90 project.

I know of very few people who ever read my *Critique*. Some of the middle echelon of people in the U.S. Department of Transportation in Washington, D.C. said that they had read it after I sent it to the Secretary. I gave copies to the Municipal, Seattle, and University of Washington Libraries. My only other I-90 activities were to prepare newsletters and flyers and from time to time to meet with fellow opponents. So how did I become the one person who delayed I-90?

I started writing this history by reading some 96 cartons of saved arterials, and selecting 14 cartons to keep. I've re-read all of those materials, and it's become a challenge to try to find out how I was chosen as the chief antagonist by the I-90 proponents.

The riddle turns out to have a simple solution: My writings were accurate and threatening, and because of them, I became the "straw man", the fictional opponent in the proponents' planned campaign to conceal their responsibility for the delays in I-90. They gained time for political action to evade the courts' mandates by continual delay, and that delay was responsible for the continuing accidents and deaths on the existing I-90. The proponents' decision *not* to make essential safety improvements continued their concealment of their delays. The fallacies in the accusations were ridiculous—impossible to believe, and I think people who actually thought about it did not believe them. The fact that the accusations were repeated as late as 1993 proved to me that the I-90 proponents still were trying to evade their responsibility for the long delay of their project and for the long-continuing accidents on the existing highway.

Throughout the years reporters have asked me to comment on the statements about me the I-90 proponents had made. I decided early on just to give the most honest answer in a few words, "The accusations are ridiculous," which they were. I thought that the language of the judges in their opinions on I-90 proved very clearly who was delaying the highway, and that I could hardly state it better than the judges had.

I decided to use my speaking time at the 1976 Federal hearing on the Seattle segment of I-90 to respond to the published accusations that I had caused the I-90 accidents (and was continuing to cause them) by my delaying of the I-90 process.

In late 1975 these were the facts which influenced my decision to talk at the hearing:

— At the November 1975, Highway Commission meeting, District Engineer Bogart had been asked what safety improvements were going to be made on I-90, and he gave the incredible answer, "<u>We haven't thought of any!</u>"

— I had obtained a peak period accident report for the years 1971-74. This very rudimentary report dated November, 1975, gave these facts: 68.7% of the accidents were rear-ends; 55% of all head-on accidents were at the beginning of the reversible lanes; there were five fatalities at the Mercer Island ramps; and four fatalities at the bulge.

— I had been present at four different meetings where Governor Evans (an engineer) said the bulge could be removed at any time, but the State continued to delay.

— The State Directors of Highways kept saying that no federal funds could be used for safety improvements on existing I-90 although federal funds were constantly being used for safety improvements like those on I-5.

My presentation at the 1976 Federal hearing on I-90 was intended to show and publicize the State's continued refusal to make safety improvements on I-90. I used photograph slides and explained how they showed the continued causes of accidents on I-90 in these categories:

>*The dangerous and reversible lanes and the signing.* I showed the poorly visible reversible signing which consisted of small, square boxes suspended above the highway with either a dim reddish "X" to show that the lane was closed or a dim green arrow to show that the lane was open. For comparison, I showed the large directional signs the State used everywhere else to close a highway lane, lighted arrows on large signs. On some of these, the lights went off and on in a sequence so that the arrow repeatedly moved away from the closed lane to a right or left lane. These signs could be placed on the pavement, on the back of a vehicle, or hung overhead.

Three years after the hearing, I wrote this letter to U.S. Secretary of Transportation Adams (on April 8, 1979), "Obviously, the safety improvements are years and years overdue. Obviously they could have been funded long ago as improvements to the existing I-90, as the improvements on I-5 are now being funded as Federal interstate projects—the *larger* reversible lane "X" and arrow boxes *are* now being funded on the Seattle segment of existing I-90. The State still has the small signal boxes on Mercer Island so that the Islanders and their friends will continue to be in accidents on I-90 and complain bitterly about the accidents being caused by the I-90 opponents' delaying the project."

>*The bulge in the middle of the Lake.* The bulge in the middle of the original I-90 bridge could be opened for ship traffic; it had two lanes in each direction around an open space, and one lane was reversed

during commuter peaks to provide for two-way traffic on one side at the bulge. My slides showed that unless vehicles traveled very slowly, their drivers could not see the other traffic due to the curvature of the bulge.

>*The on-ramp highway signing.* I showed one horrible example, a sign at the last ramp on Mercer Island to the west lane of traffic going into Seattle. The sign said, "MOVE LEFT," but if the lanes were in an afternoon reversible mode, a driver who moved left would move into traffic going the opposite direction. [Bang! Crash!]

There was a very large crowd at the 1976 hearing when I spoke and showed my slides, and people from Mercer Island were there—yet there was never any reaction to my having shown them some of the I-90 accident sites. Highway Engineer Bogart may have reduced the effect my presentation had on the audience when he said, "The safety improvements would wait for the adoption of the I-90 proposal," which turned out to be after the final Court decision in August, 1979, *three years later*! I still do no understand why some honest and intelligent Mercer Islander in the audience did not rise to protest.

The defendants said, in their answer #605 in Volume II of the EIS, "Many of the elements of this program [the major safety improvements] are eligible for Federal funding in advance of the final SR 90 design approval." This poorly printed answer is an incredible admission of the deliberate malfeasance in the State's continual statements that federal funds were not available for the needed I-90 safety improvements. It was obvious that I had proved Mercer Island did not really want a safer highway—if they had they would have insisted on immediate safety improvements.

Throughout the years I filed newspaper clippings under "Safety on I-90", but they do not really record safety because the State had done almost nothing to make the existing I-90 freeway safe during all the long periods of the 1970's. I should have filed them under "Deliberate Delays in Safety Improvements". Two sections of my *Critique* cover the State's abysmal decision *not* to provide any safety improvements on I-90 until the 1971 project was absolutely certain.

"Alleviating Safety problems: page 32

a. Numbers and causes of accidents, page 32
b. Improving safety on the Existing Facility, page 34
c. Signing, page 35
d. The Bulge—Safety Problems and Alleviation, page 35

The 1976 DEIS proved that the State did not take the first step necessary to prevent accidents; they could not identify the problems or begin to try to alleviate them until there were public records of collated accident data which could be used to discover the cause of the accidents. These records might have existed, but the information would have been so damaging that if they did exist, they would have never been disclosed.

In 1980, after the injunction on I-90 had been lifted, the State was still not trying to make the existing highway safe, and they were blaming the accidents on the I-90 opponents. On March 19, the *Mercer Island Reporter* published records of the "accidents recorded during 1979 on the Mercer Island's portion of the unfinished I-90 freeway, including the bridges, according to the statistics obtained this week from the Washington State Department of Transportation."

The article continued, "Of the 206 accidents, 204 involved injuries and five caused fatalities." Two people were killed in accidents at the bulge, one man escaped from his crashed car in the bulge and swam to safety, six people were injured and "several persons slightly injured" at the bulge. There were eight head-on collisions involving twelve injured and one fatality, 25 sideswipes, 157 "rear-enders" (76.2%), and 38 accidents in which a vehicle hit a fixed object. Five vehicles overturned.

These facts supported the material I had presented at the 1976 Federal Hearing on I-90. My later studies of 1971-74 and 1979 accident data and the information in the 1977 FEIS proved that I should have stressed the fact that the vehicles were almost always traveling too fast on the floating bridge section of I-90. These facts proved that the State had not tried to control traffic speed in the 1970 decade: the "rear-enders" were always caused by inadequate distance between vehicles traveling too fast; the side-swipes, the hitting of fixed objects, and the vehicles overturning were also caused by speeding.

In the 1977 FEIS, Vol. II, the State printed a barely-readable answer to my request for the "stopping sight driver distance" around the bulge curve—the minimum distance the driver can see around the curve—in their answer, #663. They said that the stopping sight distance for the two inner lanes was 185 feet with a safe speed of 25-28 miles an hour—and yet the posted speed and the actual speed was 45 miles per hour! Drivers traveling at 45 mph in reversible traffic around the bulge could not see the oncoming vehicles in time to avoid accidents.

The proponents' political strategy was intended to cover up their delay on I-90 by blaming the opponents of the project for the accidents on the existing highway, but this strategy had another horrible effect—the proponents actually prevented all of the needed safety improvements on the existing highway. The 23 USC Code of Federal Regulations, Ch. 1, Section 771.18 (g) (3) requires the identification of "deficiencies in existing facilities". In June, 1975, the Federal Highway Administration had approved ninety percent federal funding of these I-90 projects: new reversible signs; closure of the ramp to the west lane on Mercer Island; collision barriers on the bulge. But even then, the State never did identify deficiencies in existing facilities [or if they did, they never disclosed or used the statistics], and because those deficiencies are never listed and publicly described, the State never intended to cure the causes of accidents by either minor major changes. (See page 33, et. seq. of the *Critique*)

The information on needed safety improvements on the existing I-90 is included in the "No-Build" Alternative in my *Critique* (beginning on page 91), where I review the federally required process. Again, the State repeats its "pro-forma compliance" which Federal Judge Beeks said in 1972 "would not do." The State gave no more information about causes of accidents than they had given when they were supposed to be discussing safety—the EIS merely plods through a list of safety improvements, discussing each item separately, and never putting together several items which would act together to provide more safety..

The piling for the East Channel Bridge had been finished for years when on December 2, 1978, the *Seattle Post Intelligencer* published an article headlined, "Hang-up on I-90 Work is Blamed on Stalling". The State wanted federal court approval of lifting the injunction to allow the removal of the bulge and construction on the proposed East Channel Bridge. Quoting the article, "They are considered safety improvements' separate from the larger question of whether the final leg of I-90 should be built at all." The removal of the bulge was indeed a safety improvement needed with the existing highway whether or not the new I-90 project was built, and the I-90 plaintiffs had already stipulated to traffic improvements on I-90, "provided they would not increase the capacity beyond the present four lanes." Since our attorney was not available, I told the reporters that we plaintiffs were leery of construction on the East channel bridge at this time because we had learned that the defendants wanted to build a structure 80 feet wide[as half of the total], and the State had refused to stipulate how wide the entire structure would be and the number of lanes of traffic which could be carried on it. The State's strategy continued—the plaintiffs' protests were to be considered worthless. State Highway Director William Bulley suggested that the I-90 opponents should leave the question of the number and width of vehicle lanes to the traffic engineers, which is exactly what we were afraid of. One of the State engineers said, "The operational characteristics are best left to experts in the field of traffic engineering and not to the lawyers or students of the law."

In an April 3, 1979, letter the Coast Guard sent to Secretary Adams, they omitted the important fact that the defendants in the *Lathan* case, including the Secretary, had stipulated that the safety improvements on I-90 could be made, the plaintiffs had also stipulated, the District Court had approved the stipulations, and the bids were to be opened in a week—but Secretary Adams' office was still saying that the

Secretary will not approve any safety improvements on I-90 unless they are part of the proposed project—no federal funds were available for any safety improvements on the existing highway!

I wrote then, "These statements seem to prove the point that I have made so often when I am being accused of holding up the safety improvements on existing I-90—I think the State and federal agencies have always intended to hold the safety improvements hostage until the entire and enormous proposed project is absolutely certain to be built—a political act."

My comment was always, "HOW WIDE IS I-90?" Why should engineers have the right to decide how much traffic would come into Seattle? Why should the engineers have the right to decide how big the new I-90 in Seattle should be?

I asked a friend to read the I-90 portion of this book and to criticize it. She wrote, "You were a good target! You were outspoken in both your testimony and letters—and said things that people did not want to hear. You did not represent a political majority and were subjected to the same tactics any majority can use to overcome criticism ... why weren't your opponents smart enough to get out of being the victim? How could you have changed to assist future citizen efforts?"

She also said, "You need more analysis of the majority's tactics to help citizens in similar positions gain strength to fight the majority's statements that they repeat over and over until they begin to rewrite history."

[My advice for future citizens' actions is: More people, more time!]

My youngest son gave me the most valid perspective on my activities. He said, "You and Dad were trained in the language of the law, and you just could not believe that people would intentionally try to ignore it and persevere in ignoring it." I could not believe that the proponents would actually win the I-90 lawsuit without fulfilling the mandates the Courts had written so clearly. I could not believe that when the case was heard in the Federal District Court for Western

Washington for the final decision, Judge Thomson would write a decision which proved that neither he nor the defendants had paid any attention to the federal courts' instructions.

The "Purpose" of I-90, a Contrived Panacea

The statement of the "purpose" of I-90 kept creeping up whenever the status quo of the 1971 design of I-90 (the Plan) needed defending, whenever alternatives to the project should have been studied and considered. For example: the "purpose" was used to finalize the Board of Review project in 1973 to prevent any changes to the I-90 proponents' design by showing that the 1971 Mercer Island design (plus the two Board of Review additions for Seattle), fulfilled the "purpose". In the Memorandum of Agreement, the "purpose" was used to prevent consideration of alternatives. The "purpose" was used to evade the courts' mandates in the 1971, 1972, 1973, and 1974 decisions by eliminating any alternatives which would be different from the 1971 project, especially the alternative of keeping (not abandoning) the original Interstate-90 highway on Mercer Island.

I quote from my discussion of Section 5, "The Purpose of the Proposed Action," beginning on page 14 of my *Critique*, which is bound and shelved (I hope) next to this book for reference. My analysis is as relevant now as it was 20 years ago.

"The Secretary's Procedures require, under '3. General content [of the EIS] 'a. Description of Project, a statement of purpose.' The State has used this statement of purpose as a standard against which all alternatives are measured for adequacy."

"There seem to be no procedures for the writing of the purpose. In this case, it was done outside the Commission's formal meetings.

"The draft EIS shows that the Highway Commission had set these limits before December, 1975 [when the DEIS was published]. The purpose was then, "the alleviation of traffic congestion and safety problems in the corridor connecting Interstate 5 in downtown Seattle, the City of Mercer Island, and Interstate 405 in Bellevue to the east." The State always puts the purpose in quotes in the EIS, although they maintain that they are not quoting anything, and there is no record of any meeting in which this purpose was written.

The final EIS shows this purpose [page I-248]: "The purpose of the proposed action may be broadly defined as increasing the people-carrying capacity, alleviating safety problems, and providing transit facilities and environmental amenities in the corridor connecting downtown Seattle, the City of Mercer Island, and the City of Bellevue to the east." Note: The State has added "to increase the people-carrying capacity" and "provisions for transit facilities and amenities." Note the addition of "downtown Seattle" and "the City of Mercer Island" in the description of the corridor. This addition and the addition of "provisions for transit facilities and amenities IN THE CORRIDOR" [emphasis added] enables them to avoid studying alternatives which are not in the Mercer Island route even though I-90 is actually in the same cross-Lake Washington corridor as SR 520, the Evergreen Bridge route, and the highways around the ends of the Lake could all be used to "increase the people-carrying capacity, and alleviating safety problems" on the I-90 corridor." I wrote, "If there are alternatives which are outside the immediate corridor of those particular seven miles but which will have the net result of fulfilling all four of the requirements, those alternatives *can* be considered along with the proposed action."

Note that they no longer describe the project as the connection between I-5 and I-405, but between "downtown Seattle and Bellevue" [and they do not say downtown Bellevue]. This change enables them to avoid designing the transit termini at the east end of I-90—and hereafter their federally-required section ends a half-mile short of I-405 and is not a legal section under the Federal Highway Act definition.

Note that they have added "providing" ... "environmental amenities" which ever after means that there can be no consideration of any changes in the Mercer Island portion of I-90 because their amenities are set in the 1971 design. No cost-analysis would ever be made or required.

The "purpose" of this I-90 Section was really to build the I-90 section of Mercer Island chose in 1971 with nothing added, nothing deleted. The "purpose" was deliberately written to ensure that the Mercer Island 1971 I-90 project design and corridor would remain intact. Examples of how "purpose" was used are found in the "WHEREAS" statements and conclusions in the Memorandum of Agreement, and in Judge Scholfield's decision on Initiative 21 (See Chapter 14).

The Memorandum of Agreement

The writing called, "MEMORANDUM AGREEMENT" (MOA), looks like a very important document with its ten "WHEREASES" and thirteen pages signed on December 21, 1976, by all those important people: the Governor, the County Executive, three Mayors, the Director of State Highways (an employee signing for the Washington State Highway Commission), and an employee Executive of Metro signing for the Municipality of Metropolitan Seattle (the transit and sewer agency for King County). I immediately spent hours analyzing the process and trying to dissect out the most important features of the product, but I could not see that the parties were trying to do anything. The parties were trying to do nothing—to preserve the 1971 I-90 project without paying any attention to the facts:

— The I-90 project had long been under federal court injunction—the State Highway Commission and the Secretary of the U.S. Department of Transportation were under the court's orders to meet the requirements of the federal laws, as mandated by the judges;

— The federal law had been drastically changed by the 1976 amendment to the Federal Highway Act.

Three years ago when I began to work with the materials I had kept and to remember 1976, I realized that the Memorandum of Agreement part of the history of I-90 could be written in a very few words because nothing had actually happened. *An amorphous group had gathered together to enter into a secret so-called mediation process through which they reached unenforceable decisions they did not have legal authority to make—with the intent that the MOA would be used for political clout*, especially so that the Secretary of the U.S. Department of Transportation could use it to show that there was unified support of the political "leaders" for the 1971 I-90 project as designed, without termini on either end, or transit facilities and any design for the project in Seattle west of 23rd Avenue.

The great achievement of the MOA was supposedly cutting the ten lane project down to eight lanes. This was a fallacy perpetuated by describing the project in lanes rather than measured width—the project was to be wide enough for ten lanes, and this width would not be reduced. Important evidence is found in the Bulley deposition for the 1979 trial, where he said that the eight lane size could be converted to ten lanes, and in the drawing of the design of the "recommended" 4-2-4 project "configuration" in the September 7, 1972, *Post Intelligencer* official notice of the availability of the draft EIS. Under the title "3-2-3 configuration" they say it ... "provides for a plan similar to the recommended plan with a lane configuration modified to three lanes eastbound, two reversible lanes for exclusive transit, and three lanes eastbound. The three eastbound lanes would be placed on the existing floating bridge." Note that the designs are presented under the term "configuration", showing no intent to narrow the width of the project, only to re-stripe it for fewer lanes. This illustration was used in both the draft and final EIS—as if it were all the State had. [see page 152]

[This notice is extremely interesting because the public was told to submit comments on the pamphlet EIS which Judge Beeks had declared inadequate a month earlier, on August 4, 1972, in an opinion which recorded very good instructions for what the defendants must to write an adequate EIS—surely it was a complete waste of time to ask for comments on the ridiculously inadequate EIS. The defendants were trying to conceal their "serious delay of the project," despite Judge Beeks' warning just a month earlier.]

Unbelievably, the intent that the width of the project would not be changed was proved in this answer on page 414 of the FEIS Volume II [see the *Critique*, page 31]: "When the right-of-way for this 3-2-3 plan was established, it was determined that reductions of the right-of-way width of twelve feet [on each side] should create a hardship to many property owners by leaving undesirable remainders of land." This statement unquestionably wins the booby prize for the most stupid in all the defendants' writings—how could the State create a hardship on an abutter by building I-90, twelve feet further away? This statement is a futile attempt to conceal the 4-2-4 project.

My criticism of the DEIS is well-documented. As I read the DEIS, I put each item on a 4" x 6" card, filed the cards in categories, and wrote what I called my *Critique*. As I finished it, I mailed it to the Secretary of the U.S. Department of Transportation, beginning in October, 1977. There are 228 pages of my manuscript and some 60 pages of additional illustrating material, my letters, and letters from federal officials; the indexes in the book are adequate descriptions of the issues as I examined them. I was especially careful to write accurate citations to the DEIS to confirm my statements.

By February, 1976, the supporters of the inviolate 1971 I-90 project must have been fairly well bothered by the public and the agencies' questions at the hearing and their submitted written comments. In retrospect, it's pretty obvious that the supporters had to do something to improve their image and to burnish up a horribly expensive, badly tarnished project—so—they decided to go into hiding in a so-called mediation process ending in the production of a writing which would cure the deficiencies of the process—both by changing the facts and by filling up the blanks with promises for future actions. Judge Duniway's instructions (and common sense) required the project design to be finished before the hearings and approvals, but the parties to the Memorandum of Agreement decided that they could get by with face-lifting the now obsolete and still inadequate 1971 Mercer Island I-90 project. Their main object was to protect the status quo.

The mediation was a well-orchestrated sales campaign. The Memorandum of Agreement before us is a purely political writing, and

the forum of parties to it existed purely for political purposes. It was prepared for the sole benefit of Mercer Island and the highway builders:
— To protect the Plan;
— To keep the 1971 project intact;
— To cover up planning inadequacies identifiable in the environmental impact statement;
— To wipe out any possibility of a study of the new transportation alternatives which were available;
— To try to get the political power to force Seattle to agree to the same old highway projects that were in the Zahn offer.

From the very beginning, the Memorandum mediation process was difficult to understand. The exercise had been initiated by Governor Evans or Mercer Island's Aubrey Davis, or Metro's ex-counsel James Ellis, or the Highway Department (they all said they had). The mediators were Gerald Cormick and Leah Patton of the Office of Environmental Mediation at the University of Washington, and the mediation was to be financed with grants from the Rockefeller and Ford Foundations. Mr. Ellis was a trustee of the Ford Foundation.

The group of people in the mediation were a mixed lot altogether. My first analysis problem was to find out what this miscellaneous group of people was supposed to be doing in the mediation. [Note that the finished title of the MOA is MEMORANDUM AGREEMENT—it doesn't give a clue as to what was mediated.] When the mediation was announced, I searched the state and federal laws to see if they gave the authority to any such body, made up of parties like these to do anything; as I expected, I found nothing.

The parties in the MOA could not enter into an agreement by which transportation projects would be prioritized. Under state laws, the Washington State Highway Commission has the authority to plan and prioritize the construction and use of state-funded highways. Under federal laws *only* the four jurisdictions adjacent to the I-90 project could, with the concurrence of the Governor, withdraw the funds from the I-90 project.

Federal law does not set forth any requirements for time of or for procedures for the voting on the withdrawal of funds, but that did not stop the State Legislature from passing their own laws to amend the federal law: by requiring that the decision to withdraw funds from the Interstate 90 project be made before December 1, 1975, by all four jurisdictions, the Governor, *and* the Puget Sound Governmental Conference; by requiring the State to hold the federal hearing no later than February 1, 1976; and to submit the final EIS by May 1, 1976, just a few days before the 1976 withdraw/substitution amendment to the Federal Highway Act applied. [No one seemed to notice that the draft EIS could not be converted into a valid final EIS in three months.] The Legislature obviously wanted to be sure that the EIS could not be used as the basis of facts for choice of withdrawal of federal funds from the 1971 project as an alternative to the 1971 I-90 project and that Judge Duniway's mandates instructing the defendants to begin again in their consideration of all aspects of the problem would <u>not</u> be obeyed.

I was lobbying full time in the Legislature on transportation issues when these laws were passed, but I paid little attention to them because they were so stupid—how could the state change the federal procedures laws for decision-making on I-90 and still qualify for the 90% of federal funds? How could the state make these laws when federal laws had intentionally omitted state legislatures' participation in this process?

I tried to find out what the mediation group was doing. Since they could not take any valid enforceable actions, I waited and hoped that their meetings indicated that at last there would be some study and open discussion on the really important I-90 factors:

— The production of a valid Environment Impact Statement which would require completing the design in Seattle and Bellevue and determining the effects of the whole project;

— The complete consideration of the alternative uses of I-90 finds through the process of withdraw/transfer, with a special study of the provisions of the new May 5, 1976, Highway Act.

At the very beginning, we learned that the process of mediation would not be fair. Mediator Jerry Cormick told me that none of the meetings would be open to the public due to the objections of Aubrey Davis to open meetings. [In his *Lathan* case deposition, Mr. Davis explained why he thought the public should not be allowed in meetings—it allowed more freedom and took less time.]

Seattle Mayor Uhlman had supported the ten lane I-90 in the Zahn offer negotiations and had met secretly with the State to wipe out eight of Seattle's ten objections to design elements before the Board of Review was convened. Although we did not know until author Allan Talbot wrote later, Mayor Uhlman had contacted our lawyer to tell him that he could be part of the group IF he agreed at the beginning not to contest the final MOA. [If this is true, our lawyer refused. Mayor Uhlman had a law degree, and he surely knew that a lawyer could not make such agreements for clients without their knowledge and consent.]

I knew about some of the previous mediation team's work, where the mediation had always involved both the opponents and the proponents of the contested action. In any mediation concerning I-90, the parties should have been the *Lathan* case plaintiffs and the defendants, the Washington State Highway Commissioners, and the U.S. Secretary of the Department of Transportation, *but none of the plaintiffs were allowed to participate in the mediation, not as active parties or even as observers.* The I-90 plaintiffs had won the lawsuit in decisions which clearly told the defendants what was wrong, and the project was being delayed by the defendants' failure to meet the mandates of the Federal Courts which supported the plaintiffs' evidence. How could there be a mediation, if one of the two parties did not participate?

Washington State has an open meeting law which ensures the people's rights to attend meetings of elected officials; there were three elected mayors, one elected country executive, and one elected governor in the mediation group, but they all agreed to secrecy, and no one admitted to having kept any records at all. I concluded that the mediation process had been set up so that the parties to the process could evade responsibility for their agreement. The secrecy was already proof that the mediation was an invalid exercise that would not accomplish anything.

Public meetings ensure that all points of view have been raised and evaluated—they really protect the elected officials, but open meetings would also have protected the mediators Patton and Cormick because they knew so little about the problem when they started to work. They knew nothing about the complicated legal and engineering parameters of the I-90 decision, what the courts' edicts were, what project structure choices were engineeringly possible, whether and what alternatives were available. *The mediators allowed themselves to be led up a primrose path of misinformation furnished by the project proponents because there was no way for the highway opponents to find out what the mediators were and were not being told and no one to tell the mediators what wasn't true.* (A study of the I-90 history by Allan Talbot records that there was only one session of the mediators open to the press, but I do not know anyone who knew about it or attended it.)

From the minute the mediation began there were no opponents to a chosen outcome—the mediation group at once agreed to protect the Plan—that the 1971 I-90 project could not be changed because if changes were options, Mercer Island would probably lose the non-essential design elements—the "amenities".

The Memorandum begins with ten "WHEREAS" statements. Four of them prove that the MOA exercise was created to solidify the 1971 I-90 design—to make it impossible to study or choose any other alternatives:

#3 "WHEREAS, the decisions of the Ninth Circuit Court for the Western District of Washington have required that all alternatives to the proposed highway be studied."

There is no "Ninth Circuit Court for the Western District of Washington"! ALL of the officials had signed the MOA! They were all elected or appointed officials and were supposed to be well educated in the structure of the federal and state court systems; and if they had read the MOA, they would have caught this glaring mistake. So this WHEREAS proves that the parties to the MOA had not read or based any of the decisions on the *U.S. Court of Appeals for the Ninth Circuit's opinions in 1971, 1973, 1974,* or on the *1972 decision of Judge Beeks for the U.S. District Court for the Western District of Washington.*

#4 "WHEREAS, all parties hereto state that they have reviewed the proposed highway development and available alternatives to it, including the option of withdrawal and substitution." This was a remarkable statement for the Governor, three Mayors, and the County Executive to have signed in December, 1976, for it was a record that they had learned the provisions of the new May 1976, amendment to the Federal Highway Act and the new alternatives available under it. They would have had to read the Federal Highway Act section 103, and the administrative regulations promulgated under it. They would have had to read the federal court I-90 decisions to learn what effect the amendments had on the I-90 project decisions. They should have considered all the alternatives available in the new amendment before the MOA was signed in December, 1976! In fact, the 1971 and 1973 amendments were incorrectly stated in the 1975 draft EIS, the mistake was repeated in the final EIS, and the FEIS never recognized the 1976 amendment at all. There is no evidence that the parties had reviewed these amendments.

#5 "WHEREAS, the I-90 facility from I-405 to I-5, when constructed, must contain all of the social and environmental amenities included in the Commission's previously adopted plan and modification thereof contained in the Findings and Order of the Board of Review in order to be acceptable to all jurisdictions."

This WHEREAS refers to both the Mercer Island amenities and the 1973 Board of Review decision in Seattle, and it inters the 1971 Mercer Island project in concrete. The MOA parties had no intention to obey the Ninth Court of Appeals' mandate to begin over again to consider "whether or not the project should be built at all as well as where and as previously designed".

#7 "WHEREAS, the parties have concluded that withdrawal and substitution is not a desirable option because it would double the matching moneys required and because Mercer Island and Seattle find unacceptable a major highway transit I-90 facility without the extensive environmental which amenities might not be funded under the withdrawal and substitution alternative."

This WHEREAS comes directly from Aubrey Davis as he represents Mercer Island, where the project as designed is going to cost about fifty percent of the total cost of I-90, and remember, the State had not yet produced any evidence of the design for the Seattle segment of I-90—except for the essential moving of Colman school and the covering of the highway east of 23rd Avenue, the amenities were all on Mercer Island. Furthermore, the matching funds required for substitution projects had been reduced in the 1976 Federal Highway Act, from twenty to fifteen percent. The fact that all of the Memorandum parties signed the Memorandum despite this obvious mistake means that they either had not read and considered the new alternatives available or that they had read and considered them and decided to ignore their existence.

These defendants' comments in Vol. II of the EIS try to wipe out an consideration of alternatives by using their definition of "purpose":

—answer 582, "Funding options which involve construction outside of the SR 90 corridor are not true alternatives to the proposed project unless they serve the purpose of the proposed project."

—answer 566, "The options covered by U.S.C. 103(e)(2) and (4) [the Federal Highway Act withdraw /substitution amendments], are all uses of funds, rather than alternative methods of accomplishing the purposes of the proposed project."

[Why, I ask, isn't a different use of the interstate funds the only method for funding alternative uses of interstate funds? Answer, because the "purpose" is a description of the Mercer Island, 1971, I-90 project, and if the funds were used for any other project, they wouldn't accomplish the "purpose", so the Plan was perpetuated.]

These four WHEREASES are proof of the results of closed meetings. One mediator told us that there were not very many meetings—the mediation mostly consisted of his taking items to be considered around to the participants. The MOA process and the MOA meetings are a perfect example of why the open meetings law should be enforced. If public observation had been allowed, these WHEREASES would have been questioned and accurately criticized, with full media coverage of the meetings and the audience. And, since they are not true and cannot be defended, they could not have been included in the MOA. But, of course, that's why the MOA tactic was chosen — it's a political document.

The political document proved its value—it cast the 1971 Mercer Island design in concrete. When U.S. Transportation Secretary Brock Adams finally approved the 1971 project in 1978 (still incomplete with no transit connections and no design west of 23rd Avenue in Seattle) *he* cited the MOA to verify his actions—as if it were a valid document.

When the mediation began, the ten-lane highway <u>width</u> had been set. The mediators could not have believed that there was an alternative eight-lane *width* choice and that it had been chosen over a ten-lane *width* choice—the MOA was always publicized as having reduced the ten lane project to eight lanes. This would have been true only if the ten lane width were to be striped for eight lanes. State Transportation Department Secretary Bulley said in his *Lathan* case deposition that the I-90 Chief Project Engineer John Stephenson had come to an

MOA meeting with his drawings to show that the eight lane highway was as wide as, and could be converted to ten lanes, a fact which was known by everyone who was familiar with the DEIS or had been at the hearings.

The group must have spent some time on wall-papering over their mistakes—writing out promises to execute a whole lot of items which were essential to the I-90 process, required by law before approval of the design, and which were not done yet! Nor would they be done before the Secretary approved the project. The MOA pages outline what has not been done, by the simple process of saying it *will* be one in the future—all of parts of the project which had not been included in the design: weaving lanes for both cars and transit would be corrected; access provided to the other freeways and city streets; public transportation, the transit connections; the termini on the east and west ends, etc.—a digest of what the people said the project lacked. The only parts which were completely designed was the Mercer Island section, the bridge, and the section west of the tunnel in Seattle to 23rd Avenue.

The Attack on Seattle in the Memorandum of Agreement

When I read the MOA I found a revival of the 1970 Zahn fictitious offer—an attempt to force the same bridge and highway projects on Seattle. I found one item which is particularly scary for Seattle. On page 9 of the MOA: The "parties hereby agree that projects ... listed below are of highest priority ... The Commission and Metro shall work with the local jurisdictions in undertaking location and design studies for these projects ... Projects to be considered [See Item (e), page 10]: ... Redesign, in a manner acceptable to the City of Seattle, of the lanes where SR 520 [the Evergreen Bridge highway] meets I-5 and at the Mercer Street egress from I-5 in order to improve transit flow and reduce the congestion on I-5 between Mercer Street and Roanoke Street;"

Two Seattle Councilmen, George Benson and Paul Kraabel, were in the MOA group, although only the Mayor signed the MOA. None of the Seattle elected officials who participated in the MOA process nor any of the other Seattle elected officials should have agreed to have the Mayor sign the MOA and thus confirm those provisions. These projects were in the Zahn offer in 1970—unfortunately, these same projects keep creeping up.

In the 1975 session of the legislature, Rep. Bill Burns had opposed a bill for a study to extend the Evergreen Bridge SR 520 corridor to Redmond because the study would be of the beginning of the construction of SR 520 further east that would require additions to the Evergreen Bridge with construction and traffic damage to Seattle—a forerunner of the MOA provision. Rep. Burns was right; this item should have been deleted from the MOA because of its effect on Seattle.

The Roanoke-to-Mercer connection Seattle approved in the MOA may be dangerous in the future if it is used as Seattle's authorization to accommodate traffic from the <u>four more bridge lanes proposed</u> to be added to SR 520. This MOA project is also the crossover of I-5 to Roanoke planned to enlarge Mercer Street in Seattle. In 1994, two large highway building firms tried, with the participation of Aubrey Davis, (who had been appointed to the Washington State Transportation Commission), to start construction of an additional bridge across Lake Washington, adjacent to the Evergreen Bridge, SR 520.

The 1976 MOA project and the 1994 proposed SR 520 additions resurrect the old *1963* plan for the ring road around the Seattle business district, called "The Noose". CARHT and C.A.F. had fought the Bay Freeway on the same Mercer Street corridor in 1972 and had won both the lawsuit we filed and the city vote to use those 1960 city bond funds for other projects. I thought that any additional construction for an elevated or buried Mercer Street was forever dead because the problem is not with the present capacity of Mercer—the problem is that the connections *to* Mercer are far beyond capacity and cannot take any additional traffic coming to and from Mercer, but all the Seattle elected officials approved the Mayor's signing of the MOA. And the sensible transportation faction in Seattle had decided that the MOA was meaningless and that they would not spend time opposing it.

On the last page of the MOA, the State spells out where the power is: "The Commission will take no action which would result in a major change in either the operation or the capacity of the I-90 facility without prior consultation with and involvement of the other parties to this agreement." This statement is highway-lawyerese for, "the State will do what they darned please in the future." If "approval by" had been inserted instead of "consultation with and involvement" of the other parties, the statement would have meant that the elected officials would have some control over I-90 in the future IF federal and state laws allowed them to so do, which they don't—and if any amorphous body like the MOA group had any authority to do anything, which it doesn't.

Metro and the I-90 Decision

The most interesting fact about the MOA is that it records exactly what Metro *had not done* for public transit on the I-90 project by adding all these elements to the MOA as "work to be performed in the future." This is especially remarkable because Aubrey Davis, a voting member of the MOA group, was Chairman of the Metro Transit Committee from 1972-78, and he held other important positions involving decisions on public transportation—he should have been working to expedite the transit elements of the I-90 project and to consider building rail on it. But Mr. Davis was holding the line on the I-90 transit connections as part of the strategy of the proponents of the 1971 Mercer Island project, who believed that it would be seriously threatened by the discussion and decisions of the already-designed transit on Mercer Island.

Or, did Mr. Davis really represent Metro? The records will show that Metro Council had not taken any action to design the I-90 transit connections except on Mercer Island.

Metro had been the transit agency for King County from 1972. The early design of the transit elements of the I-90 project was essential to ensure the operation of transit on and off the project and to provide the best solutions for transit design elements to control the cost and to avoid the adverse social, economic, environmental effects of these elements.

Through the years, Metro's consistent and deliberate inaction on the design of I-90 is proved:

— In his deposition for I-90, Davis reported that Metro would finish the study of transit on I-90 in 1972.

— In 1975, when the bus tunnel proposal was unveiled, the newspapers had reported that Aubrey Davis, the Chairman of the Metro Transit Committee, said that the bus tunnel was an essential connection to the I-90 project, but this connection had not been designed by 1980.

— In December, 1976, the Memorandum of Agreement, signed by all the parties to it, recorded that the transit elements of the design of I-90 would be done in the future—this was an acknowledgment of the whole group that the work had not been done.

— In 1977, Secretary Adams warned the State that he would not approve the I-90 project until the termini and the transit connections to I-90 were designed.

— In 1978, Secretary Adams reneged when he approved the project with the condition that he would not take the final step—the P.S.&E. (plans, specifications and estimates)—until the I-90 termini and transit elements were designed.

— In 1979, Federal District Judge Gordon Thomson copied the defendants' findings and orders after the I-90 trial for his own opinion, which meant that he was declaring the environmental impact statement adequate—without any termini or transit designs or connections, except on Mercer Island, OR any design west of 23rd Avenue in Seattle!

Metro had avoided all of the I-90 project's transit decisions by the simple expedient of doing nothing at all! [Year after year.] But where were Metro decisions made? Metro decisions were not made by the Metro Council members in the meetings of the Metro Council.

Metro was founded in 1956, and, in the 1970's, when I attended Metro meetings, Metro still had no operating procedures for the functioning of the Metro Council and its decision-making. All actions of the Council were taken by vote on legal-sized multiple-paged resolutions, and Metro had no requirement that Council members should receive these resolutions far enough in advance that the council members could read what they would vote on. The resolutions were not available to the public, even at the meeting when the voting took place. Council meeting minutes were prepared by the Metro Counsel, James Ellis, and were not available at the following meeting. The Metro Transit Committee met just before the Council meeting, and previously undisclosed action was passed in Committee and sent to the Council for voting that same day. The Chairmen of the Metro committees were chosen by a small group which included the non-elected Metro Counsel James Ellis and the hired Executive Director; there was no term of office for the Chairmen—Aubrey Davis served as Chairman of the Metro Transit Committee from its inception in 1972 to September, 1978.

Early in 1974, (eighteen years after Metro had been organized), the State Auditor warned Metro that it must adopt by-laws (procedures for operating the Council). Interested Council members and the public made suggestions similar to those on this list I submitted on July 7, 1974.

"Obviously Metro procedures must be changed to give fair and adequate notice to citizens and to allow time for their participation in the process. The elected officials must also be given adequate time to familiarize themselves with the proposed action they must take in the Metro Council. Metro must make these procedural changes:

(1) Committee meetings must be scheduled for alternate weeks when the Metro Council in not meeting.

(2) Proposals for action must be submitted to the Metro Council and delegated to the proper committee for action during the next week.

(3) No action may be taken by the Metro Council unless the proposal has been introduced at the previous Metro Council meeting and has been voted at the appropriate committee meeting the previous or an earlier week.

(4) No action may be taken on any item which has not been placed on the agenda and submitted as a written proposal.

(5) The agenda, written proposals, and committee resolutions must be sent to Committee members and posted—at least five days before the meetings—in the King County office building and in the municipal buildings of all cities in the county with a population of over 30,000."

Metro did not act on the State Auditor's mandate until the Thursday before the Labor Day weekend in 1974. None of the Seattle elected officials was present. The Council needed a simple majority of the members present to take any action, it lacked one vote, the hired non-elected Executive Director voted, and Metro adopted the bare minimum of by-laws. None of the procedural defects I wanted corrected had been discussed or included.

In February, 1976, King County Council member Tracy Owen suggested that new procedures be adopted for Metro because, "new issues are now coming to the Council in final form ... and it's embarrassing to ask questions then." The Executive Director said that any changes would add two weeks to the Metro review process; he said that he would give advance notice of all committee agenda and any council members were permitted to ask that a matter be discussed by a committee!

In 1976, the Council learned that all of the actions that had ever been passed had been recorded as having been passed unanimously, regardless of votes against them. Some of the Council Members were angry, and the Council voted for a true record of votes in the future. The Council rejected a rule requiring meeting agendas to be sent to its members and the media one week in advance—thereby agreeing that they didn't really want to know what they were doing, to participate in decisions. They did vote that Metro would continue to provide a 24-hour notice of meetings as required by state law. (As my professor used to say, "Whether they needed it or not").

On May 12, in 1986, I submitted a "RESOLUTION PROVIDING PROCEDURES FOR THE METRO COUNCIL," which was almost identical to my 1974 submission, with one provision added, to provide for the selection of committee chairmen by the members of the committee and to limit their term of office to one year. My resolution was not considered or recorded in the minutes. Bob Lane, the excellent reporter for the *Seattle Times,* was present at that meeting, and I was dissapointed that he did not write about it for the *Times*–apparantely, they did not consider Metro's procedures to be news! I felt that it should be news when governments failed as Metro had, to follow the most elementary Democratic procedures. No one, not the members of the Metro Council, or the other elected officials, or the citizens had adequate notice of important decisions to be voted by Metro. And no one had the opportunity to participate. This closed process greatly jeopardized the validity of these decisions.

I kept my five pages of records of a meeting of the Metro Transit Committee on May 18, 1978, which prove how tightly the I-90 transit decisions were being controlled in Metro. The Metro Citizens Transit Advisory Council (CTAC) was a group of people who had been asked to come to regularly scheduled meetings to advise Metro. In 1978, they were concerned with Metro's failure to pay any attention to Secretary Adam's letters that he would not approve the I-90 project without the necessary transit connections. Quoting the memorandum I wrote at the meeting:

"Two months ago CTAC passed a resolution which said: (1) the transit connections were not yet designed as part of the I-90 project; (2) the Secretary of Transportation (Adams) would not approve the I-90 environmental impact statement until the transit element of I-90 was designed. This resolution was transmitted to the Metro Transit Committee, (chaired by Aubrey Davis), where it was discussed for three meetings but was never put on the agenda as an action item."

"A new item appeared on the May 18 Transit Committee agenda as an action item, 'the Kraabel resolution'. The latest version of this resolution was not handed around the afternoon of May 16—the CTAC never saw it, although two of their subcommittees did.

[Seattle Council Members] "Williams, Hildt, and Mayor Royer got their heads together, and at the May 18 Metro Council meeting they moved to have the council consider the CTAC resolution."

[continuing with a digest of my notes:] "To everyone's amazement, Mr. Ellis, the Metro Counsel, interrupted the meeting to speak as *if he were a legitimate member of the Metro Transit Committee*. Mr. Ellis tried first to have the group vote on the items in the CTAC resolution before they had adopted the "WHEREAS" statements. Then Mr. Ellis proposed that the group vote to adopt the "Kraabel resolution" he had brought with him which proved that Metro had intentionally delayed the transit portion of I-90. He said, "*The question is whether the Secretary should be allowed to approve part of the project and defer approval of the access until later—to move ahead.*"

Mr. Ellis is a highly-respected lawyer, but his proposal was pure politics, intended to get support for Metro's refusal to obey Secretary Adams' demands. "To move [the project] ahead" is based on the fiction that others, not Metro, have delayed the project's transit elements since the first District Court decision in 1972. And it is not honest to say that Metro's past and future decisions <u>not to design</u> the transit elements on the I-90 project are "moving ahead".

"The question is whether the Secretary should be allowed to approve part of the project," is based on the fiction that the Secretary's duties under the laws can be circumvented in some process not provided by law—but only the action of Congress and the President to amend NEPA and the Federal Highway Act could allow the Secretary to approve part of the project, "and go ahead."

After the intervention of Mr. Ellis, the Citizens Transit Advisory Council's resolution failed, Mr. Kraabel submitted the resolution introduced by Mr. Ellis; it passed and was sent to the Metro Council. The warning that the Citizens Transit Advisory Committee thought the transit elements should be designed with no further delay did not get to the Metro Council; the Ellis maneuver was successful; his resolution passed at the June 1, Metro meeting. Nevertheless, the members of the Metro Council should have known that the delay was continuing through the decade and that they were responsible for it. The members of the Metro Council should have known that they alone were responsible for the lack of the procedures essential to the process of their decision-making. Doing nothing is doing something, and nonfeasance becomes malfeasance.

Politics ran Metro, not the Metro Council. The strength of the political force which ran Metro was unbelievable—in Seattle, in Olympia, and in Washington, D.C. (where Mr. Ellis' firm had an office staffed by excellent attorneys). Secretary Adams had been unable to withstand the political pressure on him, and he approved the project without transit connections, including no connection to the tunnel publicized as essential by James Ellis and Aubrey Davis.

Since 1972, the federal courts had repeatedly warned the state that the designs of all the I-90 project must be finished before the environmental impact and 4(f) statements could be completed and the project could be federally approved. The effects of the project could not be determined until there was a complete design of the project. Clearly, the decisions attributed to Metro were designed to evade the mandates of the courts. The effects of this delay were far-reaching—it took away all opportunities Seattle had to participate in the transit connections decisions and to avoid the adverse effects of them.

Permanent reminders of Metro's damaging inaction are: the dangerous entry and exit of transit vehicles into and out of the transit lanes on I-90—in 1996 this built-in weave has not yet been cured; and the failure of Metro to consider rail or electric trolleys on I-90.

9. ALTERNATIVES TO THE 1971 DESIGN OF I-90

The consideration of alternatives to the 1971 I-90 project was effectively evaded by the political maneuver of writing of the purpose so that the purpose could only fit the 1971 project. The Mercer Island so-called "amenities" were very expensive, and any process which considered alternatives would most certainly wipe out at least some of them. The 1975 DEIS alternatives section was drastically inadequate: It mentions only the withdraw/substitution amendment in the 1973 Federal Highway Act. The essential changes in the 1974 and May 5, 1976, amendments were never reported in the final EIS, despite the fact that it was not submitted to the Federal Department of Transportation until September, 1977.

All of the parties must have to have known that new amendments were to be considered. The proponents of the 1971 Mercer Island project probably used one of two arguments, depending on who they were trying to influence:

(1) To the parties who were not part of the Plan, they said that any discussion or consideration of the project would only waste time and further delay the project—it must [to quote Mr. Ellis] "go ahead".

(2) To rally the forces working for the Plan, they said that any discussion or consideration of alternatives would completely stop the 1971 Mercer Island project, and all the amenities would be lost.

When the parties signed the Memorandum of Agreement on December 21, 1976, they said, [in the fourth WHEREAS], "all parties hereto state that they have reviewed the proposed highway development and all currently available alternatives to it, including the option of withdrawal and substitution."

But the fourth WHEREAS was correct, for the purpose of the project had been written and interpreted so that only the 1971 project could meet the requirements for the Mercer Island section, so that there could be no alternatives to it. The MOA signers didn't need any information whatsoever because there could be no alternative to the 1971 Mercer Island project! The "purpose" had been written to exclude any alternatives of any kind. The proponents were continuing their strategy in the MOA—that any changes in federal laws to allow alternatives were not relevant and need not be considered.

Meanwhile, in the rest of the United States, the consideration of alternatives to interstate highways had been drastically changed by the 1976 amendments. A whole new selection of options were available.

THE BILLION DOLLAR DECISION

I-90 or TRANSIT

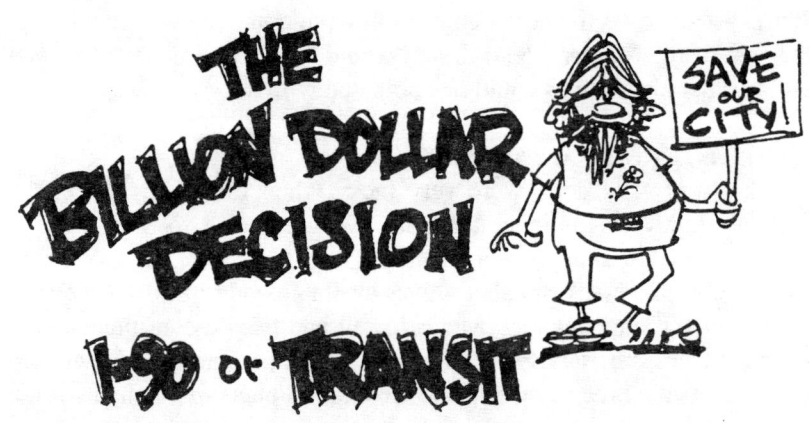

- WILL THE CITY COUNCIL FORECLOSE ON TRANSIT MONDAY AUGUST 30TH AT 2:00 PM ??

- CALL THE COUNCIL AND OPPOSE THE BENSON-KRAABEL RESOLUTION THAT WILL ACCEPT 3-2T-3 AND FORECLOSE FOREVER THE OPTION OF SWAPPING THE I-90 MONEY FOR MILLIONS IN AREA WIDE TRANSIT !!

- THE COUNCIL PROMISED THEY WOULD MEET IN PUBLIC WITH THE COUNCILS OF BELLEVUE, MERCER ISLAND & KING COUNTY TO SERIOUSLY CONSIDER A TRANSIT SUBSTITUTION AND THEY HAVE NEVER DONE IT !

The interstate funds could be used for any mixture of any kinds of transportation in the corridor or in the entire urban area-rail, highways, ferries. Cost effectiveness comparison of alternatives was required—the cost of the Mercer Island design would have to be unveiled so that all the other alternatives could be compared with it.

The 1976 Highway Act Alternatives

In April, 1977, we were very lucky when Lowell Bridwell, the Federal Highway Administrator from 1967-69, came to Seattle at his own expense to talk to Mayor Royer; he took time to talk about substitution processes and alternatives available under the 1976 Federal Highway Act amendments. Mr. Bridwell had been a consultant to the Portland elected officials and the people in the preparation of their Mt. Hood Interstate Freeway withdraw/substitution plan, and he had written the Environmental Impact statement on the Westway Interstate in New York City.

He saw many people in Seattle in addition to the Mayor; I know who some of them were: five Council members including Benson and Williams; Representatives Charnley, Sherman, Douthwaite, Al Williams, Dick Nelson; Seth Jackson, Virginia Gunby, three other citizens, and me.

Virginia and I met his plane and talked with him for almost two hours. I wrote this letter to our attorney relating some of the things Bridwell said:

" 'The 'purpose' limited the WSTC, [the Washington State Transportation Commission, the State], to the consideration of alternatives within the 500 foot corridor from I-5 to Bellevue', he said, 'Are you happy with that?'

"He felt the avoidance of consideration of withdraw/substitution was an ingenious but inadequate method of limiting the alternatives. He said they should have given us workable transit alternatives, and this is what's wrong with Westway in New York—New York City did not have good transit alternatives. [It is interesting to note that recent articles about Westway report that 1.3 billion dollars was withdrawn from the Westway Interstate project and transferred to transit improvements in the city of New York.] Bridwell was stressing the fact that we MUST have an alternative, both for political and for EIS [Environmental Impact Statement] attack purposes.

"He told us to go after the problem of what happens to the traffic after it leaves the freeway—there is no data on that.

"He said that there was not enough information about the design in the EIS that it would be sufficient.

"He warned us that the Memorandum of Agreement was devastating politically.

In re: the merits of withdraw/substitution, he said, 'If someone said, 'we will write you a check for $800 million for anything in the way of transportation, I can't imagine spending the funds on I-90 without considering the alternatives. You get down to the bottom line: what's the most efficient use of I-90 funds?'

"He reminded people that he had never yet seen a Secretary sign off a final EIS unless he intended that the project would be built."

Lowell Bridwell's description of available alternatives to I-90 under the Federal laws was: *"I can't think of any transportation purpose which could not be funded with I-90 funds—anything in and out of the corridor, rail transit, bus transit, highways—anywhere in the whole urban area.*

Bridwell was absolutely right about the Memorandum of Agreement when he said, "If I were Brock [Secretary of the U.S. Department of Transportation Adams] sitting there, I would say that all of the local officials had agreed to the project in the Memorandum." That's exactly what Adams did! He cited the meaningless Memorandum Agreement, despite all its omissions and deceptions, in his 1979 letter of approval of the 1971 I-90 project.

Re-reading my accounts of Bridwell's statements, I realize that we should have hired him to give us advice for the I-90 trial and to appear as a witness, for I can't see that any of his advice was used by the Seattle elected officials he talked to here.

The Cost Analysis of the 1971 I-90 Project

In his letter of April 26, 1976, to the Federal Highway Administration, U.S. Transportation Secretary Coleman wrote, "I believe the policy statement should establish a requirement to prepare and submit a cost-effectiveness analysis of the transportation alternatives as a condition for Federal funding of any major urban highway investment. Further, the statement should indicate that Federal project approval will be based on a careful consideration of the cost-effectiveness of the alternatives in meeting the urban area's transportation goals, together with their environmental impact and other relevant factors." The Deputy Administrator of the Federal Highway Administration answered, on September 16, 1976, that they did not believe a new and separate national policy calling for analysis of transportation alternatives is necessary. The FHWA refusal to follow the Secretary's instructions was evidence of inconsistency at the Federal level—who was running the store? Secretary Coleman? Or his employees in the Federal Highway Administration?

In 1976, I wrote 122 pages on the inadequacy of the consideration of alternatives section in my *Critique*, pages 77 to 159. I cited my comments which had been added to the DEIS, particularly Volume II, pages 555 to 562 (copies of relevant federal laws, rules, and regulations for the consideration of alternatives) and the court's instructions, Volume II pages 528-530. I suggested that interested readers should refer to these comments and the answers despite their having been reduced to quarter size and printed in poorly-inked type.

All of my 122 pages on the EIS were valuable for one reason—I proved that the I-90 defendants never intended to consider alternatives. These pages are valuable because they record the required procedure that the State ignored and constitute important evidence of how the I-90 decision was made. The index to this section of the *Critique* is:

"II. Alternatives to the Proposed Project.

A. The Role of Alternatives in Environmental Assessment.

B. The Scope of Alternatives in this EIS.

C. Federal Laws and Administrative Rules Requiring Consideration of Alternatives.

D. The No-Build Alternative.

(1) The Impact Assessment Guidelines, the Role of the No Build Alternative in the Evaluation of Transportation Projects.

(2) The No-Build Alternative in the EIS.

E. The Role of the "Purpose" in Consideration of Alternatives.

(1) Consider alternatives at every level of transportation planning to keep all options open.

(2) Consider alternatives to meet changing local policies, to prioritize funds among system and corridor alternatives in the MPO plan, considering changes in funds available regional equity, and political feasibility.

(3) Consider alternatives on a broad enough scope that the action covered will have independent significance over a long range period.

(4) Consider alternatives even if they cannot be implemented by the WSTC.

(5) Consider alternatives raised by comments on the EIS and at the hearings.

(6) Consider alternatives when the proposal involved unresolved conflicts concerning alternative uses of available resources.

(a) The project is one of four interdependent highway facilities—a solution on one will not fulfill the purpose for I-90.

(b) The project costs too much for benefits received.

(i) The design and costs estimates do not include all of the project.

(ii) The purpose definition includes

"amenities".

(c) The conclusion that all alternatives have been studied, evaluated, and considered cannot be supported by the evidence.

(i) Transit modal splits are determined by comparison with a non-build alternative which does not include any low capital and/or TSM improvements for transit.

(ii) Modal splits are based on the fiction of freedom of choice between transit and commuting by car.

(iii) The WSTC, [The Washington State Transportation Commission or the State], has not prioritized their own projects.

(iv) The WSTC has used obsolete and false interpretations of Federal funding laws to avoid consideration of jurisdictions' and citizens' alternatives.

(v) The WSTC has tried to cover up their decisions not to consider suggested alternatives by publishing false information in the appendices and informing the decision-makers that these alternatives need not be considered.

(7) Consider alternatives which might enhance environmental quality and avoid some or all of the adverse environmental effects.

(8) Consider the probable beneficial and adverse effects of and costs of alternatives."

The Discovery of the Consideration of a Real Alternative to the 1971 Mercer Island I-90 Project

Our attorney gave me cartons of materials he had accumulated for the *Lathan* case long after the 1979 trial and Judge Thomson's decision that the Final Environmental Impact, the 4(f) Statements, and the hearing were adequate, and his lifting the injunction which had stopped property acquisition and construction of the project; and—after our final appeal to the U.S. Court of Appeals for the Ninth Circuit had failed. I set the cartons aside to read later for their historical value. In 1980, I thought that the long fight was over and that additional information would not have any immediate relevance. Any further information found would have to appear as an addition to the FEIS in order that the Secretary could show that he had considered it, so the defendants would not try to find any—Secretary Adams' final approval of the project as it stood was certain.

Years later when I read the letters our lawyer received from the state and federal defendants as evidence requested for the trial, I found that many people had been actively engaged in examining the EIS in 1977 and 1978. I had gone to Washington, D.C., in March, 1978, to talk to federal employees about the project, and I had found a viable and hard-working group of young people in the offices of the Secretary of the Department of Transportation, UMTA (the Urban Mass Transit Administration) and the CEO, (the Council for Environmental quality, which has the statutory authority for environmental impact review). Later, when I saw no evidence of any results of their work, I wrote to them on April 4, 1978, various versions of this letter, inserting the name of their agency:

"It has meant a lot to me to know that there were real people in Washington working on I-90. ... I was disappointed when the FHWA, [the Federal Highway Administration] approved the EIS submissions without requiring a single change to be made. I should think that the staff would find it most disconcerting to have no evidence in the public documents of their review. Obviously the rules of the game did not allow any changes to be made, and these rules do not seem fair to those responsible for the review—it turns the staff work into a rubber stamp.

"I had the feeling in Washington, D.C. that the Federal review process was a political process and that I was being advised that our remedies lie with the local politicians and with the courts—that the DOT's decision was made before the submissions required by law had been read and evaluated.

"The Federal review should be directed to only one question: Are the State's submissions adequate under Federal Laws? The Federal reviewers' standards should be simply whether or not the State has furnished enough information about the project, its effects, and its alternatives that the decision makers can use the submissions as the factual basis for their choices.

"My voluminous *Critique* was written to prove that the State had not submitted adequate information, and we hoped that the Federal reviewing staff would recognize this obvious inadequacy, set up a process for the preparation of adequate information, and avoid the long delay which will be caused by the continuing court action. I cannot believe that the question of the adequacy of these submissions is a political issue. If it were, all of the laws which protect the expenditure of Federal highway funds would be worthless."

My letters were too severe—the people I wrote to had been very helpful to me, some of them had come to Seattle (although they apparently weren't allowed to talk to us—I think they would have if they could). They had given me materials which were very useful in writing about alternatives in the EIS. They had worked very hard on one alternative, and I did not know it. They must have been as disappointed as I was when the Secretary completely ignored their work.

In 1978, when we were in Washington, D.C. as invitees to a federal transportation meeting, the people from our nationwide coalition, CONTACT, met with Elizabeth Gray, who had been sent from the Secretary's office to hear our complaints about the failure of the Federal officials to enforce the federal laws. She summed up the meeting when she said, "You do not have any political power."

We were all too astonished to say anything, but we should have said, "We thought Congress passed the Federal laws to take highway funding out of politics." Justice Frankfurter said it so well, "The history of liberty has largely been the observance of procedural safeguards."

When I was given the federal staff people's I-90 letters long after the trial, I realized that they are an important history that the young employees wrote in their work in analyzing the cost effectiveness of I-90. They said that the Mercer Island part of I-90 would be incredibly costly—it would cost almost fifty percent of the total funds spent on the whole project! All of them had decided that the one particular alternative should be given more attention.

The earliest letter I had about that alternative was the letter of FHWA's Berube, dated December 12, 1977; he wrote, "The ... needed supplemental information includes the following:

"1. Combinations of other alternatives, such as the 2TCP-2-2 [the use of the old highway for 4 lanes (two in each direction, with the addition of 2 new lanes to be used reversibly for transit and carpools)], with one or more of the non-structural alternatives, appear to be reasonable alternatives. However the statement [EIS] does not address any such combination alternative."

I had met Ed Kussy, FHWA Acting Assistant Chief Counsel for Right-of-Way and Environmental Law Division, in March, 1978, in Washington, D.C. in a group of seven people. I talked to them about my analysis of the I-90 EIS and hearing arterials and the deficiencies I had noted in my *Critique*—he said that he had read it! He voiced some of my concerns in a letter on June 28, 1978, including this sentence: "The most serious weakness in the environmental impact statement is its analysis of alternatives".

[An interesting sidelight — when I was there in March, I was told (not by Mr. Kussy) that, "It was a lousy EIS, and if the hierarchy of the Department of Transportation decided to run with it, it was on their own heads."] Of course the defendants did so decide; they changed almost nothing for the Final Environmental Impact Statement. For example: they added a few inches to the width of the floating bridge; opposite my comment about the snide comparison of the entitlements of the wealthier people abutting I-90 in Mercer Island and the poor abutters in Seattle, the State answered that they had changed this in the FEIS, [but, I discovered, not a lot.]

A letter from Charles Grave, Director of Planning Assistant to Charles Bingham, Deputy administrator, UMTA, July 14, 1978:

"The cost of the recommended alternative is three times greater than the two lane alternative. The major cost difference is in the environmental amenities provided by the recommended alternative." (page 5).

"The total cost of the project with transit access [the 1971 design] will be nearly $600 million. With this in mind, we believe that greater consideration must be given to the cost of the recommended alternative" [two new lanes and safety improvements added to the existing I-90], (page 6).

He also stressed the importance of completing the transit terminals at both ends of the project; he said, "The incentive created by the transit lanes can be eliminated if severe operational problems exist at either end of the facility". [But of course, the EIS was approved without them.]

In 1978, Mayor Royer had written to Secretary Adams asking him to withhold approval of the EIS until mid-August to allow for additional information to be prepared on a transit access study on the I-90 preferential bus/carpool lanes between Seattle and Bellevue. Secretary Adams agreed, but the transit study was not done.

In a "Briefing Paper" from Charles Graves, Director of the Office of Planning Assistance, the Federal Department of Transportation to Charles Bingham, Deputy administrator. Under *MAJOR ISSUES:*

"1. Cost of the Proposal. There has been considerable controversy over various aspects related to the cost of the proposal. There has been a strong effort on the part of the opponents to have the section withdrawn from the interstate system and use the apportioned funds elsewhere in the metro area or to substitute the funds for use on a mass transportation system.

..."3. Transit Alternatives. Opponents to the project assert that there has not been adequate consideration of transit alternatives."

[On page 3] ALTERNATIVES, he writes about the mediation process, making the misstatement that "This alternative represents a compromise of all concerned interests and involves certain tradeoffs necessary from a political perspective." This statement was not true for two reasons:

—The I-90 lawsuit plaintiffs were certainly a "concerned interest" which was completely shut out of the MOA process;

—There was no compromise in the MOA process—the publicized compromise was not a change in the width of the project from a ten lane wide to a project which was eight lanes wide—it was merely a change in painting the ten-lane width for eight lanes. The width of the project was not changed—although it was supposed to have been narrowed by one lane in each direction, it wasn't, and the width remained the same. The 1971 Mercer Island project was never part of any compromise.

[continuing on Graves' page 4] 'EVALUATION OF ALTERNATIVES: Based on our review there appear to be two reasonable alternatives, the recommended alternative (3-2-3) and the design alternative which provides for improving the existing facility and the addition of a two lane reversible bus/carpool facility (2-2-2).

"The cost of the recommended alternative is $549 million (1976 estimate).

"The cost of the two lane reversible alternative is $180 million (1976 estimate).

"The cost of the recommended alternative is three times greater than the two lane reversible alternative. The major cost difference is in the environmental amenities provided by the recommended alternatives."

[on page 6] ... "The total cost of the project with transit access will be nearly $600 million. With this in mind, we believe that the greater consideration must be given to the cost of the recommended alternative. While the benefits noted above and the intrajurisdictional consensus arrived at in the Memorandum of Agreement are certainly supportive of the project, *its cost must be of greater concern in the final decision."* [emphasis added]

My records show two attempts to identify projects in the Seattle urban area for which I-90 substitution funds could be used, and those letters were from State Department of Transportation employees. On August 3, 1979, DOT Secretary Bulley received a letter written by Robert Nielson in his department. The letter said that the 1979 estimate of the project was $670 million, and he outlined a list of state highway projects which could be funded with I-90 withdrawn funds under the provisions of the 1976 Highway Act: $100 million for SR 18 between I-5 and I-90 and the rest for transit improvements in the urban area. Frank Maresca, the State's highway finance expert, wrote on September 11, 1978, "It is still my opinion that the financial machinations contained in Mayor Royer's report [that there was not enough State money for I-90] are secondary to the basic issue which is whether or not the concerned units of local government can agree to a less costly configuration for I-90. <u>The fact that millions of dollars could be available under withdrawal and substitution of other worthwhile projects is obvious to all. No one can argue that there are numerous major non-interstate projects that could be built under withdrawal and substitution that could not be built under the existing tax revenues from the Motor Vehicle fund."</u> Mr. Maresca listed highway projects in the area. [emphasis added]

It's worthwhile to also quote Dick Ducharme, the highway builders' lobbyist who worked in Olympia when I was there in the 1970's and is still there. He represented his clients when he said, "we don't care what we build as long as we build it."

Lynn Burkhart, Deputy Secretary of the U.S. Department of Transportation, wrote a letter to Secretary Adams on August 31, 1978; the subject: ACTION; Interstate 90, Seattle Washington, Final Environmental Impact Statement/Section 4(f) Determination.

Her Option 1A was conditional approval similar to what the Secretary did.

"Option 2 - Disapprove the proposal. [page 8] [emphasis added]

Discussion—If the Department were to disapprove the proposal, it would be primarily on the basis of the basis of the proposal's high cost and a belief that a combination of other improvements would better serve the region's transportation needs. The proposed project is estimated to cost $549 million (1976 dollars). Disapproval would nullify the State-local MOA [Memorandum of Agreement].

[on page 9*]* *"If you disapprove the proposal, it is the DOT staff's opinion that the State and local governments would be likely to withdraw the interstate segment and substitute safety and transit improvements (similar to the 2TCP-2-2 alternative [2 transit/carpool reversible lanes and 2 permanent lanes in each direction]) in the I-90 corridor, plus other improvements in other parts of the Seattle area.*

"Option 3 - Defer departmental action the I-90 proposal until completion of the ongoing transit access study." [emphasis added]

She then wrote Recommendations on page 9 which were: Option 1(A), [the 1971 project absolutely unchanged,] with conditional approval to assure priority treatment of transit vehicles.

— "The Office of the General Counsel recommends approval with the conditions in option 1A.

— "UMTA believes that the costs and benefits of the proposed 3-2-3 plans and the 2TCP alternative should be carefully weighed before a final decision is made on the proposal."

Most marked evidence in the EIS was the deliberate misrepresentation in the 1973 withdraw/substitution description and the failure to include any information and discussion of the 1976 withdraw/substitution amendment and the alternatives available under it. The purpose of the EIS is to give the essential information about the proposal to the public, the elected officials, and the administrative personnel in order that they will know the facts necessary for their decision-making. I think I had all the information which had been available to citizens during the 1970's, and yet I had no idea that there was serious consideration of the 2TCP alternative at any time, especially in 1978 and 1979, and I did not know that the 1971 project was going to cost so much. Cost-effectiveness of alternatives had never been given to the public. I could well remember that in 1973 State Highway Director Andrews had refused to answer the Seattle Council's question about the cost of the Mercer Island section of I-90, after the state kept refusing to fund the lid and school replacement in Seattle. He said, "The Seattle Council has no need for that information"! He surely knew that refusal constituted a violation of federal law, but he also surely knew he could get by with it, and he did.

In 1978, a trend appeared to employ officials who had been involved in I-90. In August, Aubrey Davis left the Metro Council where he had been Chairman of the Transit Committee since it was founded in 1972; he was appointed Director of District Ten of the Federal Department of Transportation—a well-paying political appointment that his predecessors had found to be more ceremonial than onerous.

In 1979, I received some very interesting information about the design contract on the Mercer Island segment of I-90. One of the firms that had worked on the pamphlet EIS had a contract. Two retired high-ranking officials who had worked on I-90 had been hired by firms with design contracts on the Mercer Island segment of I-90: ex-Federal Highway Administrator Norbert Tiemann; and ex-State Highway Director George Andrews. [Tiemann had been a banker in a small Nebraska town when he was appointed to the federal job; one can only wonder why he was hired by a highway construction company.]

I got more information and wrote this memo for our attorney in 1979 before the trial, "I have examined the contracts between the State and three engineering firms for work [on I-90] which began last October and is due to be finished this October. The contracts are for 'preliminary plans' ... to assist in the preparation of an overall scheduling document which will provide a detailed and comprehensive approach to the design and construction of project sequencing'. These are the firms and the contract amounts:

— For the I-5 to Lake Washington portion, Howard Needles, Tammen, and Bergenhoff got the contract and were to be paid $552,345. This firm had also been paid to participate in the preparation of the inadequate pamphlet the state submitted to Judge Beeks as an I-90 Draft Environmental Impact Statement in 1970 and again in 1972.

— For the Lake to 76th east on Mercer Island portion, Sverdup and Parcel (the firm which hired ex-highway director George Andrews after he retired) was to be paid $446.155.

— for the 76th east to the east channel on Mercer Island portion, Durham Anderson, and Freed/HJR (Hennings, Durham, and Richardson); the firm which hired ex-Federal Highway Administrator Tiemann, after he retired, was paid $1,113,315.

"I am told that the firms which get these preliminary design contracts usually get the design contracts. How much will Andrews and Tiemann get? No wonder they would not allow the consideration of anything cheaper on Mercer Island". [I do not know if these firms did get those final design contracts.]

It is of great interest that ex-mayor Uhlman moved to Bellevue, became a member of a land-developing company, First South Investments, and was in the Pacific League Foundation, an amicus for the defendants in the Thompson trial on I-90. Ulman as mayor had never tried to obtain federal and state funding to pay for the rehabilitation of the Seattle areas damaged by property acquisition and construction, and in 1995, Seattle was still faced with that tremendous expense.

10. CONTACT, THE NATIONAL ORGANIZATION PROTESTING INTERSTATE PROJECTS

In early 1978, Marian Agnew and I had been talking to each other over the telephone—she was in an organization called CONTACT, Continued Action on Transportation and the Environment, that opposed the construction of I-66 in Arlington, Virginia. When I went to Washington, D.C., in March, we met for the first time, and we rapidly decided that the organizations like ours, that were opposing the construction of an Interstate highway in their areas, should try to join together in a nationwide organization, to be called CONTACT. We decided that we would try to get all the organizations to hold a press conference on a set day in May, and I began to hunt for the organizations and to identify one person from each who could be counted on as the leader in the CONTACT effort in their area.

We set the date for a national press conference—May 8, 1978. I asked each group to send me a single page about their organization and their opposition to their interstate highway construction, and I copied and mailed these pages to each organization so that they could be copied and stapled together to be handed out at the press conference.

Each organization provided its own cover for the pamphlet.

We sent this letter to President Carter, May 6, 1978.
Dear Mr. President:

TRANFERABLE FEDERAL FUNDS *(in millions)

I-565, Huntsville, Alabama	$ 119
1-10, Phoenix, Arizona	440
I-84, Northeast Connecticut	480
1-494, Chicago, Illinois	2,033
1-35, Duluth, Minnesota	129
1-78, Watchung, New Jersey	58
1-478, New York City Westway	1,342
1-675, Dayton, Ohio	130
I-279, Pittsburgh, Pennsylvania	259

1-440, Nashville, Tennessee	120
I-66, Arlington Virginia	179
I-182, Richland, Washington	150
I-90, Seattle, Washington	900
I-105, Los Angeles, California	$1,000
14 Interstate total	$7,339

* These are local estimates.

We are angry citizens from 14 urban areas of our nation who want our tax dollars spent for rational transportation improvements to conserve energy, our environment, our cities—not wasted on obsolete, undesirable, unbuildable scraps of superhighways. We resort to the constitutional "free press" to attempt to reach our President in this time of crucial decision-making on the spending of $7.3 billion dollars. Here is our message,

"Mr. President, you have a National Urban Policy, a National Energy Policy, and a Transportation Policy for a Changing America.

"Now you have an extraordinary opportunity to do something about your policies.

"All over the country there are plans for non-essential segments and spurs of unbuilt Interstate highways, snarled in controversy and increasingly obsolete. These can be withdrawn from the Federal Interstate system, and the money can be transferred to useful transportation projects which will restore our cities—for public transit, for street and road and bridge repairs, for ferries, buses, subways and trains.

"Congress has provided the basic legislative authority for this withdraw/transfer/substitution. The necessary Federal administrative regulations are in place. Your policies are the top priority of Secretary of Transportation Brock Adams, who recently told the Association of the Bar of the city of New York that he had thousands of people working to implement them.

"But the Federal gears are not meshing. The citizens who want to uphold the laws requiring consideration of alternatives to Interstate freeways have been forced to institute and continue actions in court because they could not get administrative review and enforcement of the Federal process laws. Federal funds have been used only to ram through the original highway decisions, and no efforts have been made to publicize alternatives and to educate the local decision-makers in their options. On some occasions the Secretary has done nothing at all to require consideration of these alternatives; on other occasions he has hindered the consideration.

"We believe that the Interstate withdraw/substitution alternative will give our 14 urban areas an opportunity to carry out the mandates of Congress as expressed in the Federal laws and in the policies of your government. Billions of dollars can be mobilized to help urban areas rather than multiply their problems.

"We urge you now to continue your fine work with Congress to amend the Federal Highway Act so that the transfer of funds will be easier and the Federal matching share of substitution projects will be raised to 90%.

"We urge you now to instruct your cabinet to aggressively promote the withdraw/substitution options by carrying out your policies.

"We urge you now to meet with us as soon as possible to discuss how we can work together to transfer these Federal funds to transportation solutions which will rebuild our cities."

Here is a list of the withdraw/substitution projects in the United States as of June 30, 1994:

Interstate Substitution Funding

Under 23 U.S.C. 103(e)(4), As of 06/30/94

State (Withdrawal Area)	Base Costs	Total Amounts Being Made Available
Arizona (Tucson)	29,163,101	68,695,242
California (Sacramento)	57,737,509	96,411,661
California (San Francisco)	54,262,208	96,401,464
Colorado (Denver)	153,229,348	263,829,994
Connecticut (Bolton to Killingly)	344,616,300	404,906,511
Connecticut (Hartford-New Britain)	336,158,100	656,753,939
District of Columbia (Washington)	1,470,723,700	2,197,659,829
Georgia (Atlanta)	96,361,200	112,582,644
Illinois (Chicago)	1,464,370,200	2,576,948,996
Indiana (Indianapolis)	52,558,200	87,583,649
Iowa (Waterloo)	189,158,400	315,749,048
Maryland (Baltimore)	868,409,100	1,047,724,221
Maryland (Bowie to Millersville)	80,003,700	93,807,610
Maryland (Washington)	77,237,100	154,434,110
Massachusetts (Boston)	637,708,900	1,538,023,385
Massachusetts (Fall River to Providence)	12,183,300	14,298,237
Minnesota (Duluth)	44,672,400	74,517,657
Minnesota (Minneapolis-St. Paul)	71,163,900	121,980,663
Nebraska (Omaha)	47,022,300	78,269,086
New Jersey (New York City)	108,716,400	184,637,107
New Jersey (New York City to Trenton)	210,881,700	246,544,525
New Jersey (Philadelphia)	71,336,700	118,740,651
New York (Albany)	35,178,300	59,241,564
New York (New York City)	1,726,695,000	1,876,246,788
Ohio (Cleveland)	147,860,100	262,912,003
Oregon (Portland)	260,437,181	517,750,487
Oregon (Salem)	32,488,773	56,844,885
Pennsylvania (Philadelphia)	230,139,000	480,137,331
Pennsylvania (Pittsburgh)	39,549,600	65,976,803
Rhode Island (Rhode Island)	591,042,600	647,280,711
Tennessee (Memphis)	171,629,100	287,503,353
Virginia (Washington)	58,239,900	78,174,638
TOTALS	9,770,933,320	14,882,568,792

11. U.S. SECRETARY OF TRANSPORTATION ADAMS' APPROVAL OF THE I-90 PROJECT

On September 20, 1978, U.S. Secretary of Transportation Brock Adams signed his, "Decision on I-90, Seattle, Washington". As we had expected, the 1971 project had been approved, with the addition of three conditions:

(1) The safety problem presented by the "bulge" was to be corrected as soon as possible. Associated work including the construction of the East Channel Bridge shall be the first order of work. [The state waited until 1980 to begin this work, despite the facts that: the replacement of the bulge could and should have been done years earlier when there no longer was any need to open the bridge; the plaintiffs in the I-90 *Lathan* case had stipulated that the East Channel Bridge replacement could be done in 1978 if the capacity were not increased.]

(2) The approval of the plans, specifications, and estimates, (P.S.&E.), for the portions east of the East Channel Bridge and its temporary connection to the existing highway, and west of 23rd Avenue, will be withheld until development and necessary approvals of design and financing agreement for priority transit access into downtown Seattle and downtown Bellevue (as enumerated in paragraph 3 of the MOA (Memorandum of Agreement signed in December, 1976). [—when the Secretary wrote this letter, Metro still didn't have a plan].

(3) As provided in the MOA, public transportation shall permanently have priority use of the center lanes, and the State will assure that general Mercer Island traffic use of the center lanes is controlled to the extent necessary to maintain bus and carpool speeds of 45 mph or greater.

I found great fault with the statements Adams had written under the title, "Background and Analysis".

He said, "A wide range of alternatives was considered ... and documented in the EIS." (I could find no such consideration and documentation in the EIS.)

He said, "In addition to the proposed project, a principal alternative considered locally is ... safety improvements on the existing I-90 and construction of a new two lane roadway for transit and carpools. This alternative is identified as the 2TCP-2-2 alternative in the EIS." [But the presentation in the EIS is drastically inadequate and, if anything, based on the 1973, NOT the 1976, withdraw/substitution law. See my *Critique*, beginning on page 77 for a complete analysis of the alternatives to the proposed project. The 2TCP-2-2 alternative is attributed to Mayor Royer, but there is no cost-benefit analysis of the two alternatives anywhere except in letters written by some of the Washington, D.C., staff and not read until long after the final I-90 trial in 1979. They said that the Mercer Island segment was to cost almost half of the I-90 funds.]

Adams said that the State's proposal for I-90 would serve a projected demand in 1990 18,300 transit person trips, but that the 2TCP-2-2, [2 transit-carpool] alternative would serve only 14,900 transit person trips." [This must be wrong. The 2TCP portion would not have any single-occupant traffic so the transit would surely go faster, and since there would be fewer lanes for cars, more people would chose transit.]

He said, "The State's proposal incorporates more environmental amenities than the alternative," [—true because there had been no study or consideration of amenities on any alternative to the Mercer Island I-90 project, "but the amenities on both alternatives should be cost-effective." [There is no cost/benefit analysis of Mercer Island's amenities. Any discussion of what Mercer Island is going to get for its costly "amenities" never takes into account that the development of the island took place AFTER the present I-90 project was built, and the need to now repair damage by the highway's severing one area from another no longer exists; the costs of abandoning the old four lane freeway and adding those four lanes to the new freeway was never reported or compared.]

He said that people are worried about transit connections—the transit lanes are in the middle and have to weave over general traffic lanes at both ends to exit. But he says that the I-90 MOA commits the parties to further planning and construction. And still yet again, he says that Metro is currently conducting an I-90 Transit Access Study with the State, he has examined it and concluded that any problems of transit access to and from I-90 can be resolved by any of the alternatives under consideration. [These statements prove the inexcusable delay in designing the proposed project west of 23rd Avenue and west of I-5 in Seattle, the delay that has caused and will cause great harm to the property owners involved in what they call, aptly, the Judkins Rejected area. It is unconscionable for Secretary Adams to approve the incomplete EIS—to let the State and Metro get by without designs. The EIS did not show the actual width of the project, the right-of-way, elevations, designs of structures, etc. west of 23rd Avenue; the harm to the areas cannot be predicted. Secretary Adams' statement that he had carried out the requirements of the 4(f) law are not true; he has not provided any evidence to prove that there is no reasonable alternative to taking of parkland and that measures to reduce the harm have been carried out—there is no public record of what parkland is being taken and no record of how the project is being designed to reduce the harm to the parkland.]

He said, under *Safety* that the existing highway is unsafe. [And yet he had not required the State to give all the data on the causes of the accidents in the EIS, and he had not made the State provide essential safety items, which could be 90% paid for from the federal highway trust fund as repairs to an existing interstate freeway. [See my pages on safety, and remember that the bulge could have been removed long ago, the signs for the reversible lanes replaced, etc.].

He said, under Environmental *Considerations*, that alternative designs do not include the amenities that the 1971 project does. [As I have pointed out before, the State deliberately did NOT design the

2TCP-2-2 alternative (or any others) to find out what environmental amenities they might need and the cost of them. It's ridiculous to keep repeating that the alternatives don't have this or that when only the chosen project, designed for and on Mercer Island in 1970 and 1971 has everything the residents could think of for their amenities, and Mayor Aubrey Davis said that they never considered costs.]

12. THE DELAY OF THE I-90 PROJECT, 1972-1979

When we consider the defendants' deliberate eight year delay of the I-90 project, we can only wonder why the government lawyers chose to ignore the deliberate directions from Congress to provide the more sensible spending and the saving of federal highway trust funds. We can only wonder why they had chosen to ignore the federal court decisions. Both the State and the federal lawyers obviously were following the instructions of the I-90 project proponents: the political decision would hold; and neither the state or the federal agencies had to conform to the law as mandated by the federal courts in the *Lathan* case decisions.

Slade Gorton (now U.S. Senator) was the Washington State elected Attorney General when the State was delaying the project by completely ignoring the federal laws [When he was a state senator, he was known for his intelligence and his ability to learn the contents of every bill submitted]. He assigned lawyer Tom Garlington to the State Highway Commission, [the State]. and as I lobbied the legislators, I was constantly aware of his peculiar role. Lawyers usually are hired to help their clients by outlining the requirements of laws so that legal problems can be both avoided and solved in advance, but I never saw any evidence of the Commissioners acting on legal advice.

THE WCST Newsletter reported an interview with the man in charge of the Federal Highway Administration's group assigned to the WSHC. He said that there were 44 Federal employees working under him (in 1973) and the State had about 5,000 employees; *there were no U.S. Department of Transportation lawyers assigned to the*

Washington FHWA office in Olympia—two lawyers in Portland were available.

At one of my meetings with staff members of administrative offices in Washington, D.C., I asked them to tell me what instructions they had received from their lawyers; no one replied—they just looked blank. I had studied the draft EIS of I-90 and noted that the lawyers either had not set the guidelines for the preparation of the various items required by federal laws or that their advice at both the state and federal levels had been completely ignored.

The long delay in the I-90 project cannot be explained by the defendants' need for more time to carry out the mandates of the courts so that the injunction could be lifted. The long delay cannot be explained by the need for more time to finish an adequate Draft Environmental Impact Statement (DEIS), and/or to submit an adequate 4(f) statement, or to hold a corridor/design hearing, and/or to prepare and submit the final Environmental Impact Statement. The most unexplainable delay was the four-year delay in submitting the final EIS—up almost identical to the draft EIS—why wasn't it submitted earlier?

WHY WAS THE PROJECT DELAYED NINE LONG YEARS? BECAUSE IT TOOK THAT LONG TO BUILD UP THE POLITICAL STRUCTURE WHICH ENABLED THE DEFENDANTS TO EVADE THE ESSENTIAL REQUISITES OF THE FEDERAL LAWS, TO BE SURE THAT THE PLAN WAS SECURE.

Federal Court Decisions in the I-90 Case to 1979

The federal court decisions are reviewed here again to emphasize the judge's instructions and to make it easier to read the next materials about the final *Lathan* case decision. I will keep the titles of the original parties to the lawsuits, calling them the plaintiffs and the defendants, (although in the appeals processes both of them change back and forth to appellants and appellees).

1970, May 28, the case of *Lathan v. Volpe* was filed in U.S. District Court; Mr. and Mrs. Lathan, corridor property owners, were the lead plaintiffs, and citizens' groups are allowed to intervene—Citizens Against Freeways, was the first organization on the intervenors' list, and thus became the lead organization, called "Citizens" in the court opinions. The defendants were the U.S. Secretary of Transportation, (the name changed with new administrations), and the Washington State Highway Commission, called the WSDH in the opinions and called merely the State in this manuscript. Plaintiffs alleged that the National Environmental Policy Act (NEPA), the section 134, 4(f) and the section 128 of the Federal Highway Act, the Relocation Act and the Clean Air Act all apply to I-90, and they requested the Court to grant an injunction on the project to stop all property acquisition, design, and construction of the project until adequate environmental impact and 4(f) statements are prepared, new corridor and design hearings held, and the Federal Relocation and Clean Air Acts enforced.

1970, November, Judge Beeks' decision, plaintiffs lost, and their plea for an injunction on the project was denied. Plaintiffs appealed the decision to the United States Ninth Circuit Court of Appeals.

1971, November 15, the Ninth Circuit Court of Appeals reversed the District Court and ruled that plaintiffs are right, the defendants must meet the requirements the federal laws. They granted an injunction of further construction of the I-90 project and remanded the case back to the Federal District Court to ensure the complying to federal laws before the injunction was lifted. Defendants appealed the part of the opinion which mandated a new hearing.

1972, The defendants gave Federal District Court Judge Beeks the same items they had given him in 1970, i.e. the 16-page EIS pamphlet. Judge Beeks re-evaluated it, following the mandates of the 1971 Court of Appeals, and on August 8 he ordered the defendants to prepare a new Environmental Impact Statement (EIS), evidence that they met the requirements of the other federal laws, and to return to the court for a determination of adequacy. He said, "*THE IMPACT STATEMENT SUBMITTED IN THIS CASE FAILS TO MEET MINIMUM LEGAL*

STANDARDS. ... BY SERIOUSLY UNDERESTIMATING THEIR DUTY, DEFENDANTS HAVE CAUSED YET ANOTHER COSTLY DELAY IN THIS PROJECT" [emphasis added]. However, Judge Beeks did not order new public hearings on the project, and plaintiffs appealed to the Ninth Circuit Court for a reversal of Beeks' decision that no new hearing was required. [*Lathan v. Volpe*, Western District of Washington, August 19, 1972: 450 F. Supp. 202]

1973, CARHT and occupants of the I-90 corridor in Seattle and Mercer Island filed the *Adler v. Brinegar* case to force the *Lathan* case defendants to maintain property they had bought in the corridor. The court held for the plaintiffs, but they had to return to court many times to get court orders to force the defendants to comply.

1973, December, a three-judge panel of the Ninth Circuit Court of Appeals affirmed Judge Beeks' decision that the defendants' submitted materials were inadequate, and they ordered a new hearing on the I-90 project *WITH THE DRAFT EIS AS A BASIS FOR THAT HEARING.* Another three-judge panel of the same court handed down a decision that a new highway hearing was NOT required in a similar case—in the *Keith* case in California, (the I-405, the Century Freeway Case). To resolve the issues, both cases had to be heard by the entire Ninth Circuit Court of Appeals.

1974, September 27, the Ninth Circuit Court, en banc [altogether], affirmed the December, 1973, decision for the Seattle plaintiffs and ruled that the defendants in the *Lathan* case in Seattle and the *Keith* case in Los Angeles must each hold a new hearing as required by Section 128(a) of the Federal Highway Act and that the draft EIS would be the basis of the hearing. The two cases were remanded to Federal District Courts in their areas for a determination of the adequacy of the Environmental Impact Statement and meeting the requirements of the Federal Highway Act.

1975, December 12, the draft I-90 EIS, (DEIS). was mailed to the Federal Highway Administration but not circulated locally until later. The DEIS was an enormous amount of material—17 pounds of more than 2000 pages.

1976, January 20, the corridor/design hearing on the I-90 project was held, but when the public complained about the lack of time provided to review the draft EIS before the hearing, the State continued the hearing on February 10 and 11.

13. THE FINAL DECISIONS, 1979 AND 1981

The Seattle I-90 *Lathan* Case Compared to the California I-405 *Keith* Case

On August 24, 1974, the entire U.S. Court of Appeals for the Ninth Circuit had reviewed two opposing decisions on almost identical cases, the *Keith* case, (Century Freeway, I-405), in Los Angeles, and the *Lathan* case, (I-90), in Seattle. The Court had prepared decisions in each case, requiring each of the defendants to prepare an Environmental Impact Statement and to hold a new design/corridor hearing based on this EIS. The injunctions were continued, the cases were remanded to the federal district courts, and if the defendants had met the requirements set by the Appellate Court, the injunctions on the projects could be lifted. And here the two cases become radically different because of the two judges appointed and because the cases were decided by a completely different process, for completely different reasons.

Judge Gordon Thompson of San Diego heard the I-90 case in Seattle—no reasons were given for the appointment of a judge from an out-of-state district court to hear the case, and, oddly enough, Judge Thompson was also appointed and heard the other interstate freeway cases in the state of Washington: [the *Brooks* case (on that part of I-90 west of the summit of Snoqualmie Pass)]; the *Daly* case (the North Bend section of I-90); and the *Lange* I-80 case in the Yakima Valley.]

Judge Harry Pregerson was appointed to hear the *Keith* I-405 case in the District Court in Los Angeles as a "United States Circuit Court Judge, Sitting by Designation." Judge Pregerson must have been appointed because of his previous knowledge of the case; in 1972, he had been the Federal District Court Judge for the *Keith* case, and he had decided that a new hearing should be held with an adequate EIS as a basis for the hearing. The defendants appealed and that part of the *Keith* opinion which required a new hearing was reversed by a Ninth Circuit Court panel of three judges in 1973 only to be sustained in 1974 when the whole Court ruled on the *Lathan* and *Keith* cases together. So in 1980 Judge Pregerson was again hearing the case he had before him in 1972. In 1993, when the I-405 freeway was opened for traffic, the newspapers quoted a participant who said, "The case could have gone to a judge who would have only dealt with it as a legal issue. Fortunately it went to a judge who saw it as a way to better society."

Judge Thompson's Trial and Opinion on I-90

In Seattle in June, 1979, Judge Thompson heard the I-90 case evidence in four days, then assigned the case to a magistrate for an additional one-day hearing. From the beginning of the trial, I thought the judge was favoring the defendants—some of his rulings against the plaintiffs were incredible and could be reversed on appeal. His most bizarre error was his ruling that wiped out the plaintiff allegations and proof of the defendants' omissions in the Environmental Impact Statement, the EIS. Judge Thompson said, "*IF IT ISN'T IN THE EIS, IT ISN'T ADMISSIBLE.*" He allowed the plaintiffs to introduce evidence to show the errors in the EIS, but he would not allow them to introduce the most important facts, the omissions in the EIS!

In the trial Judge Thompson kept shifting the burden of proof from the defendants to the plaintiffs. For example, he would not allow the plaintiffs to submit the facts to prove that the EIS had omitted information on the damage I-90 would cause the residents of the corridor. He said that the demographic data the defendants had used was not obsolete because it was all they had! He said that the plaintiffs' trial evidence failed to establish that the impacts on minorities and low-income people in Seattle would be any different from the impacts on the high-income people on Mercer Island; he said that there was no evidence to show that the project was located so as to intentionally discriminate against or injure any minority or low income group.

Judge Thompson then made his most memorable remark about the people in Seattle who might suffer damage from I-90. He said, "*IF THEY WANT TO LIVE BY A FREEWAY, LET THEM LIVE BY A FREEWAY!*" [I thought of the French Revolution Queen, Marie Antoinette, when she was told that starving French people had no bread, and she said, "Let them eat cake."]

Before the Judge left the courtroom the final day of the trial, (and before the magistrate heard the evidence on an additional day), he gave each litigant a minimal time to submit findings of fact and conclusions of law, before they had access to the court reporter's transcript of the trial. When his opinion was published, we were amazed to find that Judge Thompson had adopted the defendants' submission almost entirely. Such changes as were made consisted of deletions of repetitious materials and immaterial changes in tense, length of sentences and paragraphs—changes which could be made merely by paraphrasing paragraphs and the insertion of a few quotations. The opinion even copied the defendants' errors!

After the plaintiffs had read Judge Thompson's decision, we found three important categories to be covered in our attempt to get the decision reversed: Must a judge? Does a judge have the duty to do more than virtually copy the findings of fact and conclusions of law of one opponent in a trial—here the state and federal defendants' submitted findings and conclusions in the I-90 case? If the judge's opinion records none of the plaintiffs' evidence in the trial, is there adequate evidence for an appeals court to consider, review, and rule on the fairness of the trial judge's opinion? Did the defendants carry out the mandates of the federal courts?

The Judge Has the Duty to Judge

Appellate courts in all of the jurisdictions have had to deal with the problem of a trial court judge's adopting the prevailing party's findings of fact, conclusions of law or opinion, and judgment—or a combination of two or all three. After the Thompson decision came down in August, 1979, I read many cases on the subject and briefed some 23 of them for my own use. I will quote two of them, as examples of the rule of law on the issue.

"Certainly, the fact that the trial judge has adopted proposed findings does not, by itself, warrant reversal. But it does raise the possibility that there was insufficient independent evaluation of the evidence and may cause the losing party to believe that his position was not given the consideration it deserves", (*Photo Electronics*, 1977).

"In the instant case, a comparison of the findings with the opinion seems to show that the findings proposed by the defendant were mechanically adopted, with the consequence that some of the findings made by the district court are not supported by the evidence and not substantially in accord with the opinion." (*U.S. v. Forness*, 1942, opinion by Judge Jerome Frank).

Appellate courts have asked two questions in trying to ascertain whether or not the adoption of the prevailing party's submissions are the "product of the Judge's own independent thought and research:"

— Were the findings and/or conclusions "mechanically adopted"?

— Was there good evidence of the trial court's mental involvement in reviewing and adopting the material?

Obviously, the Thompson I-90 opinion failed to meet both tests, the plaintiffs should appeal the Thompson decision, and this is the outline I wrote:

"The plaintiffs in this case have carefully studied the District Court's [Judge Thompson's] opinion. We find continued evidence that there was "insufficient independent evaluation of the evidence" which leads the plaintiffs to believe that their case was not given the consideration it deserves.

"The plaintiffs find no evidence that the Federal District Court Judge was mentally involved in the findings of facts and in reaching the conclusions of law despite his mechanical corrections to the defendants' submissions. We find no modification of the Federal/State argument. We find no evidence of painstaking and time-consuming study.

"The plaintiffs find that the Federal District Court Judge's adoption of the defendants' submissions has resulted in the presentation to this court of a record which is so inadequate that it is not subject to adjudication. The appellate court cannot tell what has happened or what the issues raised by the plaintiffs were."

The Defendants Did Not Carry Out the Mandates of the Courts

Judge Thompson's decision did not prove that the state and federal defendants had met the requirements of the federal laws per the mandates of the federal courts. This section will have two parts:

The 1976 hearing was not valid.

The 1978 Final Environmental Impact and 4(f) Statements were not adequate.

The 1976 I-90 Hearing Was Not Valid

The defendants did not meet the U.S. Court of Appeals for the Ninth Circuit's mandates that the defendant must hold a new corridor/design hearing and that the new EIS should be the basis for that hearing. Despite all their allegations that the plaintiffs had delayed the project since they filed the original lawsuit in 1970 and the 1971 ruling, the defendants did not finish their Draft Environmental Impact Statement and distribute it until early January, 1976. The defendants' decision to hold the hearing less than one month after the huge draft EIS was available and before people could read it violated the Circuit Court's instructions and intent that the people should have the DEIS in time to read it and learn what the proposed project was and what effects it was going to have while there was still time for changes in the plans to be made. Congress had passed the Federal Highway and the National Environmental Policy Acts to ensure the wise and valid spending of federal funds on capital projects so that the people making the decisions could have adequate facts available. The defendants' decision to hold the hearing before the DEIS could be read was a deliberate evasion of the intent of Congress and an evasion of the Ninth

Circuit Appellate Court's instructions. The Thompson decision should have been reversed on this one issue alone.

The I-90 Environmental Impact and 4(f) Statements Were Not Adequate

Evaluation of the adequacy of the EIS is difficult because the defendants alleged that it was adequate in their findings of fact and conclusions of law, and when Judge Thompson adopted the defendants' submissions, he adopted all of the defendants' statements and their excuses. His opinion proves that he had not given any attention to either the plaintiffs' evidence presented in court or to their findings of facts and conclusions of law. Since the evaluation of the adequacy of the EIS was based on the evidence in the submissions the Federal and State defendants wrote and Judge Thompson adopted as his decisions, the Appellate Court had no evidence in his opinion of the plaintiffs' issues and argument. [I should title this Thompson writing "the Judge/defendant's opinion to distinguish it from a judge's opinion.]

The requirements for the contents of the EIS are found in the original laws, and in the very good administrative regulations adopted by the federal agencies, and in the clarifications as they appeared in the opinions in cases decided under the laws and regulations. They were the basis for what I wrote in my *Critique,* and I considered them to be as clear as crystal. One Judge had written succinctly, "NEPA is a procedural statute. It's purpose is to assure that, by following the procedures it prescribes, agencies will be fully aware of the impact of their decisions when they make them."

I had read and briefed the applicable laws, and I had continued to read the changes in the laws, the administrative regulations, and many relevant case decisions. I could not understand why the defendants did not use them when they were preparing their EIS. I could not understand why the defendants were not paying any attention to the mandates of the courts. *I didn't realize, until I read the opinion in the I-90 case in August, 1979, that the defendants had decided that they could get by with the EIS they wrote and never changed despite the valid evidence that the EIS was fatally inadequate.*

From the beginning, the proponents had decided to build only the Mercer Island 1971 project and that there was one way they could keep their project intact and meet the requirements of Federal laws and the instructions of the courts: they took eight long years to evade the laws by political processes. When Elizabeth Gray was sent by the Secretary of Transportation to meet with the CONTACT people when we were in Washington, D.C. in 1978, she had told us outright, "You have no political power," meaning that we could not rely on the protection of the federal laws and court decisions. She was right. The plaintiffs' case was finally heard by Federal District Court Judge Thompson from San Diego, who accepted all of the defendants' arguments and ruled for the defendants. The political pressure on Secretary Adams was so great that he finally accepted the drastically inadequate EIS and said that he had fulfilled the essential 4(f) procedures to protect the parkland in Seattle, when he hadn't.

In their four decisions on I-90, the Federal Court judges had written full instructions for the preparation of the environmental impact and 4(f) statements. Judge Beeks had said in 1972, "Defendants have simply failed to meet the minimum required standard. By seriously underestimating their duty, defendants have caused yet another costly delay in the project.." In 1974 Judge Duniway wrote for the U.S. Court of Appeals for the Ninth Circuit, "*WE CANNOT IGNORE, AS JUDGES, WHAT WE KNOW AS CITIZENS. THE KNOWLEDGE AND ATTITUDES OF THE PUBLIC, OF THE CONGRESS, AND OF THE STATE AND LOCAL GOVERNMENTS ABOUT THE ENVIRONMENTAL AND SOCIAL CONSEQUENCES OF FREEWAY BUILDING HAVE DRASTICALLY CHANGED WITHIN THE LAST DECADE. WITH THAT KNOWLEDGE HAS COME CONCERN, AND THAT CONCERN IS REFLECTED IN THE 1968 AND 1970 AMENDMENTS TO SECTION 128(A), (THE HIGHWAY ACT), AND IN NEPA. THE PROPOSED SEGMENT OF I-90 IS TO BE BUILT IN THE FUTURE, AND DECISIONS ABOUT IT ARE TO BE*

GOVERNED BY THE LAW AS IT READS NOW, NOT AS IT READ IN 1963." [emphasis added]

The first problem in evaluating the I-90 EIS is trying to determine what IS the EIS. After the 1976 hearing on I-90, the defendants published another set of books—they had added a volume of the comments of the various governmental agencies and the people and the state's answers [defenses?] to these criticisms and comments. These pages of comments were greatly reduced in size and the printing was poorly-inked, which made it hard to read—my submission was reduced to one-quarter size. The covers of these books labeled them as the "Final Environmental Impact Statement for I-90", but the defendant's original 1975 draft EIS had not been changed materially in the final EIS (FEIS) which they submitted to the U.S. Department of Transportation in September, 1978. It may have been the defendants' intent that these virtually unreadable comments and answers were part of the FEIS, to be added to the EIS, but that was impossible. The officials who were supposed to use it in making the I-90 decisions could not possibly have spent the time necessary to read these materials. However, this volume is very good proof that much of the essential material was omitted in the EIS and that more of the EIS was wrong.

On August 24, 1979, I wrote, "Federal District court Judge Gordon Thompson's decision on I-90 in Seattle sets an incredibly dangerous precedent: State highway builders can use federal funds for any highway project they want as long as they won't let the public or the local governments know what they are building. Judge Thompson had validated the state's 1971 strategy adopted for political purposes. Judge Thompson had ruled that the State can avoid the requirements of the federal environmental and hearings laws and the mandates of the courts interpreting them merely by sticking to the 1971 10-lane width design, assembled by and designed by Mercer Island, and concealing enough relevant information about the Seattle section that no one had:

— facts to determine its effects on Seattle;
— facts to determine how these adverse effects could be alleviated;

— facts to determine whether or not the chosen project was the best alternative use of the I-90 federal funds."

One of the worst defects in the whole I-90 process was readily confirmed by the defendants and the Judge when they read, admitted, and excused their abysmal failure to include designs for the part of I-90 west of 23rd Avenue in Seattle that was to include the taking of land from Judkins Park in Seattle. Federal law, referred to as the 4(f) of section 138 of Federal Highway Act, [it is also in NEPA], prohibited the taking of parklands unless the United States Secretary of the Department of Transportation had signed a statement that there were "no prudent and reasonable alternatives to the taking of a parkland and that all possible measures to minimize harm were going to be taken." The defendants had neatly circumvented this requirement by not designing I-90 west of 23rd Avenue in Seattle in the Judkins Park area! And the Secretary backed them up with his unsubstantiated statement. The Judge, in adopting the defendants' submission, agreed with them that this omission did not invalidate the EIS and the 4(f) statement.

[At the end of this writing, I discuss the effects of the failure to design I-90 in Seattle in the report of the Judkins area damage still not repaired in 1996.]

The defendants also said that it was not relevant that no highway widths were given; they said that their statement that there would be eight lanes was sufficient. But State Transportation Department Secretary Bulley had testified in his sworn deposition for the I-90 1979 trial that the project was to be adequate for ten lanes. When the Judge/defendants said that the project could be described by lane configuration (the number of lanes the State might stripe on the pavement) instead of by actual physical characteristics, they proved that the defendants never intended to and did not describe the project—a complete violation of the mandate of the Ninth Circuit Court of Appeals to provide an adequate EIS.

Two most peculiar results came out of the so-called Memorandum Agreement. In 1976 Metro still had not designed, and had promised in the Memorandum of Agreement, to design the transit elements of I-90, but nothing happened. For years U.S. Secretary of Transportation Adams persisted in his demands that the transit portions of the project should be designed as well as all of the project west of 23rd Avenue in Seattle, but nothing happened, and he finally acknowledged these defects when he qualified his approval of I-90 by stating that he would withhold plans, specifications, and estimates [P.S.&E.] approval until the transit termini were designed. This qualification was ridiculous because it merely repeated the obvious fact that a project HAD to be designed before there could be any plans, specifications, and estimates for the Secretary to approve!

Since Judge Thompson adopted the defendants' allegations that the FEIS was adequate in all respects and since the I-90 plaintiffs thought the FEIS was woefully inadequate, this analysis cannot begin to cover the defects I found in the EIS; I refer the reader to the *Critique*. Here my analysis will be confined to the main categories of defects:

The Project was Only a Segment of the I-90 Highway Section

The defendants described their project as being 6.7 miles long between I-5 in Seattle and a half-mile west of I-405 in Bellevue, less than a highway section as required by law because the I-90 project had no ends. The Code of Federal Regulations for the Highway Act states: "A 'highway section' is a highway development proposal between logical termini (population centers, major traffic generators, major crossroads, etc.) as normally included in a location of multiyear highway improvement program". ... "the total length of highway between logical termini." The EIS was inadequate because the project was divided into two separate segments throughout the entire design process and throughout the preparation of evidence required to prove that the defendants had met conditions written in federal laws and court decisions. *THE TWO SEGMENTS, THE SEATTLE AND THE MERCER ISLAND PARTS OF I-90, COULD NOT BE EXAMINED, PLANNED, OR DESCRIBED INDIVIDUALLY.* The federal aid section was the complete interstate highway from I-405 in Bellevue over I-5 to touchdown near Elliott Bay in Seattle. The EIS did not cover the east and west ends of the project—the entrances and exits from I-90 had not been designed, except on Mercer Island. There was no design at all of that part of the project west 23rd Avenue in Seattle. There were no connections on the west end beyond I-5 in Seattle (and there was no capacity for I-90 traffic on I-5): the EIS did not include the proposed Connecticut Viaduct over the railroad tracks to a touchdown near Elliott, although it was on the maps as part of I-90, the EIS predicted the volume of traffic on it, and the Federal Highway Administrator had said that it was part of the project and could be funded with federal interstate funds.

Highway Commissioner John Rupp and I had engaged in what turned out to be a happy, but ineffectual, fun game during the 1971 hearing. I had asked the Commissioners and received assurance that the I-90 highway description included that portion of the road to be built west of I-5, which had been called the Connecticut Viaduct when the 1960 bond funds were voted for it. I asked the Commissioners present at the hearing if they had or were going to apply for the federal funding available for the Connecticut Viaduct as part of the I-90 project. Commissioner Rupp suggested that I telephone Federal Highway Administrator Frank Turner in Washington, D.C. to find out whether or not those funds were available for that purpose. I did phone Mr. Turner and found him very knowledgeable about the Seattle I-90 project. I told him that a California highway employee had told me that federal funds were available for the "touchdown"—the end of the highway—and I asked Mr. Turner if federal funds were available for the Connecticut west end of I-90. He answered that these funds were available. He knew exactly the project he was talking about because he said that *when a highway terminus had to be built over railroad tracks, that portion was funded as part of the highway.* At the hearing the next day, I reported to the Commission and the audience what Mr. Turner had told me. Did the Commissioners jump with joy at the news of getting millions for the I-90 West terminus? You guessed it—no mention was ever made of it! The design of this part of the project would require an amendment to its EIS, and they did not want to risk it. This west end of the I-90 project was never built—the truck traffic has to go over local streets to reach the port facilities.

The illegal division of the I-90 section did not deter the defendants and Judge Thompson, for they said, (in their finding 13) "The I-90 project described in the FEIS ... is of independent utility, is long enough to ensure adequate consideration of alternatives, and fulfills important State and local needs." They said that the State is still studying parts (the west and east ends) and will include them in the I-90 design later; all of the designs the state is considering for these parts are compatible with the middle part of the project, but the project is complete and will function without any of these parts! Secretary Adams approved this substitution of promises of future performance for the required complete description of the project when he approved the FEIS, but to this day, I wonder how the middle of the project could have functioned without entrances, exits, or the portion between 23rd Avenue and I-5 in Seattle.]

Judge Pregerson's Opinion in the Keith (I-405) Case. Comparing the Seattle and Los Angeles Decisions

The defendants in the I-90 case in Seattle and the defendants in the I-405 case in Los Angeles had been given the same instructions in the 1974 U.S. Court of Appeals for the Ninth Circuit's decision which required each of them to submit evidence to their federal district courts of the adequacy of their Environmental Impact and 4(f) Statements and the new corridor/design hearing based on them. Judge Gordon Thompson from the Federal District Court in San Diego was assigned to the Federal District Court in Western Washington to hear the *Lathan* I-90 case; Judge Harry Pregerson, a Ninth Circuit Court of Appeals Judge "Sitting by Designation" was assigned to hear the *Keith* I-104 case.

I think the difference in the trial procedures for the I-104 and I-90 cases was due to the difference in the judges' pre-trial decisions about what they would try to do. Judge Thompson's goal was apparently to come to Seattle for as short a period as possible and to submit an opinion in the easiest way—copying the defendants' findings of fact and conclusions of law to submit them as his opinion. Judge Pregerson's goal was entirely different. He was the Federal District Court Judge in 1972 who had given the original opinion which was finally affirmed by the Ninth Circuit Court of Appeals, and he had apparently been interested in the case ever since. He began a totally different process by listening to and trying to reconcile the litigants, and his final opinion was his 1981 'AMENDED FINAL CONSENT DECREE". He said, "I stuck with this case because I had a lot of my own time invested in it. I could see that if this project was done properly, if the proper tone could govern, like emphasizing the human aspects of building a freeway, ... the project could have very beneficial consequences for Los Angeles."

Judge Pregerson began his work on the I-104 case by listening to and trying to reconcile the litigants. The *Keith* defendants were the state transportation agency Caltrans, and the U.S. Secretary of Transportation; they firmly believed that the Century Freeway should be built. The *Keith* plaintiffs were citizens and citizens' organizations; they said that over seventy percent of the right-of-way had been purchased, some buildings had been moved and others were the source of local problems with vagrants, vandals, and crimes—they wanted to repair this damage and to use the I-105 federal interstate funds to build public transit instead of a freeway; they said that the I-105 Century Freeway was being built to connect on the eastern end to two north/south freeways which were already full; they said, "Construction of the Century Freeway would be a criminal use of public funds in view of Los Angeles' great need for public transit, our air pollution crises, the energy crisis, and the other enormous burdens imposed by the automobile."

Judge Pregerson's 24-page opinion is completely different from Judge Thompson's. Judge Pregerson said the defendants had prepared an adequate EIS, had held the required hearing, the mandates of the

Circuit Court had been carried out, and both the plaintiffs and the defendants had agreed to settle all claims in this action. His decree permitted the I-405 freeway to be built, and the injunction was to be lifted if the project incorporated the design features and support facilities described by the Decree, including six lanes for general traffic and a separate median for transit/HOC (high occupancy vehicles), called a transitway, not to exceed 64 feet in width. The connections of I-405 to other freeways and roads were completely spelled out. He gave complete instructions for the amelioration of the right-of-way damage, for funds for building, employment, and to pay for damage to the area. One newspaper reported that almost half of the I-105 funds were spent for the non-highway purposes set forth in Judge Pregerson's opinion.

Although the Century Freeway transitway was initially designed for buses and carpools, the opinion required it to be designed to be convertible to rail; the stations, pedestrian access-ways and park-and-ride lots were also to be convertible, and they were to be 90% funded with federal interstate highway funds.

The decree *gave* all property acquired by Caltrans for I-405 "which had become or is to become vacant" to the State for "replacement housing obligations". The decree provided for "Rehabilitation [of housing] in excess of HUD standards where a determination is made that the long-term benefits of such higher standards will outweigh any additional costs." *The decree said that the federal funds already spent on I-405 need not be repaid. The decree said that the federal funds given to the state did not have to be repaid.*

And finally the Decree stated that defendants must pay the plaintiffs' court costs!

The I-405 freeway was opened on October 15, 1993 with one very significant change: in 1984 all the parties had agreed to convert the transitway to rail. It was named "The Green Line", and it opened on August 12, 1995. It extends beyond I-104 on the east end and three miles were added on the west end, turning south near the Los Angeles Airport to service the high tech area there.

The Plaintiffs' Appeal of Judge Thompson's Decision

The I-90 *Lathan* case plaintiffs lost in August 1979. They had been in court for nine long years. Judge Thompson declared that all the conditions in the 1974 U.S. Court of Appeals for the Ninth Circuit's decision had been met, and he lifted the injunction on acquisition of property and construction of the Bellevue I-405-to-Seattle-Elliott Bay section of I-90, although this description of the section was incorrect because the project did not go to past Interstate 5 to Elliott Bay in Seattle.

The plaintiffs had all the evidence for a successful appeal of Judge Thompson's decision on the grounds that the judge had copied it from the defendants' findings of fact and conclusions of law:

— There was no evidence that he had considered the plaintiffs' evidence in the trial or their submitted findings of fact and conclusions of law.

— The hearing was illegal because the DEIS was published too late for it to be read before the hearing.

— There was no design for the complete 7.2 mile project, there were no designs for the freeway and the transit terminals at both ends or for the transit elements in Seattle.

— The taking of land from Judkins Park was illegal because the State had not recorded the land to be taken and the harm that would be done because they had no design for I-90 there, and there was no factual basis for Secretary Adams' 4(f) statement that there was no reasonable and prudent alternative and that all possible harm had been ameliorated as required by the Federal Highway Act and NEPA.

— The EIS published false as well as inadequate material on the option under federal law to withdraw the I-90 funds and use them for any area wide transportation alternatives which would fulfill the real purpose of the project.

— The defendants' "purpose" had illegally limited the project to the crossing of the Lake at Mercer Island when the corridor should have

included any projects [including rail] affecting all of the Lake crossings and traffic around the Lake.
— The EIS had published false as well as inadequate material on the options available under federal law to withdraw the I-90 funds and to use them for any area wide transportation alternatives that would fulfill the real purpose of the project.

The plaintiff's attorney appealed the Thompson decision. I did not see the appeal brief nor did I see the Ninth Circuit Court's opinion or know who heard our appeal and who wrote the final decision—if anyone did more then say "Denied".

14. NEIL GOLDSCHMIDT, UNITED STATES SECRETARY OF TRANSPORTATION, 1979

Neil Goldschmidt, an ex-Mayor of Portland and longtime friend of Seattle Mayor Royer, was appointed by President Carter to succeed Brock Adams as Secretary of Transportation in 1979. The I-90 plaintiffs were delighted with the choice because Neil Goldschmidt had shepherded the Portland area through the long process of deciding to withdraw the federal interstate funds from the Mt. Hood freeway project and to fund substitute highway projects and the Banfield rail line. Despite the Thompson decision in 1979, Secretary Adams had *not yet* given the final Federal approval of the I-90 project, and that decision would have to be made by new Secretary Goldschmidt.

When I met Secretary Goldschmidt in Seattle, I told him that we opposed the I-90 highway as planned. I asked him if he would read a letter from me if I wrote it. He assured me that he would, and I sent a three-page letter dated February 16, 1980. I said, "As Secretary you have inherited a hot potato in Secretary Adams' "approval" of the plans location, design, and of 4(f) land taking in Seattle. The Adams' approval was merely a political fiction which requires important steps to be taken to ensure the validity of the I-90 project, steps he was afraid to take but imposed as a condition of his approval as follows:

"In his September 20, 1978, letter and subsequent approval of the project, Adams stated that he would withhold the Federal Highway Administration approval of the plans, specifications, and estimates [P.S.&E.] of those portions of the project west of 23rd. Ave. S. in Seattle and east of the East Channel Bridge in Bellevue UNTIL the "development and necessary approval of design and financing agreements for priority transit access into downtown Seattle and Bellevue."

I wrote that the delays in the designing process were not due to lack of time but to the political pressure to preserve the 1971 Mercer Island project intact with no changes, not even essential additions. I ended the letter with:

"Now, as Secretary, you are faced with two important decisions:

"(1) What will your office do to ensure the completion of the action required by the Adams' conditions?"

"(2) How much more money will the Federal Department of Transportation be willing to spend on I-90?"

My letter was mailed, received by the Secretary Goldschmidt's office, and Goldschmidt sent it over to the Federal Highway Administration proponents of the I-90 project to answer for the Department of Transportation. I was appalled. When he passed my letter on to the FHWA, Secretary Goldschmidt had ordered the most thorough rejection the project opponents received in all of the I-90 process! In effect he had given the FHWA permission to ignore any of the content of my letter, which meant that he was validating the FHWA decision to evade all of the required laws, administrative rules, and court mandates in the long I-90 process. IN EFFECT, GOLDSCHMIDT TRANSFERRED HIS DUTIES AS SECRETARY TO THE I-90 PROPONENTS.

I met Secretary Goldschmidt again at a meeting in a private home on the Lake Washington shore that was almost under the existing I-90. Our invitation specified that we could not discuss I-90 at the meeting, and so we sat there—it was a far cry from the many, many meetings in Portland when Neil Goldschmidt had worked to withdraw federal interstate highway funds and to substitute the Banfield rail line for the Mt. Hood Freeway.

In my last re-reading of my newspaper clippings filed under "Goldschmidt", I noted that when his appointment was being considered, he had solicited support from our local "leaders" who were very influential in Washington.

15. THE LAST CHANGE: INITIATIVE 21, 1979-1980:
The Withdraw/Substitution Alternatives as the Basis for an Initiative

When Judge Thompson handed down his decision on August 6, 1979 in the I-90 *Lathan* case, he ruled that the defendants had met all Federal law requirements, and he lifted the injunction that had been placed on I-90 in 1971. Since his decision was merely a paraphrasing of what the State had submitted in their findings of fact and conclusions of law, he had followed the defendants' instructions, he had completely ignored the plaintiffs' arguments, and he had paid no attention to the abysmal failure of the State to meet the federal law requirements for the consideration of alternatives: despite new amendments Section 103 to the Federal Highway act in 1973, 1975, and in May, 1976; despite the mandates of the U.S. Circuit Court of Appeals for the Ninth Circuit in the 1971, 1973, and 1974 decisions and the mandates of the U.S. Court for the District of Western Washington in 1972.

By 1973, many of the unfinished urban sections of interstate highways were obsolete as solutions of transportation problems, and *Congress began to try to regulate sensible spending of the highway trust funds by allowing the states to reconsider their decisions to build non-essential interstate highways so that they could take advantage of the new opportunities to withdraw funds planned for those urban interstates, and use those federal funds for substitute rail and highway projects.* When the amendment to the Federal Highway Act Section 103(e)(4) became effective on May 5, 1976, Congress gave the states full latitude to use these interstate funds for any transportation purpose—as former Federal Highway Administrator, Lowell Bridwell said, "it's impossible to think of any purpose these funds cannot be used for, rail or highways, anywhere in the area". Nevertheless, the State did not consider alternatives to their 1971 adopted design of I-90, or did the State alter the 1975 Environmental Impact Statement to show that they had so done—the 1978 Final Environmental Impact Statement was the 1975 version virtually unchanged.

The amendments to the Federal Highway Act provided that the decision to withdraw the interstate segment was to be made only by the local jurisdictions adjacent to that segment with the approval of the governor of the state. Seattle, Mercer Island, King County, and Bellevue were adjacent to the Bellevue I-405 to Seattle I-5 section of I-90, and the decision to withdraw the federal funds from the I-90 project could be made *only* by the elected officials of those jurisdictions and the governor. The state legislatures were deliberately excluded from the law. When Congress passed the withdraw/substitution amendments to the Federal Highway Act, Congress obviously decided to require local decisions in which the state legislatures would play no part.

The Mandates of the Federal Courts Required Consideration of 1976 I-90 Alternatives

I wrote a section for my *Critique*, 'ALTERNATIVES TO THE PROPOSED PROJECT" (pages 77 TO 159). This review of the essentials of the 1974 court decision is a basis for the plaintiffs' decision on what we could do after we had lost our case and our appeal.

In the September 27, 1974, the U.S. Court of Appeals for the Ninth Circuit, (in a decision written by Judge Duniway, who had also written the 1971 and 1973 I-90 decisions), ruled that the State must prepare and circulate a new and adequate Environmental Impact Statement and that a new corridor/design hearing must be held. The opinion was a clear and concise direction to the defendants:

Judge Duniway wrote, "*We cannot ignore, as judges, what we know as citizens. the knowledge and attitudes of the public, of the congress, and of state and local governments about the environmental and social consequences of freeway building have drastically changed in the last decade. With that knowledge has come concern and that concern is reflected in the 1968 and 1970 amendments to section 128(a) of the Federal Highway Act and in NEPA [The National Environmental Protection Act]. The proposed segment is to be built in the future, and decisions of it are to be governed by the law as it reads now, not as it read in 1973. [506 F. 2d. page 689].*

"In short, we hold under the facts here that the policies of NEPA and section 128(a) must be construed together and that section 128(a) provides a public forum at which, among other things, the NEPA required EIS will be the basis for the hearing.

... "With respect to ongoing projects, section 128(a) and regulations which implement it must be interpreted and administered, to the fullest extent possible in accordance with the policies of NEPA. In appropriate cases, this may mean total reassessment of the project in light of its potential environmental impact, i.e. the consideration of its wholesale alteration or abandonment."

[AT PAGE 890] *"We stress that the hearing under section 128(a) must take into account factors that are now outlined in that section and in NEPA. It will not merely be a new 'corridor' or 'location' hearing although, of course, what was considered at these hearings can be considered. The major focus must be on the total impact of the project as a whole, including whether it should be built at all, as well as whether, if it is to be built, it should be built where and as previously planned."*

The City of Seattle Initiative 21

Judge Thompson's August, 1979, opinion said that the I-90 defendants had met all the requirements of the federal laws and the injunction on I-90 was removed. On appeal, the decision was confirmed by the U.S. Court of Appeals for the Ninth Circuit, and the opponents of I-90 had only one available remedy to try to get consideration of the alternatives to the Mercer Island I-90 project—an initiative to be submitted to Seattle voters with the hope that they did not approve the planned I-90 project and wanted an alternative to it.

SR-520
I-90
ROANOKE REEF
WHY ARE CITY KNIGHTS SO SLEEPLESS?
BECAUSE WE'RE UP TO OUR ASCOTS IN DRAGONS
THAT'S WHY
KILL 2 WITH ONE STROKE
SUPPORT INITIATIVE 21 AND
TRADE THE I-90 & 520 BRIDGE MONEY
FOR A GREAT TRANSIT SYSTEM

A new group formed immediately to frame the initiative and to collect the 21,000 signatures needed to put it on the ballot. They named themselves the I-90 MAJORITY, with John Barber, Chairman, and in September they drafted Initiative 21 to be submitted to the people (with all petitions to be handed in by January 14, 1980). They circulated this flyer:

"INITIATIVE 21"

"FOR Better Public Transportation,"
"NOT more highway lanes across Lake Washington.
"Fact: The I-90 highway will cost more than $1 billion.
"Fact: Under Federal Law, I-90 funds can be used instead for public transportation.
"Fact: Many cities, including Portland, have substituted public transit for highways."

"Shall Seattle be prohibited from involvement in expanding existing Lake Washington Bridges or constructing new bridges except for public transportation?"

The collection of signatures on the initiative petition went very well. When it was certain that the initiative would be on the ballot, a lawsuit was filed against the City of Seattle to quash the initiative. The suing plaintiffs were the same pro-highway group that had lobbied through the 1975 State law, RCW 47.20.645, which provided specific state deadlines for these I-90 processes: finishing the study to withdraw the interstate funds; the corridor/design hearing; the submission of the environmental impact statement.

The federal law had not set any requirements for the local jurisdictions' voting on withdrawing an interstate project, but state law RCW 42.20.645 required three adjacent jurisdictions to vote for withdrawing the I-90 Federal funds, and for the approval of the governor and the Puget Sound Governmental Conference. This PSGC requirement is particularly noteworthy because the backers of that state law had simultaneously passed a bill abolishing the PSGC! These two bills are the ones I named the "silly bills" during the session because they attempted to pass state laws which would supersede federal laws. The federal law had not provided any requirements for voting power. In fact, I had a copy of a letter that Lynn Burkart in the office of the Secretary of the U.S. Department of Transportation, had written to tell Secretary Adams that the people in his offices working on I-90 had said that if Seattle ONLY were to vote to withdraw I-90, it would probably be withdrawn.

I had been lobbying in the state legislature in 1975 when these bills were introduced—it was an incredible attempt to use politics as a smoke-screen. I thought that the bills were meaningless and not worth lobbying against. I was sure that if the State Legislature passed the bills (which they did), they would be absolutely unenforceable because the State Legislature and the Governor had actually tried to amend the Federal Highway Act! Washington State had set deadlines for the various actions required by the federal laws—where the federal laws had not set any—and the state law had limited the voting power of the jurisdictions. The federal share of the I-90 project was to be more than 90%—it seemed incredible that a state legislature and governor could believe that the state could qualify for and obtain federal highway funds in spite of their passing state laws contrived to allow the state to evade the requirements of federal laws attached to those federal funds.

These state laws were obviously drafted in what I began to call the "highway/engineers-highway/contractors' legalese." If any of the lawyers in the state Attorney General's office had participated in the writing of the laws, they had either decided to try to evade the federal laws, OR they had just written down what they were told to draft by the pro-I-90 people.

It just occurred to me that the Attorney General, (now U.S. Senator) Slade Gorton, some of his assistants, and some legislators probably knew that there were some Superior Court judges in the State of Washington who would use laws like these as if they were valid. They could predict that some Washington state judges would ignore the fact that the Washington law in question was rewriting a federal law to evade the required procedures for ensuring the wise spending of federal funds on highway. This had already happened in 1976 in the I-90 *Leschi* case in Seattle, when neighborhood organizations and citizens sued the State alleging the inadequacy of the EIS under the State Environmental Protection Act (SEPA) which was almost an identical copy of the National Environmental Protection Act, (NEPA). The defendants had submitted the same pamphlet EIS which Federal District Court Judge Beeks had already found inadequate in 1972 under the National Environmental Protection Act. Washington State Superior Court Judge James Dore heard the case and completely ignored the federal court decisions in his opinion. He upheld the validity of the original 1970 EIS because, he said, it had been prepared pursuant to the provisions of the *State* Environmental Protection Act! (although SEPA was a copy of the National Environmental Protection Act!).

When the I-90 defendants had not met the deadlines in state law RCW 47.20.645, I mentally erased the state law: the State had not finished the withdraw study; they had not submitted the environmental impact statement in time so that it could not be read before the corridor/design hearing; and the local jurisdictions had taken final acts negating any alternatives according to that state law even though the date it set for the hearing was before the DEIS was even available. I thought the state law had died a natural ridiculous death and would not be heard from again. Little did I know!

The Initiative 21 Lawsuit and Judge Scholfield's Decision

The case was heard by State Superior Court Judge Scholfield, from, of all places, Mercer Island!—and he decided for—guess who? The plaintiffs! He said that Initiative 21 was illegal. He cited the 1975 State law, RCW 47.20.645 as his authority! He cited the Memorandum Agreement as if it were a valid instrument! He held that the Board of Review had ended all possibility of any changes to the project by their 1973 decision—nothing could change the I-90 project after that.

THE DECISION OF JUDGE SCHOLFIELD, A WASHINGTON STATE SUPERIOR COURT JUDGE, HAD AMENDED THE FEDERAL HIGHWAY ACT!!

On August 1, 1980, I wrote the following memo and sent it to the city Attorney Doug Jewett, Mayor Royer (via Hugh Spitzer), Seattle Council President Paul Kraabel, and City of Seattle lawyers Phil Mortenson, Jorgen Bader, and John McKay:

"Judge Scholfield's decision seems to contain two 'rules of law':

(1) The state, in RCW 47.20.645, terminated the City of Seattle's' right to make a choice on the spending of available Federal funds on I-90, although that choice was provided for local jurisdictions only by Federal law and was in no way derived from state authority, (the right to withdraw the Seattle segment of I-90 from the Federal Interstate system was established by Congress in the Federal Highway Act, 23 USC, Section 103(e)(4)).

(2) The design of the Seattle segment of I-90 had been set pursuant to state law providing for the limited access Board of Review process, and no design changes could be made after 1973, [After the Board of Review decision].

"Judge Scholfield's decision, if allowed to stand, could be used as precedent to seriously jeopardize all of the billions of dollars of federal-aid grants which Congress has decided should be transmitted directly to cities by Federal processes without the interference by the states—such funds as the millions Seattle now receives each year directly from the Federal government (i.e. under the laws providing for revenue sharing—HUD, CETA, UMTA, etc.)."

RCW 47.20.645 as interpreted by Judge Scholfield effectively foreclosed Seattle's opportunities in January, 1976: under that law, the state could and did terminate any rights the city of Seattle had thereafter to study, advocate, and/or join with less than two of the other abutting jurisdictions in alternative pending of the I-90 funds for anything but 1971 project as supplemented by the 1973 Board of Review decision.

"Judge Scholfield's decision also erased any right the city of Seattle might have had under federal laws and mandated in the various *Lathan* case decisions requiring a valid environmental impact statement for the use of the people who would make the decision on the spending of the I-90 funds."

I added, "A reading of the state law will show clearly that it had no legal validity and could not and did not actually terminate any rights the local jurisdictions had under federal laws. These processes, all required by federal laws had not been completed by the state's deadlines, ... and the project had been enjoined by the federal courts until these laws were met:

— the National Environmental Protection Act (NEPA), the Federal design hearing and approval processes (23 USC Section 128(a);
— the taking of Seattle parkland (23 USC Section 138);
— the protecting of city neighborhoods from damage by the construction and use of the project selected (23 USC Section 109(h), (i), (j) and the Clean Air Act.

"In effect, Judge Scholfield's decision meant that the state could and did wipe out all of the federally-required processes as set forth in laws, regulations and the federal courts' interpretation of those laws and regulations as they applied particularly to this project. Judge Scholfield had ruled that the state could and did erase the mandates of the Federal Ninth Circuit Court of Appeals."

Judge Scholfield's decision was appealed to the Washington State Supreme Court. I did not read the brief the appellants submitted, but I was present when the case was argued. I could not see that there was any attention paid to what I thought was the real issue, the validity of Judge Scholfield's decision that state law superseded federal law. During the hearing, Washington Sate Supreme Court Chief Justice Utter asked different versions of the same question three times—I thought he was raising the issue of the conflict between state and federal laws—but the appellant's attorney's answers to these questions did not pertain to this issue, he did not raise it in the argument at all, and the final decision did not refer to it.

We appellants lost, Initiative 21 was quashed, and we will never know what Seattle voters thought about withdrawing federal funds for I-90 and using them for substitute projects, highways or transit, in or out of the corridor, anywhere in the urban area.

Law decisions are supposed to be based on a theory called "stare decisis": legal questions are decided on precedent—what was decided in previous comparable decisions. Has the Scholfield decision been used in our state as a precedent to allow subsequent issues to be decided using his theories? If a strong political force in our state does not want to perform federal procedures required to qualify for federal funds can they merely pass a state law to supersede the applicable federal laws?

16. SEATTLE 1996

Judkins Rejected - 1994

On July 13, 1994, the *Seattle Post-Intelligencer* published an article under the headline, "THE NEIGHBORHOOD THAT TIME FORGOT." It reported the increasing rage of the Seattle people who called themselves "the Judkins Rejected" area, because of the city's continued failure to rehabilitate their community, located immediately north of I-90 between Martin Luther King Way and 23rd Avenue. Since 1968, for twenty-six long years, they had lived among the hundreds of unsightly vacant lots and derelict buildings left when the State bought property not needed for the I-90 project—property the state still owned! They said that in 1989 the city had finally adopted a development plan for the Judkins Rejected area, but that in the next four years, the city had built only six houses with two more under construction.

The newspaper article said that the City of Seattle had agreed to PAY for the Judkins area rehabilitation by BUYING the lots from the State at the assessed price at the time of the sale, plus the cost of the assessment when the lots were sold, and then selling the lots! The rehabilitation was to cost the State absolutely nothing!

This Judkins' protest added to the record of the abysmal and continued deliberate refusal of the elected officials of Seattle to care for the people of Seattle. The history of I-90 in the Judkins area is marked by one overriding fact: the elected officials of Seattle had not made the essential policy decisions required to protect the Judkins area. By the early 1970's there was enough evidence to prove that the city should design the I-90 project through Seattle, find what the harmful effects would be, and how they could be eliminated. When the elected officials did nothing at all, the citizens had filed two lawsuits.

In 1970, the *Lathan v. Volpe* case had been filed by city residents against the State, (the Washington State Highway Commission) and the Secretary of the U.S. Department of Transportation to force them to comply with the federal laws which would protect area residents from damage. In 1972 the Federal District Court had stopped all work on I-90 until the defendants complied with the laws.

In 1973 the residents had filed the Adler *v. Volpe* case to force the State to take care of the derelict property bought in the I-90 corridor; the court ruled for the plaintiffs, but they had to return to court several times because the State was still not taking care of the property.

The worst result of the failure of the Seattle Mayor and Council to act for Seattle was that Seattle lost all of the federal funds that should have been available to rehabilitate the Judkins area and the area south of the freeway—to replace housing and repair damage. *More than ninety percent of the cost should have been paid from federal Interstate funds for I-90, and the remainder should have been paid by the State. The city of Seattle should not have paid anything at all!*

While Seattle's elected officials were doing nothing to protect property owners affected by I-90, the State had provided all of the "amenities" on Mercer Island, and the property damage on the I-405 corridor in Los Angeles had been completely erased. (See the CONSENT DECREE in the *Keith* case). The California state transportation authority, Caltrans, spent about 18 percent of the $2.2

billion total cost of the I-405 project on corridor rehabilitation and housing—the federal share was ninety percent or about $324 million, the state paid the rest. In Seattle, the elected officials did nothing about the Judkins' rehabilitation, and the state and federal defendants paid absolutely nothing.

If there had been timely designs of I-90 to show the harm which would be caused by the project in the area west of 23rd Avenue in Seattle, and if there had been plans to eliminate that damage, Seattle could have had a development plan for the Judkins area before 1976, and the development plan could have been funded and finished long ago. As the design work on the freeway began, the work to protect the adjacent areas could have begun. It would have been funded, as it should have been as part of the I-90 project. The development plan would have been finished and Seattle would not have paid for any part of it.

By April, 1996, Seattle had bought fifty-one lots in the Judkins area at the current assessed price plus the cost of the assessment. Seattle funds are being used to build fairly undesirable houses which are then sold to buyers under an unusual financing scheme; close examination of the entire process will show that the new buyers of those properties are paying for the restoration of the Judkins area!

It is not too late for the present Seattle elected officials to act to get the funds for rehabilitation owned the residents of the areas damaged by the construction and use of the I-90 project. They can force the State pay back all the money the city has paid for the Judkins property so far and to give them the remaining I-90 purchased property and to pay for its restoration:

The elected officials should:

— Demand information about each property they have already bought and each property they need to acquire from the State: When was it purchased? What was the price paid? Were federal funds used?, and, if so, how much? Were state funds used, and if so how much? What is the asking price for this property now? Did the State pay

Seattle property taxes through all these years, and if so, how much did they pay?

— Ask if federal funds were used for the acquisition; ask if the State returns them to the federal government when the State sells the property in Seattle, and if so, when? I-405 in Los Angeles was built at the same time as I-90 in Seattle, and the U.S. Secretary of Transportation agreed that the State of California did not have to pay back the federal funds spent for properties bought earlier for the project and not used. Point out that the federal defendants agreed that almost $360 Million dollars would be spent on the I-405 in Los Angeles project to restore the residential areas affected by the highway.

— Ask if state and federal highway trust funds were spent for housing rehabilitation on Mercer Island? Since almost half of all the money spent on the Seattle-to-Bellevue I-90 project for the Mercer Island segment was used for that 3 mile-long almost-flat section of I-90, a high percentage of the total cost must have been spent for the abandoning of the existing freeway (which furnished land for the business district) and the "amenities" in Mercer Island. Who owns the land which was available when the old highway was removed? Who did they pay for it, and how much did they pay?

— Calculate and demand retribution funds.

The people of Mercer Island designed their part of I-90 with all the damage "amenities" they required, and the funding for that part of the project was never questioned. Seattle was treated very differently than Mercer Island: the I-90 decisions in Seattle were made behind closed doors in an entirely political process; decisions were not made on the basis of what was good for Seattle and those who live here, and the people who care about Seattle were and are still being ignored.

The Judkins area people suffered great damage from I-90 from the State's acquisition and destruction of property as they virtually laid waste to the area and throughout the building of the highway. Many people who live there will always be affected by the traffic noise and pollution. The people in the corridor of I-405 in Los Angeles and of

Mercer Island were protected from freeway damage—why do Seattle residents still have to live with it?

There is an added problem: A map recently published shows that land between Judkins Park and I-90 will be developed for commercial use. The original 1960 bond park drawings show that Judkins Parkland is bounded on the south by I-90—the city owns that undeveloped land, and it must be kept as a park per the 1960 bond promises to the voters. [It would be interesting to know if the city got paid for the parkland in that area which was used by I-90].

Seattle Transportation 1996 - Nothing Changes!

I decided to write this book when I realized that the materials I had saved provided an important history of the 1968 to 1980 transportation decisions in greater Seattle and in the state—if it were not put into a readable and usable form, that history would be lost forever.

Those who do not know history are doomed to repeat it. And now, in 1996, the Seattle elected officials are repeating all the old mistakes which have cost billions of dollars and caused great damage to Seattle by construction and traffic on highways and bridges—and accomplished nothing for the residents of Seattle.

The subtitle of this book is **"Fighting Fiercely and Winning Sometimes"**, and it records the twelve long years when the citizens were fighting fiercely. It records the victories of the citizens against freeways in the Settle area from 1968 to 1972—stopping the R.H. Thomson and Bay Freeways, years after final decisions had been made to build the projects. This book records the 1971 to 1977 years when the statewide Washington Coalition for Sensible Transportation was able to make only a few changes in the state laws: to delay additions to the state motor fuel tax; and to make important additions (for essential planning processes and for citizens' participation) to a Department of Transportation bill that did not change the old Highway Department. This book records the abysmal failure of the citizens of Seattle to convince the Governor, and the state, county, and Seattle elected officials to take the action required by federal laws as conditions precedent to federal funding of I-90; for nine years, they bowed to the political powers that supported the continuing action which enabled them to ignore the federal courts' mandates on the I-90 project.

The citizens of Seattle cannot continue to fight freeways one-by-one as we did in the 1970's. They must use the power of the electorate on the legislators to change the obsolete transportation laws. They must use the power of the electorate to require Seattle elected officials to make future decisions on transportation that represent and protect the people of our city.

Mandatory Changes in State Laws

In 1975, Governor Evans said, "I believe the Secretary of Transportation should be appointed by the Governor, so that maximum responsiveness to public opinion is built into the Department. Each new administration should be able to review the question of appointing the Secretary. ...Otherwise the Government is unresponsive and isolated from the people."

The electorate of the state, the residence, must insist on this immediate action.

>>>Washington state legislators must amend the existing law to establish a Department of Transportation under the administration of the governor and with a secretary appointed by the governor. In the same law, the legislators must abolish State Transportation Commission, the facade that prevents any participation by the governor or the electorate in transportation department decisions and operations.

>>>Washington state legislators must repeal the state laws controlling the state, county, and city transportation planning and the spending of their share of the state's transportation funds; these laws perpetuate an obsolete process which promotes large highway projects at the expense of sensible transportation. New laws must be passed to

allow the counties and cities full freedom to make their own decisions for spending these funds for transportation.

>>>Washington state legislators must abolish the Transportation Improvement Board law—it was established in 1967 (as the Urban Arterial Board) to raise more funds for costly projects by the sale of bonds.

AND

>>>Washington state legislators must refuse to consider any increase in taxes on motor vehicles and motor vehicle fuels until the above reforms have been completed. Without sensible transportation laws, the people have no way to determine what funds are needed for what purpose. Using our existing laws for processes which have excluded the electorate and the governor, the State will spend $1,321.5 billion for *1995-7*, and *they* want an additional $850 *million* for 1997-1999, 60% more!

Mandatory Changes: Goals and Policies of Seattle Elected Officials

The electorate of Seattle, the residents, must pass new ordinances that require the city council and the mayor to develop and adopt policies and goals for our city and the procedures necessary to implement them. The mayor and the council must make transportation decisions for the city based on their duty to act for the people who elected them, the residents who want them to preserve and protect homes and the environment—to preserve the people's rights to clean air and water, to freedom from noise and danger, to parks, schools, police and fire protection—and most of all, to preserve the people's rights to keep their neighborhoods intact and safe from the damage caused by highway construction and traffic. Seattle elected officials must adopt goals and policies that will prevent all planning and construction of more commuter vehicle highway lanes into Seattle because they must protect the residents of their city.

In the writing of my book, I learned that Seattle elected officials' transportation plans and project decisions are always political decisions made by people outside Seattle for their own benefit. There is never any evidence that any of the commuter-based transportation decisions the Seattle mayor and council agreed to are for the benefit of the residents of the city—the horrible example being the I-90 project. There is no evidence that the elected officials of our city ever developed policies and goals as a basis for transportation decision-making for the benefit of the residents of Settle, the people who elected them.

Seattle is now severely threatened by eastside commuters who are still intending to build these freeway projects that the citizens stopped in 1972!

>>The 1970 SR 522/R.H.Thomson freeway for commuters from Woodinville and north Bothell into Seattle. The elected officials of Seattle removed this part of the project from the city transportation plan in 1972.

>>Additional lanes on the Evergreen Bridge and SR 520 from the Redmond area into Seattle and its connector through the Portage Bay area, over I-5, to Mercer Street on an elevated highway—like the Bay Freeway! This proposal was part of the 1970 Zahn proposal; a law was passed in 1975 for a study of the 520 corridor, east of 148th Street, in Bellevue; a study of the Evergreen Bridge SR 520 proposal and the construction of the connector in Seattle were part of the Memorandum of Agreement signed by the mayor for the city in 1976; in 1993-4, private construction companies were trying to build additional vehicle capacity of the Evergreen Bridge into Seattle—the legislature had (with no real notice to the people) passed a new law allowing the private financing and building of the highway facilities in the state of Washington!

Seattle's transportation plans are based on the obsolete state laws and city plans dating from before 1956. Neither the state nor the city has ever tried to consider the essential interdependence of the public transit and travel by private cars. Decisions are never based on the consideration of whether a prospective transportation project is an alternative, supplement, complement, or a substitute for other parts of the existing and/or planned transportation system.

In 1996, the Seattle elected officials are still intent on implementing elements of transportation plans that are obsolete because the planning process is backwards. They are not planning future transportation for commuter transit development in the greater Seattle area—*they are bowing to traffic demands on a prediction of future auto-oriented needs*. Seattle elected officials do not use the basic information they already have that obliterates this demand; they know that the suburbs have been and are continuing to be built for two, three, and even four-car commuting families; they know that suburbia's appetite for more streets, highways and parking places in Seattle is insatiable; they know that the city of Seattle is two narrow peninsulas between Puget Sound and Lake Washington, they know that residents of Seattle suffered greatly from the construction and continuing travel on highways in the city. They know that there is no longer any space for parking and highways in the city and that additional vehicular traffic capacity on bridges and highways into the city cannot be tolerated. Nevertheless, at the same time, they profess to be fostering public transit, the elected officials are planning to furnish additional capacity in the city for suburbanites' trips by private cars.

They are building more parking garages in Seattle. They are supporting the 1996 Regional Transportation Plan that harms Seattle residents;

—The bus lines in the proposed RTA plan are all to be built as an addition to existing highways, freeing the existing bus lanes for more commuter vehicles.

—Some of the new bus lanes are to be built <u>with</u> additional highway lanes.

—The elected officials have agreed to the RTA rail plan in the city despite the horrible damage to be caused in the building of the Capitol Hill tunnel—despite the horrible damage caused by the building and operation of rail transit-bus connection facilities in the University District.

—The elected officials have agreed to the RTA plan which actually promotes the demand of the eastside commuters for more highway lanes into Seattle.

.....THEN AT 75 MPH I COULD SAVE 5 MORE MINUTES PER DAY

This fall area voters are asked to approve the spending of 3.9 billion dollars on the RTA plan that will not work. The eastside suburbanites' threat to build more highways into Seattle is a prediction that they will not use bus transit. The area east of Lake Washington has grown rapidly, and development consists mostly of private residences with garages for several vehicles, businesses surrounded by parking space (as required by local law), and wide new streets connecting to inadequate highways. The express bus transportation on I-90 has not worked, and the suburban bus transit planned for the 1996 ballot issue will not work in these suburban areas because the residents of these scattered developments are auto-dependent, and they think that the bus transit is not a substitute for the additional commuter highways, bridges, and parking they demand.

Railroads concentrate land development—one has only to look at the results of existing rail and subway systems, the San Diego line east from the city is a good example. In 1976, the greater Seattle area had the choice of using all of the I-90 federal funds for a highway to connect with the tunnel for a freeway/bus tunnel transit project which does not work, or for an I-90 freeway/rail project substitute, connecting rail to the tunnel rail, which would have worked to concentrate eastside suburban development and give fast access to Seattle.

I just found an April 24, 1970, *Seattle Times* map showing the connection of the proposed Forward Thrust rail to Third Avenue tunnel rail and on to rail on the proposed I-90 project! Part 3 of my book proves that Seattle had the same option that Los Angeles, Portland, and many other areas had to use interstate funds to build rail with the I-90 highway, but the Seattle elected officials allowed the politicians to make the decisions in a forum which did not allow consideration of any alternatives. The $3.9 billion "transit" system on the November, 1996, ballot continues this obsolete decision—it does not include rail on I-90 connecting to rail in the downtown tunnel, although both the tunnel and I-90 were built for it. The eastside bus transit system in the $3.9 billion plan is merely a red herring to prevent rail on I-90; *if bus transit does not work on the eastside (and it won't), the eastsiders will justify their demands for highway additions into and through Seattle.*

Seattle elected officials have been selling out to suburbia by making transportation decisions completely ignoring the factual evidence we citizens have provided: the Seattle-to-Issaquah rail line can be laid on the present I-90 right-of-way and in the tunnel and would not cause any social, economic, or environmental damage from construction or more vehicle traffic into Seattle; this rail system would cost less and would be a substitute for additional vehicle capacity into Seattle. The argument that the distance from Redmond and Woodinville is too great to use I-90 rail, is not valid; commuters could

8 The Seattle Times Wednesday, April 29, 1970

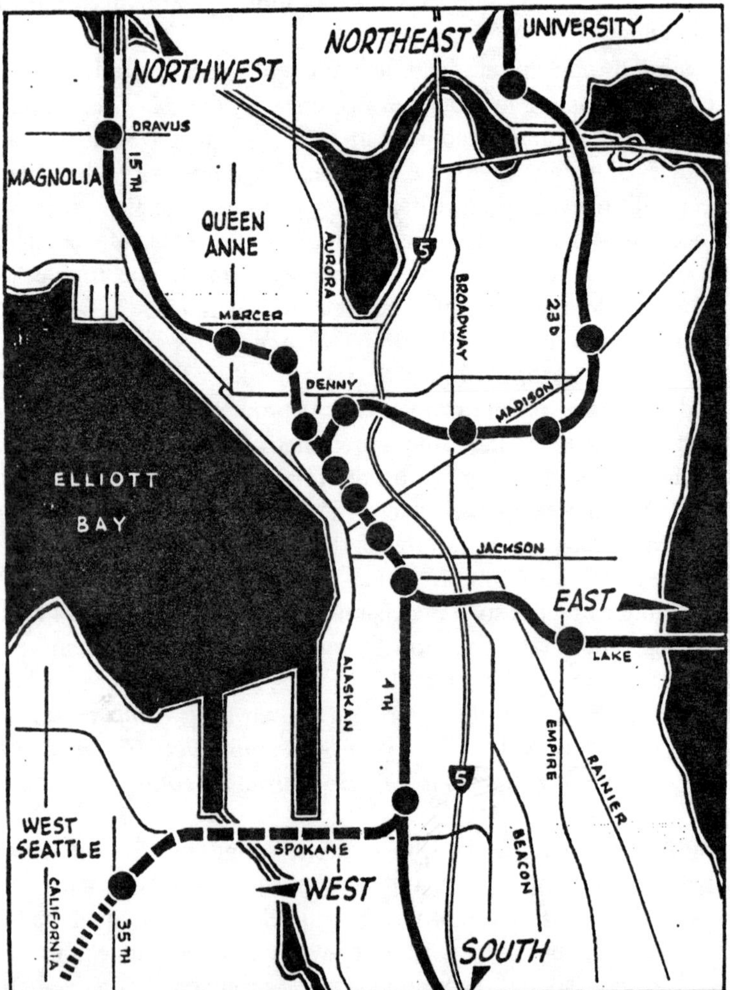

Choice of Third Avenue Transit Line Explained

Seattle Citizens Against Freeways

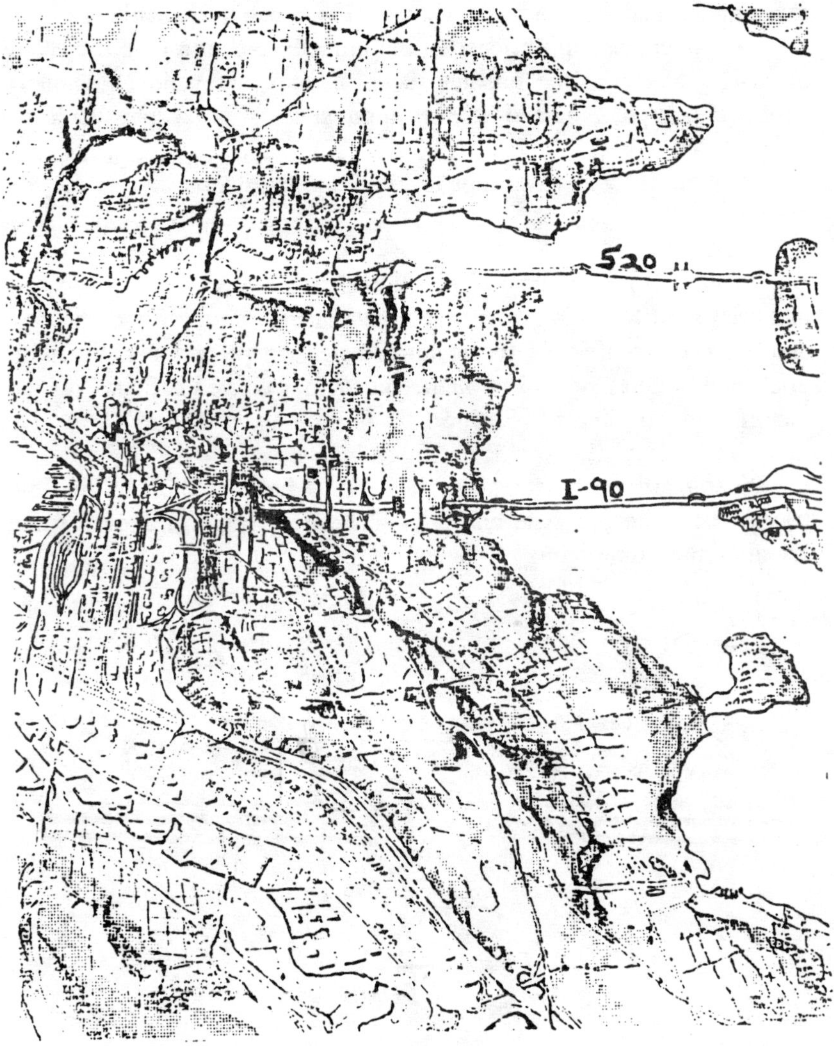

drive from the SR 520 Evergreen bridge route to I-90 rail in less than four minutes and make a faster, cheaper, easier trip into Seattle.

Seattle citizens must insist on the immediate action by our elected legislators to repeal the obsolete laws that prevent valid and honest transportation planning and funding in our state. A good start would be to read the current laws, draft new bills, and form a statewide organization of citizens' groups to lobby the legislators to vote for the changes.

Seattle citizens must use their power as the electorate to organize and prepare effective arguments and materials to convince both the new and the present officials to act immediately to protect our city with goals and policies set and implemented by our elected officials for the benefit of the residents of Seattle.

Seattle citizens must take all the action necessary to obtain sensible transportation in our state and city—instead of fighting freeways and winning only sometimes.

EVEN IF
YOU'RE ON
THE RIGHT TRACK
YOU'LL GET RUN OVER
IF YOU JUST
SIT THERE